Jimmy Carter as
Educational Policymaker

JIMMY CARTER

AS EDUCATIONAL

POLICYMAKER

Equal Opportunity and Efficiency

DEANNA L. MICHAEL

STATE UNIVERSITY OF NEW YORK PRESS

Published by
STATE UNIVERSITY OF NEW YORK PRESS, ALBANY

© 2008 State University of New York

For information, contact State University of New York Press, Albany, NY
www.sunypress.edu

Production, Laurie Searl
Marketing, Michael Campochiaro

Library of Congress Cataloging-in-Publication Data

Michael, Deanna L., 1961–
   Jimmy Carter as educational policymaker : equal opportunity and efficiency / Deanna L. Michael.
     p. cm.
   Includes bibliographical references and index.
   ISBN 978-0-7914-7529-4 (hardcover : alk. paper) 1. Educational equalization—Government policy—United States. 2. Educational equalization—Georgia. 3. Education and state—United States. 4. Carter, Jimmy, 1924– I. Title.

LC213.2.M53 2008
379.2'60973—dc22

                                                                                            2007037592

10   9   8   7   6   5   4   3   2   1

Contents

Acknowledgments

As I have read so many times in acknowledgments, but now understand completely for the first time, no one writes a manuscript alone. Many people have supported me through this process and for all of them, I am grateful. First, I would like to thank the archivists at the Jimmy Carter Library for their help and support in my search for documents. They were patient teachers and guides through the innumerable documents available at the library. The archivists at the Georgia Department of Archives and History and the librarians at Georgia State University Special Collections were equally supportive and patient. Phillip Kovak, then a graduate student at Georgia State University, ran down documents for me. His efforts saved me trips to Atlanta and enriched chapters 3 and 4. Lauren Kent-Delany at the Carter Center of Emory University helped me find the answers to questions that were pivotal for the development of chapter 6. She generously sought out the people who could answer my questions. I am grateful that she gave her time to help me. The Sumter County Public School District gave me access to the school board minutes and thoughtfully found me space to work. Mr. W.W. Foy, the superintendent of Sumter County schools when Jimmy Carter served on the school board, graciously spent an afternoon answering my questions. Through our conversation, I learned about the consequences of racial moderation in the 1960s.

I also wish to thank Georgia State University for a dissertation grant that supported my research expenses and travel to Sumter County, and the family of George M. Stansbury for their generous award for the dissertation that began this study. Dean Vivian Fueyo of the College of Education at the University of South Florida St. Petersburg provided release time from classes and much emotional support, which was invaluable for the completion of the manuscript. Additionally, the support and encouragement of my friends at the University of South Florida St. Petersburg, in all the colleges, but particularly in the College of Education, made writing this manuscript an enjoyable process.

The members of the Southern History of Education Society, the Southeast Philosophy of Education Society, and the History of Education Society have supported the development of this manuscript and its thesis with their thoughtful comments when I presented yet another paper on Jimmy Carter's involvement in educational policymaking. Wayne Urban, Philo Hutcheson, and Gary Fink began this road with me and helped me along it. I will always be grateful for their support. Kathy Borman and Sherman Dorn both encouraged me in this process through our work on Florida educational policy.

I believe with any manuscript there are individuals who go above and beyond the call of duty. Ellen Hufnagel read and critiqued the chapters many times. Her patience was only exceeded by her ability to stay focused on the thesis, especially when the details demanded my attention. Throughout, she demonstrated what a mentoring relationship should be. Catherine Lugg also read chapters and encouraged me to follow where the material led. Greg Seals, my comrade from our days at Georgia State University, read the final manuscript and made many thoughtful suggestions about its themes and how to enhance them. I also wish to thank the anonymous reviewers from the State University of New York Press for their constructive criticisms. The manuscript is much stronger from all the suggestions and probing questions of these individuals. Naturally, any mistakes are my own and my responsibility.

My editor, Lisa Chesnel, demonstrated great patience when circumstances in my life demanded my attention. Lisa, Llewellyn Somers, and Laurie Searl made the publication of this manuscript possible.

I have special thanks to the people who have been on this journey with me from the point when I decided to spend my life in higher education. The women of St. Paul's Episcopal Church have supported me emotionally and given me their support through the ups and downs of this long writing process and my career. Finally, I am most grateful to my family, especially my parents, Anne and Edward Michael, for their unshakable support for my dreams and ambitions.

Introduction

IN 1955, two unrelated events occurred that would have far-reaching effects on educational policy in the United States. The first received national attention: on May 31, the United States Supreme Court issued its second decision in the *Brown v. Board of Education* case, which ordered the end of racial discrimination in public schools "with all deliberate speed." The second was hardly noticeable to anyone outside of Sumter County, Georgia, where the grand jury, the local governing body, appointed Jimmy Carter to the Sumter County Board of Education.[1] As Carter's political career unfolded in the decades that followed, culminating in the presidency, the equal opportunity mandate articulated in the *Brown* decisions would significantly alter the shape of education policy in the United States, challenging the emphasis on efficiency that had guided educational policymakers for decades.

In the 1950s and 1960s, as the nation struggled to desegregate and provide equal access to education for previously underserved minority groups, Carter developed both a personal commitment to equal opportunity in education and a fundamental belief that the efficiency of our educational system would be improved by applying the principles of scientific management. As his political influence grew and his sights shifted from local to state and federal educational policies, Carter became increasingly involved in the debate over the future of public education as he sought to reconcile these often conflicting objectives. Combining his talents as an administrator, businessman, and humanitarian, he pursued new policies that expanded access to education, but he also supported efficiency measures such as the placement of students in classes based on intelligence tests and centralization of policymaking, contributing to the legacy of tension between equal educational opportunity and efficiency that continues to influence the structure of educational policies in this country today.

As the twenty-first century begins, the nation is once again actively pursuing educational reform with the expressed goals of increasing efficiency and improving the quality of education, while leaving no child behind. Although these themes have been recast in contemporary terms, they are in many ways a continuation of the educational efficiency movement that began in the early 1900s and reemerged during the Carter administration. Thus, reflecting on Carter's role in the history of education is both a vehicle for exploring the tensions that exist when efficiency and equal opportunity are juxtaposed, as in the accountability movement of the 1970s, and a lesson in reconciling these seemingly incompatible objectives. Because of his involvement in educational policy on all governmental levels, Carter's political career also offers a unique opportunity to study the formation and implementation of educational policies on the local, state, and federal levels and to witness the centralization of educational policymaking on the state and federal levels in the latter half of the twentieth century.

THE EDUCATIONAL EFFICIENCY MOVEMENT

Educational policymakers seldom begin their work with a clean slate.[2] Instead, educational policy typically evolves over time in response to a host of external influences, including political, economic, and social pressures that may have little to do with specific academic goals and objectives. The educational efficiency movement is a good example. Early in the twentieth century, Frederick W. Taylor introduced the business world to a new management approach that he designed to eliminate waste and increase productivity by applying a set of principles that came to be known as "scientific management." These principles involved using time and motion studies to analyze work methods, systematically selecting and training workers for specific jobs based on their aptitudes and abilities, and controlling all aspects of the production process.[3] Taylor and his followers had a substantial impact on industrial management, developing the concepts of work design and measurement, production control, and other efficiency measures that completely changed the way industry organized and managed labor.

Impressed by the industrial reforms that scientific management triggered, education administrators, professors, and socially prominent school board members looked for ways to adapt Taylor's principles to school administration. For example, education administrators, who typically lacked the training, time, and money "for painstaking, thoughtful, thorough research,"[4] analyzed the function of schools and looked for ways to test and place students based on their abilities and to exert greater control over the educational process. Many of their studies centered on the cost of teaching a class rather than on how students learned or how teachers taught, leading to the use of cost accounting procedures to establish optimal student–teacher ratios and intelligence testing to sort students according to their talents.[5]

Although the industrial use of scientific management had waned by the mid 1920s, dramatic changes had already occurred in the organization of schools. Graduate schools of education had trained a generation of new school administrators under the supervision of professors like Ellwood P. Cubberley, a prolific writer of textbooks, who supported the use of industrial methods in managing schools. In a discussion of special classes for gifted students, those with special learning needs, and those with special interests, he explained that "to reduce waste, speed up the rate of production, and increase the value of the output of our schools" districts needed to design specialized classes. Continuing the analogy, he outlined the problems with the public schools in terms of running a factory. He explained,

> the waste of material was great and the output small and costly—in part because the workmen in the establishment were not supplied with enough of the right kind of tools . . . largely because the establishment was not equipped with enough pieces of special-type machinery, located in special shops or units of the manufacturing plant, to enable it to work up the waste material and meet modern manufacturing conditions.[6]

Teachers needed the correct tools—specialized classes—to produce the desired output—students who understood their place in business and society.

In the march toward the efficient use of taxpayer monies, many new administrators turned to statistical studies, surveys, and the adoption of routine intelligence testing to measure students' inherent abilities.[7] Advocates of such testing argued that IQ tests would enable educators to use science to predict more accurately the results of education before the public made an investment. Furthermore, because students were the "products" of the schools to be molded according to their measured abilities, prudent placement would result in the best use of scarce resources.[8] Advocates stressed that because student ability was the basis of the placement in academic or vocational curriculum, the use of the tests followed democratic principles.

Critics protested the blanket application of scientific management in public education and pointed out that intelligence tests tended to reflect existing racial and economic divisions in society and, therefore, increased discrimination rather than alleviated it. For example, those who scored highest on these exams were typically white males from the Northeast, who had the greatest access to educational institutions, while those who scored lowest were generally black southern males, who had the least access. John Dewey criticized such classification of individuals as a violation of the democratic ideal in its attempts "to fit individuals in advance for definite industrial callings, not on the basis of trained original capacities, but on that of the wealth and social status of parents."[9] Both critics and advocates sought to define the place and the purpose of the public school in American society. The advocates of scientific management viewed the schools as gatekeepers with a responsibility to train students to fill their place in society. For the critics of efficiency, the public schools served communities as a source of education. By the middle of the 1950s, however, placement for efficiency became less important than placement for separation.

After the 1954 *Brown v. Board of Education* Supreme Court decision ordering the desegregation of public schools, intelligence testing continued to be used widely in the South and elsewhere for many years, providing support for both the notion of white supremacy and the continued segregation of the school systems. During Jimmy Carter's service on the Sumter County Board of Education, even this small school district with fewer than 2,000 students voted to adopt scientific management principles, using intelligence testing for student placement in programs. While the members of the board made few statements regarding the purposes of this testing, the decision to administer intelligence tests throughout the district occurred in 1957 as school districts across the South struggled to maintain segregation at all costs.

During the 1960s when Carter served in the Georgia state senate, support for scientific management dwindled briefly in the face of mounting demands for equity in education. In contrast, as the governor of Georgia early in the 1970s, he and the member of the Georgia General Assembly joined the "back to basics" movement, with its focus on accountability and minimum competency testing, and brought the principles associated with scientific management into the limelight once again. According to policy analyst Arthur Wise, state politicians designed their educational policy mandates emphasizing accountability to "reveal how to make students learn."[10] As with the early efficiency studies, policymakers sacrificed the process of teaching and learning to the end product. As president, Carter continued his strong support of both the "back to basics" movement and the use of testing to increase accountability within the public school system. He believed that programs such as these would not only improve the efficiency of the schools themselves, but also eventually offer equal educational opportunity for all children.

EQUAL EDUCATIONAL OPPORTUNITY

Although one of the frequently cited justifications for the use of scientific management in student placements was its theoretical impartiality, the *Brown* decision with its declaration that "separate was inherently unequal" galvanized the leaders of the civil rights movement to demand equal access to educational facilities and resources. Like the scientific efficiency approach to education, the decision ordering the desegregation of public schools had strong and powerful supporters. However, southern politicians and school officials resisted the desegregation of school systems segregated since the 1870s. Throughout the southern states, black children often attended substandard schools with fewer materials than their white peers and, in rural areas, where funding for education was low, boards often reserved high school education for white students.[11]

Despite resistance to the *Brown* verdict and its supporting decisions, educational opportunity slowly expanded in both urban and rural areas across the nation. In anticipation of court challenges to their segregated public schools, southern governors and legislators sought to shore up the equal provision of the earlier Supreme Court ruling, *Plessy v. Ferguson* (1896), which had enshrined segregation in education and other social arenas through the "separate but equal" doctrine. As the pressure to desegregate garnered increasing attention in the federal courts, southern politicians began to build new schools for African American children in the hope that more genuinely equal facilities for black and white students would mitigate the mounting court orders pursued by the National Association for the Advancement of Colored People (NAACP).

Despite the efforts to equalize educational facilities by state legislatures and public school officials, the demands by black citizens and other groups for equal access to education continued until they gained at least a token response. School districts began various plans that allowed small numbers of black students access to facilities intended for white students. Against the backdrop of this crack in the wall of segregation, Jimmy Carter's exposure to politics at the state level increased dramatically. Following his election to the Georgia state senate in 1961, he focused his efforts on educational policy as a member of state senate education committees and the Governor's Commission to Improve Education. Through these activities, he gained a broader perspective on educational policy, using it as a key issue in both of his gubernatorial campaigns—the one he lost to segregationist Lester Maddox in 1966 and the one he won in 1970.

While he was governor, the NAACP returned to court to protest the meager desegregation efforts in Georgia, and other places, citing the slow pace and small numbers involved. In response, the federal courts endorsed more sweeping measures that included the use of busing. In Georgia, a federal judge answered the resistance of the Richmond County School Board (Augusta) with an order to desegregate the district through busing. In Atlanta, however, Judge Griffin Bell allowed the NAACP and the school district to reach an agreement to hire more African American administrators and teachers in exchange for busing students for racial parity. Governor Carter's reactions to these decisions—support for the local agreement in Atlanta and rejection of the court-ordered busing—reflected the national political response to the involvement of the federal court in the desegregation of schools and to later court decisions concerning equity for other groups. He believed that the laws mandating equity addressed the civil rights of minorities and that the equalization of access through the distribution of funding and services would provide for their needs. The movement of students to desegregate schools reflected an ideal that, in his opinion, was detrimental to public schooling.

As president, Carter faced a crumbling economy and many social demands from the public. Because of his belief that the federal government's fiscal responsibilities were limited by its ability to pay for them, his administration focused on rationalizing and expanding existing federal programs. Although he began new programs in energy and environmental protection, in education he advocated the equitable distribution of funding for existing compensatory programs intended to offer all groups equal educational opportunity. He also attempted to begin voluntary national standardized testing to encourage student achievement and increase accountability for teachers. His administration dropped voluntary national standardized testing from its legislative agenda, but Carter believed that such a program would increase achievement for students who were failing. For students attending institutions of higher education, he increased the amount of student loans and expanded the base to include more of the children of middle-class parents. Through these programs and the creation of the United States Department of Education, Carter believed existing federal programs could serve the needs of citizens more equitably.

After his defeat by Ronald Reagan, Carter turned his attention to the development of the Carter Center of Emory University (CCEU). Although the majority of the programs of the CCEU focused on international poverty, health, and agricultural development, the project coordinators often invited Atlanta teachers to participate in panels and curriculum development. After Atlanta won the 1996 Summer Olympics, he used the international attention that the city received to initiate The Atlanta Project (TAP), which he intended to address the conditions of the urban poor in the same manner that the CCEU concentrated on poverty in other countries. Through TAP, he began to see that education depended as much on the ability of a community to support the children living in it as on the programs implemented by the state and local educational bureaucracies. For children living in poverty, the lack of economic opportunity for their parents weighed as heavily on their shoulders as poorly furnished schools.

ORGANIZATION OF THE BOOK

Can equal opportunity and educational efficiency be reconciled or are these goals so antithetical that the achievement of one requires substantial compromise on the other? This book will explore the interaction and potential conflict between these objectives during the turbulent years following the *Brown* decision when our nation struggled to redefine its educational priorities. Because Jimmy Carter was an advocate of both, analysis of his actions as a school board member, state official, and ultimately president provides a lens through which the issues surrounding these objectives can be explored on several levels. The goal of this analysis is to better understand how educational policy evolved under Carter's leadership and how his efforts to reconcile these often conflicting priorities shaped its development. The lessons that can be learned from such an investigation are not strictly historical. The insights gleaned from this examination of Carter's development as an educational policymaker have implications for today's educational policymakers insofar as his actions and beliefs highlight many of the fundamental issues and conflicting priorities that continue to challenge efforts to reshape our schools.

The chapters of this book are arranged chronologically to follow educational policy development and Carter's development as an educational policymaker in a period of enormously complex social and political realities. Certain topics and issues appear in each chapter because of their continuing importance in the southern states and in the nation as a whole during this period, including desegregation and racial awareness, funding and school efficiency, social and racial stratification, and equal opportunity. These topics offer continuity to the narrative and the opportunity for analysis of how Carter's views changed as his understanding of the issues as well as his political influence grew.

Before the 1950s, educational experts and officials described educational opportunity in the language of scientific efficiency. The schools sorted the students by their potential talents and the needs of society.[12] Once the desegregation of the public schools loomed before southern legislators and school officials, educational opportunity acquired its own status as an educational goal. In chapter 1, Carter's experiences as a school board member in Plains, Georgia, offers a view of a local school board's response to the political resistance that ensued following the court order to desegregate. It also establishes a foundation for his interest in and attention to scientific efficiency and educational opportunity as his political career unfolded. At this level of educational policymaking, Carter believed that the efficient use of community resources was the surest road to equal opportunity. His view of resource management reflected the national movement toward the consolidation of small school districts.

Although little attention has been given to Carter's service in the state senate, his term of office began at the conclusion of southern massive resistance to desegregation when most southern states, including Georgia, passed laws reducing the state's financial support for the public schools if they were desegregated. In chapter 2, this last act of overt resistance and Carter's role in it are examined along with his participation on Governor Carl Sanders's blue-ribbon education commission to reform education in Georgia. Although desegregation is ignored in the commission's report, the document does reveal the fundamental problem of social and economic stratification in southern education in the early 1960s. In his initial exposure to state policymaking, Carter began the process of separating fiscal efficiency from social and political equal opportunity.

While the problems of high dropout rates and drastic differences in funding in the stratified southern school systems were still present when Carter became governor, he faced the additional political issue of metropolitan busing for school desegregation. Whereas the early resistance to desegregation was concentrated in the Georgia legislature, the response to busing was local, emotional, and squarely in the national spotlight. As a politician with a growing reputation for progressive thinking on racial issues, Carter's position on court-ordered busing cast doubt on his sincerity. In chapter 3, his indirect encouragement of resistance to busing and his support of the out-of-court desegregation agreement in Atlanta are analyzed within the national debate on busing.

In the 1970s, educational accountability began to appear as part of reform packages that increased school funding and services. Carter's Early Childhood Development Program and his Adequate Program for Education in Georgia (APEG) reflected this national movement as well as his belief in planning and efficiency, equal opportunity, and educational excellence. In chapter 4, these programs along with his position on access to higher education place Carter within the national movement for educational accountability and increased access to higher education. His often tense relationship with the state superintendent and the teachers' union provides different contexts for efficiency. Both the state superintendent and the teachers' union viewed teacher benefits and salary increases as the most effective use of funds, while Carter believed that the expansion of the state educational system to include kindergarten better served the people of Georgia. These different interpretations reflected two technocratic approaches to educational efficiency, one emphasizing personnel and the other programs.

As the president of the United States, Carter continued Lyndon Johnson's legacy by increasing funds for equal educational opportunity programs. He also continued his policies supporting efficiency. Chapter 5 focuses on his attempts to reorganize educational programs to increase access, which culminated in the creation of the cabinet-level Department of Education. While the establishment of the department was his most visible and political educational reform, he also added a basic education title to the Elementary and Secondary Education Act, attempted to begin voluntary national standardized testing, and increased access to higher education through loan and grant reform. Examination of his policy initiatives—both those that were successful and those that never left the planning table—provides insights into his priorities in federal educational policy.

The sixth chapter addresses Carter's continued involvement in education after his unsuccessful bid for a second term as president. Through TAP, he attempted, with mixed results, to coordinate educational, social, and economic reforms for people living in poverty in the Atlanta metropolitan area. The Carter Center of Emory University, however, represents a successful attempt to offer education as a tool for social change in an international context. While some might argue that the mission of the Carter Center is a departure from educational policy and planning, Carter has repeatedly claimed that educating both leaders and the general populace in countries where the center operates is one of its most important missions. Hence, the work of the center represents the final stage of Carter's development as an educational policymaker. It is also an example of the limitations imposed on efficiency by the traditions and needs of communities. By examining the community context rather than merely the programs offered through TAP, the relationship between efficiency and equal opportunity becomes apparent. The abandonment of communities in the name of progress caused the conditions of the urban poor in Atlanta. The reform of schools in Atlanta offered little to the students living in poverty in the city.

The implications of Carter's policies on the local, state, and federal levels and the lessons that can be learned from them are examined in the conclusion. His twin commitments to efficiency and planning on the one hand and to equal educational opportunity on the other are reflective of a larger national movement in educational policy. When these commitments came into conflict, his attempts to reconcile them reveal both his own shifting priorities and the complex social and political obstacles facing educational policymakers both then and now.

ONE

The Resistance to
Equal Opportunity and Efficiency

═══════════

IN NOVEMBER 1955, the Sumter County Grand Jury appointed Jimmy
Carter to the Sumter County Board of Education, beginning a political
career that would span twenty-six years. Although this rural area of Georgia was far from Washington, D.C., the *Brown v. Board of Education Topeka,
Kansas* (1954 and 1955) decisions had changed the mission of the board
and the state's role in education. From these decisions, which declared "segregation inherently unequal" and mandated the end of racial discrimination in public schools "with all deliberate speed," Carter learned that fear
could frustrate efficiency and that the illusion of equality could replace
equal educational opportunity. How the state and local resistance to desegregation averted his efforts to reform education in Sumter County requires
an understanding of the southern social and political milieu of the 1940s
and 1950s and the issues facing local school boards in the wake of the
Brown decision.

SEPARATE AND UNEQUAL

For most of the twentieth century, the Democratic Party was the only active
political party in the South and segregation was firmly entrenched in the
political structure of the southern states. Only whites voted in elections, and
the winner of the Democratic primary typically became governor. Among the
key campaign issues in nearly every election was white supremacy—an issue
that often paved the road to political office. As V. O. Key explains, "In its
grand outlines the politics of the South revolves around the position of the
Negro."[1] In this political environment, white politicians and educational officials dismissed the need of African Americans for an education.

Throughout the South, schools reflected the social and political environment surrounding them. In urban areas like Atlanta, African American students had access to school facilities and materials similar to those provided to white students, although seldom new or in the same quantity. In rural areas, such as Sumter County where Jimmy Carter lived, white children attended school in buildings designated for that purpose with adequate materials to support the limited curriculum the rural districts could afford. The black children, however, typically only attended school between harvest and planting seasons and went to school in community churches so that the local board could avoid providing transportation or buildings. African American teachers were often overloaded with students and just as often lacked the necessary materials to teach them.[2] Although the United States Supreme Court had justified separate facilities for black and white Americans with the "separate but equal" doctrine in *Plessy v. Ferguson* (1896), separate was the only part of the phrase most southern policymakers acknowledged—until the threat of desegregation and the desire to attract industry made equalization more attractive.

In the late 1940s, the poor conditions of the schools in Georgia concerned both the relatively small segment of the white population interested in economic growth and the even larger segment that wished to maintain segregation. Earlier in the decade, the Legal Defense Fund for the National Association for the Advancement of Colored People (NAACP) had begun a series of court cases concerning higher education and teacher pay to prove that racially segregated schools were unequal. In 1944, Gunnar Myrdal, a Swedish economist, published *An American Dilemma*, a two-volume work on the "mistreatment and evident hatred of the Negro" in the United States.[3] This work shed light on the deplorable conditions that black children and their teachers endured in their schools and their communities.

In response to the mounting pressure, the Georgia General Assembly turned to one of the tools used by proponents of efficiency and appointed a committee to survey the public schools in 1946. The survey confirmed the existence of racial and geographic differences in public school funding and recommended that the state provide the necessary assistance for the equalization of Georgia's schools. In 1949, the General Assembly passed the Minimum Foundation Program for Education (MFPE), which incorporated many of the recommendations from the survey. This legislative package distributed more state funds to poorer districts to compensate for lower local revenues. It also included raises for teachers, both black and white, a building program, transportation for all county district students, and a 180-day minimum school year. Through this educational reform legislation, the General Assembly not only addressed the needs of African American students, but also those of rural white students.[4] Such a massive equalization program, of course, required a tax increase.

With these state-funded improvements came more state supervision. In the past, when the State Board of Education had made funds available for a nine-month school year for black children, some county boards had not requested the funds because of the seasonable absences of the black children.[5] The MFPE was a way to offer both black and white children in rural areas an equal educational opportunity, but it was up to the state government to mandate equal schooling for both black and white students—and to enforce it. Unfortunately, many doubted, with good reason, the will of the state to equalize educational opportunity. For example, Richard O. Johnson, a professor of education at Atlanta University, described MFPE as a "nondiscriminatory basis for allocating state funds for education to local districts with certain guarantees that these funds would be spent on a racially nondiscriminatory basis by local school boards." Despite the nondiscriminatory design of the program, he questioned whether it could in fact "provide for the removal of the wide differentials which existed in educational opportunities between the races which had been built up by a policy of rank discrimination against Negroes."[6]

As Johnson pointed out, although state leaders used the language of equalization in MFPE, they could not so easily rectify the history of discriminatory policies. The "equal" part of "separate but equal" would not be specifically addressed until August 1949 when the NAACP of Irwin County, Georgia, and parents of black school-age children filed suit over inequality in education. The parents claimed that the white school facilities were more valuable and that white teachers received higher salaries than black teachers. The suit demanded that the school board equalize the educational facilities and materials as well as teacher salaries and benefits. Although the suit did not demand desegregation of the public schools, the governor of Georgia, Herman Talmadge, denounced it, claiming that the NAACP was attempting to place "Negro children into the nearest most convenient white schools."[7] A year later, the NAACP and 200 black students in the Atlanta Public School District filed *Aaron v. Cook*, which demanded either the equalization of schools for black children or the admission of black children to the schools traditionally reserved for white children.[8] This case, with its ultimatum to equalize educational facilities or allow desegregation, added to the urgency of funding MFPE.

Events outside of Georgia also pushed the General Assembly to increase state funding. Two Supreme Court decisions in June 1950, *Sweatt v. Painter*, which desegregated the University of Texas Law School, and *McLaurin v. Oklahoma*, which opened the University of Oklahoma graduate programs to African American students, alarmed southern segregationists.[9] Talmadge spoke for many white politicians when he responded, "As long as I am Governor, Negroes will not be admitted to white schools."[10] Despite his strong rhetoric of resistance, Talmadge used the pressures for equalization from both internal and external sources to push the legislature to raise taxes and support the equalization of schools in Georgia.

The legislative package, however, came with a price potentially higher than the necessary increased taxes. Spurred by the cracks in the wall of segregation, the General Assembly attached a condition to the appropriation bill. In reaction to *Aaron v. Cook*, the General Assembly passed legislation to cut state funding for any public school intended for white students that admitted a black student. The same consequence would occur if a black student attended one of the white institutions within the university system.[11] If the public educational institutions in Georgia could not remain segregated, then they would be closed.

By the opening of the legislative session in 1953, the idea of replacing the public school system with a private one gathered strength. In an address to both chambers of the legislature, Governor Talmadge declared that Georgians were in "grave danger" and a plan had to be prepared. The danger was the *Brown v. Board of Education Topeka, Kansas* case on the Supreme Court docket. A private school plan would be a means to maintain segregated schools in the event of a "calamitous decision."[12] Talmadge's administration began to move toward the creation of a constitutional way to fund private schools in case of desegregation. It was in this tense environment that Jimmy Carter resigned from the navy and moved his family to Plains, Georgia, for "a potentially fuller opportunity for varied public service."[13]

EQUALIZATION AND RESISTANCE

When Jimmy and Rosalynn Carter returned to Sumter County in 1953, following his tour of duty with the U.S. Navy, theirs was a stereotypical 1950s middle-class white family. They had three children and actively participated in the life of the community. Jimmy focused on building the seed business his father had started, joining community organizations like the Lions Club and the hospital planning board, and teaching Sunday School at the Plains Baptist Church. His activities were those of a young man building a business and becoming known in his community. Rosalynn managed their domestic life and eventually the bookkeeping, billing, and posting of sales for their growing businesses.[14] While her activities at the seed warehouse were not stereotypical for a 1950s housewife, they reflected the Carters' moderate views on social issues such as women's rights and race.

Jimmy Carter also differed from many of his neighbors in his approach to solving problems. As a naval officer assigned to submarines and under the command of Admiral Hyman Rickover, he routinely studied manuals and took courses to earn promotions and learn about his assignments. Through Admiral Rickover, he learned to be efficient in his work and to have high expectations for himself. He brought these experiences in efficiency and excellence home with him and used them to learn about the farming business, which had changed dramatically since he had worked with his father as a teenager. Taking courses through the county extension agency of the University of Georgia, Carter learned new farming techniques and business practices that he shared with his customers, especially those who were poor.[15]

Because of their experiences in the navy, both Jimmy and Rosalynn considered themselves moderates in their beliefs about desegregation. During Carter's tour of duty, President Harry Truman had ordered the navy and all the other armed services desegregated. Truman also called for drastic changes nationally through a host of federal initiatives, including a ban on poll taxes, the desegregation of accommodations for interstate travel, the creation of a federal civil rights commission, and legislation making lynching a federal offense.[16] The federal legislation pertaining to the armed forces allowed black servicemen to serve in the same capacity as white servicemen and, through his contact with them, Lieutenant Carter began to question the segregated social and political structure of the South.

The Carters had been in Plains less than a year when the Supreme Court handed down the *Brown* decision. Rosalynn Carter recalled,

> Jimmy was listening to the radio when the boys and I walked into the office the day of the decision. He worried about the reaction among our neighbors. "I don't know what's going to happen around here," he said. Then we watched as little knots of people began to congregate on the sidewalks, in the stores. And for some time—not only in Plains, but across the South— wherever two or more were gathered, integration was the primary and, more often than not, heated topic of conversation.[17]

Her memories of that day in May and her classification of herself and her husband as moderates on racial issues gave the impression that they supported the desegregation of the schools. However, she also recounted the social pressure they felt not to support the *Brown* decision. "There were few people with whom Jimmy and I could talk openly about the issue. I could count them on two hands—the liberals in the community." They did not consider themselves liberals at the time, but rather "realists" who knew that "desegregation was a foregone conclusion." What they wanted was to find a way to desegregate the schools "in the least harmful way" for their children.[18]

In November 1955, the county grand jury, the governing body for the county, appointed Jimmy Carter to the board of education. James "Earl" Carter Sr. had served on the board for more than ten years. The younger Carter, literally taking his father's seat, remained on the board until January 1963, when he resigned to serve in the Georgia state senate. His appointment to the school board could have thrust Carter and his family into the middle of the growing controversy over desegregation. The Sumter

County board, however, focused on the equalization of facilities for black students and ignored the issue of desegregation until the county schools desegregated in 1964.[19]

As a school board member, Carter witnessed the inequalities between black and white schools and the backlash of the white community in response to the state legislature's clumsy equalization attempts. After he joined the board, matters pertaining to educational efficiency—consolidation, planning, testing, and surveys—became more prominent on the agenda of the Sumter County Board of Education. He remained silent, however, about his opinions on desegregation. In the Georgia of the 1950s, equity consisted of equalizing facilities and expanding access to programs. While Carter served on the board, it completed a building program to upgrade the educational facilities for black students and established a classroom for white children with special needs. Yet, despite the *Brown* decision, the schools in Sumter County remained segregated.

Two events occurred soon after Carter joined the board that brought his attention to the discrimination that black children in the county district suffered. One concerned the conditions of the schools that served the black community and the other their transportation to and from school. At his second board meeting, Carter suggested that the board members visit all the schools under their supervision. According to Carter, the visits to the two high schools and three elementary schools for white children went well. The board members were proud of the achievement of the students and felt that the facilities were adequate.[20]

The schools provided for the African American children in the county, however, embarrassed the board members. W. W. Foy, the county superintendent, described the conditions at those facilities: "We had . . . five fair, and I just say 'fair,' elementary schools for [black] children in the county. And then we had about thirty-two or three, one and two teacher schools in churches."[21] The one- and two-teacher schools held in churches were "firetraps" with "potbellied heaters in the middle of the building, and on cold days, everybody would crowd up next to them."[22] Carter remembered that "classes were held in various places, including the Sunday school classrooms of black churches and even private homes." His most vivid memory of the visits was of "large teenage boys trying to sit on chairs designed for children of kindergarten age."[23] The tours stopped before the board members had seen all the sites serving African American students.

The state had approved a new building program to provide safe schools for the African American children before Carter joined the board. It provided four new elementary schools and a high school, but it placed the schools in central locations and required the county to provide buses to transport the children. Carter wrote that he "was actually a member of the county school board for several months before it dawned on [him] that white children rode buses to their schools and black children still walked to theirs!"[24] The minutes of his first meeting, however, reflected that the education committee of the county government met with the board members to discuss the transportation of black students. The legislature had funded transportation for black students for 1955, and the county committee recommended "adequate transportation be provided as early as possible."[25] Nevertheless, the board postponed making a decision on the purchase of buses until the completion of the new schools two years later.[26]

Although the board initiated planning the new elementary schools in 1953, opposition over their placement developed when construction of the buildings began. Leslie, a town about the size of Plains that had an elementary school and one of the high schools for white children, was selected as a location for one of the new elementary schools. However, once construction began "about twelve citizens" objected to the placement of the school because "the children, both white and black, would have to travel the same streets and roads in order to reach their respective schools."[27] The board members argued that the waterlines had already been placed on the property and would be expensive to move. After further discussion, the board decided to move the school "to avoid the possibility of future trouble between colored and white people in the communities."[28] Carter made the motion to notify the state about the opposition of the white citizens and the reluctance of the board "to locate the Negro school building in the wrong place so that friction might arise later."[29] The protesters from Leslie agreed to pay for moving the waterlines. Within two weeks, however, the board received notice that the state had denied its request. At the next meeting, Carter made a second motion rescinding his first one to move the elementary school.[30]

The irony of the protest was that the black and white children in rural areas often lived in close proximity. Thus, the protest may have been more about the school than about the children walking on the same roads. Although Carter's actions appear to support the prejudice of the white citizens more than the needs of the African American children under his supervision, he may have believed that the protesters from Leslie would be overruled once the township received the estimate for moving the waterlines. He and the other board members may also have wanted to simply keep civil peace. As Rosalynn Carter explained, both she and her husband sought to prevent harm to their children, and he may have believed that the black elementary schoolchildren would have borne the burden if the board had insisted on keeping the school at the planned location.

The building program continued to completion without further protest from the white residents of Sumter County, but did not succeed in creating equal facilities for the black population. The board built a high school for the black students near the county seat of Americus and consolidated the many one- and two-teacher schools into four buildings spread throughout the county, but the number of students per elementary school classroom was almost double that of the white schools. Furthermore, the new schools were furnished with used materials handed down from the schools for white children.[31]

While the board pursued the building program, it also addressed requirements of students with special needs. None of the districts surrounding Sumter County had a special education classroom and County Superintendent W. W. Foy believed it was important to serve this population of students. The discussion that led to the establishment of the classroom for exceptional children centered on the personal memories of the board members. Most remembered that older boys who were "slow" had started the fires in the morning and cleaned the erasers. Because these boys could not perform academic tasks on the level of their peers, teachers assigned them menial chores. Foy believed that the board needed to create a special class for these students so that they could be productive once they left school.[32]

The main obstacle to establishing the class was that a special education teacher was beyond the number of teachers allotted by the state. To designate a special education classroom and hire a teacher, the board would have to pay for it out of local funds. Carter supported Foy's proposal and, on May 1, 1956, made a motion for the "use of a classroom . . . for a teacher of exceptional children, if it is not needed for the regular school program."[33] Although the board had to use local funds for the extra teacher, Foy believed that Carter's sense of fairness brought his support for the classroom. His sense of fairness, however, was limited. The board made no effort to use local funds to establish a classroom for exceptional black students.

As the board addressed equal educational opportunity by building schools and creating classes for students ignored in the past, the language of scientific management began to appear in its minutes. From 1957 on, terms like intelligence tests, standards, studies, and surveys appeared with increasing frequency. These topics were also discussed in the *School Board Journal*, which the board members had access to as members of the American School Board Association. In July 1957, the board requested that Superintendent Foy "investigate the possibility of a testing program for the schools."[34] Four months later, the board voted to purchase "IQ Tests . . . as a beginning for a county wide testing program."[35] The following year, Foy was "instructed to put into effect a complete placement testing program during the coming school year for all grades from the 4th grade up in all county schools."[36] To support the use of the tests, Carter made a motion to pay the expenses for five teachers, one from each school, to attend a workshop on testing in Macon, Georgia.[37] At the time of his motion, there were ten schools in Sumter County, three elementary and two high schools for white students, and four elementary and one high school for black students. It is likely that only white teachers attended the workshop.

In the summer of 1958, the board changed the standards for promotion in the county schools and the grading scale to raise academic standards. For elementary grade promotion (grades 1–8), students could only have one failing grade unless the student had already repeated the grade. In those cases, the teacher might "advance the pupil to the next grade if the teacher believes it to be the best interest of the pupil; whether or not the pupil passes the required work."[38] High school standards specified the number of units for promotion and graduation. As with the elementary students, after a student had spent a year in the same grade, the principal had the discretion to advance the student.

The grading scale for fourth through twelfth grades had been a ten-point scale with 59 percent representing a failing grade; the new standards established a seven-point scale: A = 100–93, B = 92–85, C = 84–77, D = 76–70, E = 69–65 with 64 and below considered failing. The E grade was a failing grade with the privilege of making up examinations at the discretion of the teacher.[39] By changing the scale, the board could claim that it had raised academic standards without additional costs or changes in teaching methods or curriculum. Of course, the burden for meeting these new standards fell completely on the students.

Nationally, the debates in education focused on the threat of the Soviet Union and its space program. After the launch of the Soviet Union's satellite Sputnik in 1957, Congress passed the National Defense Education Act (NDEA) to support instruction in science and mathematics. In rural Georgia, NDEA meant that districts could apply for federal grants to purchase laboratory equipment to update their curriculum. The Sumter County high schools offered only business math, algebra I and II, and plane geometry. Science courses were limited to general science, biology, chemistry, and physics. The biology and chemistry labs were substandard in the high schools for white students and unfurnished in the new high school for black students.[40] In its discussion of the grants, the board decided to apply for $1,500 and split it between the high school for black students and the two for white students. With approval from the state department of education to use capital funds to match the federal monies, they applied for funds to purchase science equipment.[41]

Once the funds were awarded, the board decided to use the majority of the $1,500 in the two high schools for white students and to apply for more funds for the high school for black students. Despite the funding acquired under NDEA, the high schools for white students still could not offer the higher level science and mathematics courses that had become the norm in larger urban high schools. The inability of the board to provide the advanced courses for the white students, much less laboratory equipment for the black students, began to convince Jimmy Carter that the county needed to consolidate its school system with that of the wealthier city, Americus. Before the two boards could pursue a merger, however, resistance to desegregation in the area substantially increased and created new barriers for this act of administrative efficiency.

Resistance to the *Brown* decision took the form of private school amendments in many southern states. Georgia's version became law six months after the *Brown* decision, when the Georgia legislature passed bills that would close the public schools in the case of desegregation. Following what he believed to be the leadership of then Senator Herman Talmadge, gubernatorial candidate Ernest Vandiver pledged, "Neither my child nor yours will ever attend an integrated school during my administration—no, not one."[42] His statement was in response to the continuing desegregation case, *Aaron v. Cook*, that challenged the segregated status of the Atlanta school district.[43] After Vandiver won the election, Senator Hermann Talmadge summoned the governor-elect to his home in Lovejoy, Georgia. There in the presence of several black community leaders, Talmadge informed Vandiver that he "would be responsible for desegregating the public schools."[44] Although he had promised white Georgians that the schools would remain segregated, Vandiver now was responsible for finding a peaceful means to accomplish desegregation.

His opportunity to fulfill Talmadge's charge came in the form of a court order for the Atlanta Board of Education to submit a desegregation plan by the end of January 1960. Vandiver called for the legislature to create a citizens commission to hold hearings in all ten congressional districts to allow citizens to voice their opinions on desegregation. He intended the commission to accomplish two things: to allow the public "to blow off the steam of their frustrations" and "to carefully study their alternatives."[45] John Sibley, a prominent Atlanta attorney, agreed to serve as the chair of the commission, which was later known by his name. Sibley interpreted his charge as asking white Georgians (although black Georgians also testified) to decide how much, if any, desegregation of the public schools was acceptable. Very deliberately, Sibley focused his questions on two options: to allow local school boards to decide whether to desegregate on a limited basis or to maintain segregation even if the public schools had to be closed. On March 3, 1960, the commission held its first hearing in Americus, near the Carters' home in Plains. Sibley began here because of the large African American population and the potential for white resistance. All of those who spoke at the hearing supported the continuation of segregation, even if it meant closing the public schools.[46]

Jimmy and Rosalynn Carter attended the hearing and heard their neighbors support the closing of the public schools. Although he was a member of the Sumter County Board of Education, he was silent at the hearing. Neither Jimmy nor Rosalynn Carter explained their silence in their memoirs, but it may have been that he was not invited to speak or that he disagreed with the majority of his neighbors. Whatever the reason, he did not speak at the hearing, and the Sumter County School Board remained silent in its minutes on the issue of segregation and desegregation.[47]

The Sibley Commission continued its meetings around the state. The testimony at each one mirrored the percentage of the black population in that area: where black citizens were the majority, the whites who spoke at the hearings supported segregation at any cost, and where white citizens were the majority, the white speakers supported local desegregation decisions. The majority report issued at the end of the hearings favored changing state laws to allow each school district to decide how it would cope with desegregation. The commission also released a minority report, which received very little press, supporting the continuation of segregation and the Private School Amendment, even if it meant closing the public schools. After these reports were released, the federal judge presiding over *Aaron v. Cook* issued an order for the desegregation of the Atlanta public schools to begin in May 1961.[48]

Three months after the Sibley Commission held its first hearing in Americus, Jimmy Carter became the chair of the Sumter County School Board, although he was the youngest and probably the most moderate member. This position did little to encourage Carter to voice his private feelings about the desegregation of the schools. The unanimity in the testimony during the hearings told him the sentiments of his neighbors.

At the first meeting he chaired, Carter faced a potentially explosive situation. At the meeting the month before, the board decided not to renew the contract of William Powell, an African American math teacher, because they had received a report from the State Security Office that he participated "in certain meetings and activities undesirable to [the] board and community," but had tabled further discussion until it had "complete information on him."[49] The evidence presented was a "report and a picture of a colored woman . . . from the State Security Office." The issue was whether Powell had associated with members of NAACP or not. At the next meeting, which Carter chaired, the board decided that Powell was innocent of the charges and renewed his contract "upon the recommendation of the principal."[50] Because of the involvement of the State Security Office and the heightened community awareness from the Sibley Commission hearings, the board faced few repercussions from dismissing Powell, but could have faced an investigation for renewing his contract in the tense political climate of the times.

In its resistance to desegregation, the governor's office had created the State Security Office to investigate potentially subversive organizations and individuals, bypassing the official investigative offices of the state. At the top of the State Security Office's list was the NAACP. During the 1950s, the attorney general of Georgia had investigated the state branch of the NAACP as a subversive organization.[51] Although no charges were brought, many white community leaders in Georgia (and elsewhere) viewed the NAACP, and other organizations that promoted the integration of the schools, as subversive. The charges against Powell were vague, but both black and white teachers understood that membership in or even open sympathy with organizations like the NAACP could cost them their jobs.[52]

RESISTANCE TO EFFICIENCY

Increasing services to the Sumter County students was the focus of Carter's leadership of the board. In preparation, he read reports written by John Gardner, president of the Carnegie Corporation, and James B. Conant, former president of Harvard University, on improving American high schools. Gardner published reports in 1958 and 1960, which addressed excellence and equity in education.[53] In the second study, *Excellence*, he asserted that the United States needed talented and motivated students to meet future social, political, and economic demands. The sorting of these students in a democracy, however, had to be tempered by the necessary balance between excellence in achievement and equality of opportunity. In his description of the barriers to equal opportunity, Gardner explained, "Many bright young people do not continue their schooling; others are ill-trained. Too high a proportion of Negro children grow up in circumstances which are such as to smother talent rather than to nourish it. We make wholly inadequate use of the talents of women in our society."[54] For the United States to reach excellence, these injustices had to be rectified.

James B. Conant's study, also sponsored by the Carnegie Corporation, supported the creation of comprehensive high schools through the consolidation of schools of less than 1,000 students, or with fewer than 100 students in the senior class, to support a broader curriculum and more services. He also suggested a standard curriculum for all students and advanced classes in science, mathematics, and foreign languages for talented ones—both boys and girls.[55] The two high schools for white students in Sumter County had around 411 students combined, and the city high school had around 600 students.[56] The only way that the county white students could have the curriculum suggested by Conant and the equality of opportunity Gardner proposed would be to combine the two districts.

Over the next two years, the state department of education did two surveys of the county to promote the consolidation of county and city districts. Outside events, however, complicated the issue of consolidation; as the two boards pushed for a single high school for white students, desegregation became a reality in Georgia. These events would intertwine, much to Carter's surprise, resulting in the failure of measures designed to expand the services available to the white students across Sumter County.

The Georgia Department of Education completed the first survey, which was of only the county district, in late 1960. At a special meeting of the board, Chairman Carter explained the results of the survey to the principals of the white schools. The state department of education recommended the consolidation of the two high schools for white students. The projected school population was 425 students with fifteen to eighteen classrooms and an expanded curriculum that included electives.[57] He stressed that the board intended to build the high school to offer more classes to the students in the county, not to move it toward desegregation. However, the ability of the county to support the construction of the new high school was in question. At the next board meeting, the members decided to discuss the recommendations of the county survey with the Americus board.[58]

Carter chaired the joint meeting and a representative of each board presented the existing conditions of his district. Local taxes only supported 12 percent of the funding for the Sumter County schools, while 24 to 25 percent of Americus school funding came from local taxes. The city district was overloaded with 370 students more than it could accommodate, and it needed thirteen more classrooms to adequately house them. Sumter County suffered from the opposite problem. Only 411 students attended the two high schools for white students. The small student body divided into two schools prevented the board from providing many electives or curriculum alternatives for students. Because state funding was based on Average Daily Attendance (ADA), the more students were dispersed around the county, the fewer teachers the county district could afford to hire. The solution to the problems that both the city and the county districts faced was to consolidate the districts and construct a single high school for white students. In anticipation of the decision, the city superintendent had requested a second survey from the state department of education that would include both the county and the city districts to establish the "best type of system for the county as a whole."[59] While the survey would include many numbers about the students and the existing schools, it would omit the prevailing political climate in Georgia and the opposition of the county residents.

As Carter led the county and city districts in discussions about increasing services through consolidation, the desegregation of the public schools in Georgia became a reality. Before the 1961 session of the General Assembly met in January, a state representative called for the repeal of the Private School Amendment that would close the public schools if desegregation occurred. His proposal supported the Sibley Commission's majority report by creating a freedom of choice plan alongside the existing tuition grants for private schools to allow parents to choose the school that their children would attend in districts where a final court order demanded desegregation.[60] It would also keep the Atlanta public schools open after the implementation of the desegregation order in May 1961.

Within a week of the publication of the proposal, the state's laws closing the public schools in case of court-ordered desegregation were challenged at the University of Georgia. On January 9, the Sumter County newspaper, the

Americus Times Recorder, carried the story that U.S. District Judge William A. Bootle granted Charlayne E. Hunter and Hamilton E. Holmes entrance to the state's flagship university. Governor Vandiver knew that the 1958 laws passed supporting the Private School Amendment dictated that he close the University of Georgia, and he did. At the same time, the state attorney's office requested a stay of execution for the order, which Bootle granted. The Fifth Circuit judge, however, overruled the stay. Before the Georgia attorney general could get to Washington, D.C., to plead the case, the United States Supreme Court ordered Hunter and Holmes admitted to the University of Georgia. Riots at the university caused the administration to suspend the two black students on Wednesday, January 11. The next day, Bootle ordered them back at the university by the following Monday.[61]

In response to these court decisions, the Georgia General Assembly struck down the laws that closed the public schools or denied them funding if they desegregated. It did not, however, repeal the legislation that allowed the state to dispose of public school property if the federal courts ordered desegregation. To maintain at least the image of resistance to desegregation, Vandiver requested that the legislature replace the repealed laws with legislation to allow freedom of choice plans and preserve the tuition grants for children to go to private schools.[62] Thus, while the immediate threat to the public schools had ended, the ability of the state to suspend public education in favor of private schools remained.

These events served as the background for the meeting of the second survey committee with the superintendents of Sumter County and Americus school districts. The committee and its subcommittees focused on the curriculum offered by the two districts and its costs. After the subcommittees submitted their reports on March 10, the reviewing committee planned to give its recommendations to the two boards at a meeting on March 28. On the same day, the two boards scheduled a public meeting at the local two-year college, Southwestern College, to discuss the reviewing committee's recommendations.[63]

At the meeting on March 28, the two boards accepted the reviewing committee's report and that evening presented the findings to an audience of about 600 at the local college. With Jimmy Carter acting as the moderator, the meeting began with a statement by the coordinator of the survey that "the purpose of the reports . . . centered on the combining of the schools and the approach used was to consider every advantage of the student."[64] The major benefit of the consolidation for the reviewing committee was a comprehensive high school for around 1,000 students that would

> First . . . give a good general education to every child in the county. Second . . . provide good elective courses for those who would want to use their education on finishing high school to go into a selective field. Third, satisfy all the needs for those students wishing to attend the college of their choice.[65]

The survey team and the board members realized that the rural residents of the county were the largest and strongest obstacle to the consolidation of the two districts. To reassure the county residents, one committee member, Paul Carroll, dean at Georgia Southern College, assured the audience, "Whether such a program [was] put into operation in Sumter County depended on the belief of the people as to the need for such a program."[66] Addressing the potential resistance, the committee and the board members focused their remarks on curriculum opportunities, the steps involved in the merger, and the administration in the consolidated district.

The administrative structure had prevented the merger of the two districts in 1953 when the county board had begun to plan the new schools for the African American children. Before embarking on such an ambitious project, the county had proposed a consolidation plan to the city district that included a seven-member board with three members from State House of Representatives District 27, which encompassed Americus and parts of the Sumter County school district, and four members from outside of District 27, which included the remaining areas of Sumter County. Because this structure favored the county district residents and did not guarantee that any member would actually be from Americus, the city board had rejected the plan and the idea of consolidation.[67]

The present reviewing board also recommended a seven-member board, but suggested that the Americus City Council appoint two members, the Sumter County Commissioners appoint two members, and the county grand jury appoint two members. The appointed members would select the seventh member. This organizational structure gave the city and the county the potential for equal representation because the county grand jury consisted of residents of both the city and the county. The board would appoint the superintendent of the consolidated district. To head off criticisms, the coordinator of the survey told the audience, "A board of education should represent no one but the children of the county."[68]

After the reviewing committee completed its presentation, Carter listed the problems that confronted the city and county districts. These consisted of "crowded substandard classrooms; insufficient library, science and athletic facilities; inadequate science, music, art, foreign language and vocational courses; small classes causing two grades per teacher, and duplication of facilities."[69] He explained to the audience that the current arrangement to relieve the overcrowding in the city and the empty classrooms in the county through an exchange of students was merely a short-term solution to the problems. The long-term solution, in his opinion, was consolidation. He assured the audience that the county board would hold local meetings to discuss the procedures and that many steps were necessary before the merger happened: approval by both boards, the legislature, and the residents of the Americus and Sumter County districts.

The questions asked by the audience reflected their concerns. The first one reported by the *Americus Times Recorder* was whether the new high school would be integrated. Carter confirmed that the new high school was for white students only. Others expressed their fear that the city would dominate the new district to the detriment of the county parents and students. In their answers to the questions, the reviewing committee stressed the need for more classrooms and programs, but the audience concerned itself with the loss of influence and local community. By the end of the meeting, it was clear that the majority of those who asked questions opposed consolidation.[70] During the following months, this opposition grew in the county.

In their attempt to persuade the residents of the county, the board followed a strategy similar to one described by C. O. Fitzwater in a 1957 *American School Board Journal* article. Fitzwater explained that the foundation for successful consolidation was legislation from the state mandating the consolidation of small school districts because of the state's responsibility for funding and building construction in the created districts. Local leadership was important as well. Grassroots opinion determined the success or failure of any consolidation, even with supporting legislation. Fitzwater suggested the creation of reorganization committees to plan the new district and procedures for consolidation. Studies of the current conditions of the schools and the needs of the students were vital because they would shape all of the planning and could be used to gain public support for the proposed consolidation. Public meetings and a newspaper campaign would help keep the public informed of the efforts of the organizers and would increase local support.[71]

There was little leadership for district consolidation from the state level in Georgia; therefore, the school boards found themselves alone in leading the change. As outlined in Fitzwater's article, the boards had requested surveys of the county and city educational services and the needed improvements. They had presented the findings of the survey at a public meeting and followed it with smaller meetings to present the advantages and disadvantages of merging the two systems. Less than a month before the election, they began a newspaper campaign to inform the public of all the issues and to convince the county and city voters that approval of the consolidation of the two districts was in the best interest of the students.[72]

Prior to the election on July 18, Carter actively campaigned for the consolidation of the districts, making many appearances at civic clubs and writing a series of articles for the *Americus Times Recorder*. In a speech at the Americus Kiwanis Club, he explained why both boards had approved the merger unanimously. He pointed out that the population of the county was decreasing and that the population of Americus was increasing. Because the state appropriated school funds on the basis of the number students regularly attending each school, the Americus school district received more

funding than the county district. These demographic trends and the necessity to expand curriculum were the reasons that the county board supported
the merger.[73]

In his analysis of the opposition to the merger, Carter acknowledged
their sincerity and stated that he would address their main arguments. The
first was a desire to preserve the status quo of small schools and the close relationship between teachers, students, and parents. While he expressed his
understanding of this reservation by the parents, he ignored the relationship
among the participants in schooling in his answer. Instead, he pointed out
that the larger school would offer a broader curriculum and other programs
for students. Second, he addressed those who claimed that the loss of the high
schools would hurt businesses in Leslie and Plains (the towns with the two
county high schools for white students) by pointing out that the losses would
be short-term ones. In the long run, the larger, centralized high school would
benefit all the businesses in the towns. How a larger school in one part of the
county would benefit small businesses located elsewhere he neglected to
explain. Although he had stated that he would address the opposition to the
merger, the focus of the rest of his speech was that both boards believed that
the time for the merger was before either district began expensive building
programs alone.[74]

The week before the election, the *Americus Times Recorder* began a
series of articles written by Carter explaining why the school systems
should merge, how the new system would be run, the cost of the system,
the arguments of the proponents, and those of opponents.[75] He began by
repeating the financial reasons for the merger that he had explained to the
Kiwanis Club, but he gave many more details about the consequences of
the decreased funding for the county residents. Through the construction
of two high schools, the city and the county districts would duplicate services, but the county, with its decreasing population, would have far less
support from the state than the growing city. In addition, the Sumter
County residents would have to pay the majority of the cost for the new
high school from local funds and a bond issue. Finally, even without the
merger, the necessary construction of a single high school for the county
students would still remove the high schools from Plains and Leslie, which
would then suffer both the problems of losing the high schools and the
burden of the added costs.[76]

On July 13, he addressed what he referred to as the "reasonable" arguments against the merger. Repeating the statements of the state department
of education's reviewing committee, he acknowledged that the conversion
into a single district would not be easy, but it could be done through the
"combined efforts of school teachers and officials, the Board of Education,
PTA groups and the people of the county." The arguments that teachers and
students have a closer relationship in a smaller school and that larger schools

have more discipline problems were again left unanswered. Instead, he pointed out that special programs could be created for "problem" students to keep them "better satisfied in school and less restless and mischievous." After pointing out that the curriculum would be expanded to address the needs of problem students, he addressed the emotional opposition from the rural communities that would lose their high schools. He viewed their resistance to the idea of the merger as "real and justifiable" and went so far as to say, "no one should be criticized for being interested in his local school and wanting his children to be educated near home."[77] After his acknowledgment that his neighbors' opposition to the merger was reasonable, he returned to his theme of the advantages of the consolidated district.

In the last article of the series, Carter addressed the ability of the new consolidated district to expand the curriculum offerings and services for the county students. The curricular changes he presented corresponded to those suggested by James Conant for a comprehensive high school. Through the use of technology, tape recordings and records, the foreign languages offered would increase from only one year of Latin to two years of Latin, four years of Spanish, and four years of French. The curriculum for mathematics and science also included advanced courses. Through these additional offerings in the school, students would have individualized programs in academics that included electives in advanced work for college preparation or vocational classes for employment after graduation.[78]

Carter did not quiet the opponents of consolidation with his articles. The day before the election, Sumter County Citizens Opposed to School Consolidation, led by his cousin Hugh Carter, ran an advertisement in the local paper listing eight disadvantages to the merger. The most significant objections were the appointment of the superintendent by the board, the increased possibility of desegregation, a heavier tax burden for county residents, loss of the close student–teacher relationship, and the potential of a higher dropout rate.[79] The first three may have been the unreasonable arguments that Jimmy Carter had ignored, but with the imminent desegregation of the Atlanta public schools, the opponents of consolidation appealed to the fears and prejudices of the white rural residents.

On July 18, the voters in the rural areas and Americus went to the polls to decide whether the two districts would merge. The city residents voted overwhelming to merge the districts, 786 to 172. The rural residents rejected the proposal narrowly, 502 for the merger and 586 against it. As expected, the major centers of opposition were the towns of Plains and Leslie, the locations of the two county high schools. In Leslie, only 52 voters approved the merger while 213 voted against it. In Plains, where the Carters lived, consolidation met the same fate—with only 33 approving the merger and 201 opposing it.[80]

When asked for a comment, Carter's response was surprisingly accepting of the defeat. He told the reporters,

Although many of our citizens are disappointed, we believe that the interest of everyone in better schools has been awakened, and that through
democratic procedures and with the cooperation and good will of all our
communities, many improvements can still be made.[81]

He later claimed that the rural residents of Sumter County defeated the proposed merger because of their belief that the change was the first step toward
the desegregation of the local schools.[82]

Other explanations were that the smaller communities feared the domi-
nation of the larger city of Americus and that the high schools were the center of these small communities. If all the decisions were made for Americus,
then the children from the county communities would be lost in the district.[83]
Superintendent Foy explained that he believed that the rural communities
opposed it because those "who had the voting power could not accept the loss
of their schools, which at that time were larger than they had ever been. Yet,
[they were] too small to meet the demands of the recommendations for the
standards of the state."[84]

All of the interpretations of the defeat are plausible, but what was not
discussed in the newspaper articles or at the reported meetings was that many
of the facilities for African American students were already consolidated and
the county high school for black students was near Americus. Those opposed
to desegregation saw the consolidation of the schools for white students as
the first step toward the desegregation of the schools. Finally, the night after
the election, the Carters found a crude, hand-painted sign on the door of
their warehouse that said, "Coons and Carters Go Together."[85] Thus, the
political and social climate in Georgia in 1961 and his own experiences supported Carter's explanation that the fear of desegregation was the primary
reason the rural residents rejected consolidation.

While the loss of the consolidation election was a "stinging disappointment" for Carter, he found the campaign exciting.[86] The voters defeated the
idea to make the school system more efficient, but he remained chair of the
board after the election. For the next year, he turned his attention to the
African American students of the county where he faced increasing frustrations in his leadership toward a more efficient school district because of the
tradition of "rank discrimination against Negroes."[87]

In rural areas throughout the South, parents and their employers pulled
black children out of school in the spring and the fall to work in the fields.
Landowners in Sumter County followed this tradition, and before the high
school had been built in 1958, the majority of black teenagers had dropped out
of the school after the eighth grade. After the construction of the high school
for African American students, the board realized that this tradition compromised the funding for schooling in the county. Because the state allotted funding and teachers to the districts based on the Average Daily Attendance of

students, the county's funding suffered when the African American students dropped out or skipped school to work. While the board members understood that most African American families in the county depended on agricultural work to support their families, the members also knew that the students' absences cost the entire county state funds.

In February, Carter suggested that the board "write a letter to [each] landowner, explaining to him how much it cost us each day a student is not in school, and ask for his cooperation in getting the students who live on his place to attend school."[88] He understood the power that the landowners had over the sharecroppers and their families from his own businesses and from observing the relationship between his father and the tenant farmers when he was a boy. Because of the consolidation campaign the prior year, the board could appeal to the landowners' knowledge of the financial needs of the county school system. At the March meeting, Foy reported to the board that since the letters had been sent to the landowners, attendance for African American children had improved.[89]

This improvement was only temporary. The following fall semester, Foy reported that enrollment in the county schools had dropped, but that "the enrollment will climb considerably . . . after crops have been harvested since colored pupils have not yet enrolled."[90] More than letters were necessary to challenge the neglect of the educational needs of the African American children in the county.

In addition to the seasonal absences of the African American children, both the county's high school and the junior high school in Americus that served all the African American students lacked accreditation. This lapse in equality in the educational facilities left the Sumter County school district open to legal action. The major obstacles to accreditation were the condition of the high school's library and the lack of classroom space, library books, and a gym at the junior high. For the high school to gain accreditation, the city board had to correct these deficiencies at the junior high. Although the districts remained separate, the city board wanted the county to contribute financially for the improvements, in particular for the new gym. The county board sympathized with the city board's financial problems, but for such a large project, it had to issue bonds, which could only be used on county school district property. The location of the school on city property prohibited the use of county funds for the construction of the gym.

The county, however, could participate with the city in construction of a recreational center that included a football field, baseball field, and a field house at the high school that black students attended. These facilities would be used by the high school during the school year and by the Recreation Commission on the weekends and in the summer.[91] The joint effort gave the black students the facilities needed at the high school, and the city the opportunity to have a recreation area for black citizens. The construction of these facilities supported the idea of separate but equal and their very existence denied the right of the black citizens of Americus and the nearby county areas to use the same city facilities as the white citizens.

Within a month of the decision to participate in the recreational center building project, Carter decided to enter the race for the state senate. Because the structure of the state senate had changed and the Democratic candidate for governor, Carl Sanders, had pledged to support education and other social welfare services in the state, Carter believed that he could accomplish more on the state level than he could as the chair of the Sumter County Board of Education. In December 1962, Jimmy Carter resigned from the Sumter County Board of Education to take his seat in the Georgia state senate.

CONCLUSION

From the beginning of his service on the board of education, Carter witnessed the efforts of the state government to counter the *Brown* decisions and their implementation on the county level. The building program for schools for African American children that the county board intended to derail desegregation fell far short of equality. The buildings may have been new, but the board used secondhand furnishings and neglected to equip the science laboratory or stock the library with books. Equalization of facilities between black and white students was fundamentally a political ploy to maintain white supremacy, and the board members, including Carter, knew it.

The failure of the consolidation of the county and city districts demonstrated the resistance to scientific management by the residents of the small towns who wished to keep their high schools despite the costs to themselves and, according to those who supported it, to the students. Carter also believed that the fundamental reason that the rural residents opposed the merger was the belief that the consolidated high school was the first step toward integration. Thus, he asserted that selfish, local interests and the fear of desegregation, which he considered a foregone conclusion, blocked the board's efforts to improve educational services through the more efficient consolidated district.

Finally, Carter saw that the economic pressures on the impoverished agricultural workers in his district often denied them and their children access to even the limited schooling provided by the county. In the case of Sumter County, the poor were usually African American tenant farmers, who believed that they had to keep their children out of school during the spring and fall farming seasons for the family to survive. The willingness of landowners to keep African American students out of school to work reflected the negative attitude many of them had toward the education of black children. Carter acknowledged this attitude when he appealed to the landowners to send their young, black workers to school because the district lost state funding when they were absent. He did not address such issues as fairness or the ability of an educated adult to better him- or herself in his letter to them.

Georgia and the other southern states, however, were changing. Segregation was still supported by the majority of politicians and white voters, but those interested in economic expansion were growing in numbers. It was in this climate of transition that Jimmy Carter began his terms in the Georgia state senate, where he would learn about the educational needs of the entire state and would witness the conflict within the southern states as equal educational opportunity became a national goal.

TWO

The End of Open Resistance

IN 1962, JOHN F. KENNEDY was president of the United States and the civil rights movement was gaining momentum. The Freedom Riders, black and white college students who mounted an organized challenge to segregation in public transportation, were met with violence in Birmingham and Montgomery, Alabama. The federal Interstate Commerce Commission responded by banning segregation in all interstate travel facilities. In Georgia, there were marches in Albany that resulted in beatings and arrests; in Mississippi, white students rioted to prevent James Meredith from enrolling in Ole Miss. Although the students killed two men and wounded many federal marshals and Mississippi highway patrol officers, Meredith enrolled unharmed after the violence abated.[1] These actions signaled the beginning of desegregated facilities in the southern states. Most of the school districts in the southern states, however, remained segregated, and state legislatures, including Georgia's, continued to support private schools by providing tuition grants, or vouchers, to parents who wished to remove their children from court-ordered desegregated public schools.

In Georgia's gubernatorial election that year, a majority of voters cast their ballots for moderate Carl Sanders, who promised to reorganize state government, increase education and mental health budgets, remove the highway department from politics, establish a fair election code, and provide more effective rehabilitation for criminals.[2] Sanders offered a new brand of politician to Georgia voters; he pledged to support public education for economic development rather than destroy it for racial segregaton.[3] In that same election, the voters in the newly formed Fourteenth District elected Jimmy Carter to the Georgia state senate.

Many years after his first campaign for statewide office, Carter asserted that education was his major concern when he decided to run for the Georgia state senate.[4] Based on his experiences as the chair of the Sumter County

Board of Education, he had developed a local perspective on the educational issues facing the state; in the upper house of the Georgia legislature, he learned to look at education from a state perspective. In this environment, he heard different interpretations of Georgia's educational needs and various proposals for addressing those needs. He also broadened his understanding of efficiency and equality and developed a new appreciation for the relationship between the two. Through his work on the Senate Education Committee and on Governor Carl Sanders's Commission to Improve Education, he observed the interplay between the state and federal government in matters pertaining to educational policy, developing a new perspective that would ultimately shape the educational policies he advocated as governor of Georgia and later as president.

In his efforts to improve educational quality in Sumter County, Carter had become increasingly frustrated by both the willingness of the state legislature to sacrifice public education in its resistance to desegregation and the narrow self-interest of the county's rural residents. In 1961, two events served as catalysts for his decision to run for the state senate. First, Carl Sanders, who had at that point won the Democratic primary, seemed to have progressive ideas and had pledged to improve education in Georgia. By becoming a state senator, Carter felt that he could help shape educational policies in the new administration.[5] Second, a federal court had ordered the reapportionment of the Georgia state senate districts, changing the political structure of the state government.

Prior to 1962, each Senate district consisted of three counties, which rotated electing a state senator for a two-year term every four years. As a result of this rotation, state senators seldom served a second term and honorary politicians predominated in the upper house. This process kept the Senate politically weak because there was little continuity in leadership—the hallmark of legislative power. The reapportionment of the state upper house created districts based on population rather than geography and mandated that all voters in the district vote in each election, making multiple terms (and hence seniority) possible. Because of the changes to the districts and the election process, the courts ordered another primary election for October 16. With the new structure in place, Carter announced his candidacy on October 1, 1962, his thirty-eighth birthday.[6] Coincidentally, this was also the day that James Meredith enrolled in the University of Mississippi. Because of the national visibility garnered by the riots at Ole Miss and Meredith's enrollment, Carter's announcement of his candidacy was effectively buried in the local paper.

In the sixteen-day campaign that ensued, Carter pledged to support the elevation of Georgia Southwestern College in Americus from two-year junior college to four-year senior college status. Because there was not a four-year college within a hundred miles, students who earned their associates' degrees at Georgia Southwestern had to leave the area to complete their bachelor's degrees. In addition to his promise to expand higher education opportunities, Carter felt the need to justify his campaign because his opponent had already won the first Democratic primary, only to have to run again because of reapportionment. Carter did so by noting the addition of counties to the new district and the court's decision enabling all registered voters in the new district to participate in the election.[7] In his opinion, all the voters in the new district deserved to exercise their right to select their senator.

During the race for the state senate seat, Carter began to develop his campaign style of meeting as many voters as possible. His leadership in civic activities and his training in the Baptist tradition of witnessing about his faith to people in their homes helped him to overcome the awkwardness of meeting new people and asking for their vote. His leadership of the consolidation campaign also paid off in Americus, where voters had overwhelmingly favored the merger of the two school districts. In the rural areas, the consolidation campaign hurt him, but his activities in the seed business and as a landowner helped gain him support there as well. By the day of the primary, he felt confident that he could win the primary, which would mean that he would win the election in November.

Although Carter won the second Democratic primary, he nearly lost it due to corrupt state politics. In one county, the local political boss blatantly coerced voters into casting their ballots for Carter's opponent, and then proceeded to stuff the ballot box—a plain cardboard box with a hole cut in the top of it. Following a recount, Carter was declared the winner in the primary, but was then forced to appeal to the winner of the gubernatorial primary, Carl Sanders, and other newly elected state officials to have his name put on the ballot in the November election. This issue remained unresolved until after midnight on the night before the statewide election on November 6, when a judge demanded that the voters write-in their choice for the office on the ballot. Despite these obstacles, Carter won the election. At the next meeting of the Sumter County Board of Education, he tendered his resignation to assume his hard-won seat in the Georgia state senate.[8]

THE LAST GASP OF LEGISLATIVE RESISTANCE

Before the legislative session began in 1963, Carter went to Atlanta to ask lieutenant governor-elect Peter Zack Geer, who was responsible for committee assignments in the Senate, to place him on the education committee, any committees that dealt with the university system, and the agricultural committee. Carter's request surprised Geer because few new senators had shown any interest in education. Furthermore, in the tense political climate surrounding desegregation, membership on an education committee had the potential to destroy a budding political career. When the federal courts had desegregated both the University of Georgia and the Atlanta Public School District the year before, many supporters of segregation believed that the state's politicians had surrendered to desegregation because the University of Georgia had remained open following the enrollment of Charlayne Hunter and Hamilton Holmes.[9] Continued federal court activities and the growing militancy in the civil rights movement promised continuing controversy in the schools.

Despite the risks involved, Carter's desire to serve on the education committee outweighed his fear of political danger. From his experiences on the Sumter County board, he understood the problems facing the rural school districts and he felt that the tuition grants for private schools legislation should be repealed. He had seen the results of inadequate funding for public education, especially in the rural counties. Allowing funding to move from the public schools to private schools would mean even less for the children in the public schools. For him, the appropriate use of tax monies was to support the consolidation of small school districts, which was expensive, but offered more to students and taxpayers alike. His interest in higher education stemmed from his campaign promise to make Georgia Southwestern College a four-year institution.[10]

Geer had no problem putting Carter on the education committee, but his request for a seat on a committee for higher education was more difficult to grant because none existed. Encouraged by his success in getting appointed to the education committee, Carter asked if a subcommittee for higher education could be established. Geer contacted the chair of the education committee, who agreed to form the Subcommittee on Higher Education with Carter as its chair. Because of the traditional weakness of the Senate, the creation of this new subcommittee would have been virtually meaningless in the past. Because of reapportionment, however, Carter's position as chair had the potential to increase his influence on higher educational policy.[11]

During his first term in the Senate, the General Assembly focused considerable attention on education. Newly elected Governor Sanders's budget proposal for the first two years of his administration included raising teachers' salaries $100 the first year and $200 the second, hiring 1,275 additional teachers for elementary and secondary schools, and building trade schools in different regions of the state. Higher education received $4.3 million in additional funding during his first year and $3.3 million in the second. He also promised the Board of Regents of the Georgia University System extra funds for building programs. Through these increases, Sanders designated 56.1 percent of the entire proposed budget his first year and 56.9 percent the second year to education.[12]

Carter supported the governor's legislative programs and his actions in the Senate attracted little attention from the newspapers. The education committee's actions, however, proved controversial. In the first session, Senator Garland T. Byrd led an effort to repeal the tuition grant legislation, which had been part of pro-segregation Governor Ernest Vandiver's legislative package to keep the public schools open in the face of court-ordered desegregation. By using taxpayer-funded grants, parents could send their children to nonsectarian private schools if the federal courts ordered the desegregation of the local public schools.[13]

As lieutenant governor under Vandiver's administration, Byrd had supported the tuition grant compromise. But his support for these grants changed to opposition when he observed the way the state department of education actually distributed them. For the school year 1962–1963, 1,756 students received a grant of $178.65 for private school tuition. Although Byrd agreed that the distribution of the grants was legal, he was disturbed to learn that 83 percent of the students using the new grants already attended private schools. According to Byrd, the $300,000 of the state education budget allocated for the grants had become a giveaway for the rich and "was not doing what it was supposed to do."[14]

The *Atlanta Journal* predicted a "spirited discussion" of Byrd's bill when the Senate Education Committee met the following week. The bill's supporters, however, felt that the measure would "get a fair shake in the committee" due to the fact that a large number of the committee's membership consisted of senators who were "intimately connected with education."[15] The following week, the education committee approved Byrd's bill repealing the tuition grant legislation in a vote of fourteen to three, with Senator Jimmy Carter voting with the majority.[16]

Lieutenant Governor Geer immediately held a press conference to announce his opposition to repealing the law and challenged the education committee's obvious retreat from resisting desegregation. Geer characterized Byrd's bill as "breaking faith" with the public. The next day, Geer submitted an alternative version of the bill to the Senate, explaining that he agreed that the abuses of the grant had to be stopped because they took up too much of the state's education budget. His version of the bill gave the local board of education, along with the county commissioners, the power to decide if conditions in the school district demanded tuition grants. Once these two governing bodies decided that local conditions merited distribution of the grants, the local board of education would accept applications, review them, and select those they deemed worthy. Once approved, the funding for the grants would come from the local board's budget using both state and local funding.[17] Because Geer's alternative bill placed responsibility on the individual school district to establish the need for the grants and finance them, Byrd agreed to postpone the vote on his bill until the Senate had an opportunity to consider both versions.

On February 20, the Georgia state senate approved Geer's substitute bill to change rather than repeal the tuition grant legislation. The bill passed without debate by a vote of forty-eight to three. Leroy Johnson, the first black state senator since Reconstruction, voted against it along with James Wesberry of Atlanta and Kyle Yancy of Cobb County.[18] Senator Carter voted for the Geer bill.

In his memoirs, Carter fails to mention his vote on the tuition grant bills, despite his statements that the repeal of private school tuition grants was one of his original motivations for seeking the state-level office. Although his vote for Geer's bill seems inconsistent with his support of Byrd's bill in committee, this contradiction might have been more apparent than real. When interviewed by the *Atlanta Journal*, local school superintendents declared their opposition to using local public school funds to support the many private schools that had been established throughout Georgia in response to the *Brown* decision and the court-ordered desegregation of the Atlanta public schools. Because the local boards had to agree to the grants, the superintendents believed that there was little chance that the grants would be found necessary in any district. Thus, they believed that the Geer bill had repealed the tuition grant law by "saving it."[19] This operational repeal of the tuition grants allowed a senator to vote for the Geer bill without actually supporting the tuition grants. Carter's vote for the bill may have reflected this belief.

Carter may have also been responding to the tense situation in Sumter County and the surrounding area. Two weeks after he was elected, hundreds of black citizens demonstrated in Albany, Georgia, over the segregated bus station waiting rooms, and Martin Luther King Jr. had been held in the Sumter County jail. The heightened racial tensions in the area continued through the spring of 1963.[20] His knowledge of the tensions in Sumter County may have pushed him back into the rank and file of south Georgia politicians. The misuse of the funds by the parents whose children were already in private schools justified his vote to repeal the tuition grants and he had voted with the majority. Lieutenant Governor Geer's denunciation of the repeal brought attention to the vote. The political risk involved in voting alone against a bill that nullified the grants may have been too great for him, especially when superintendents throughout the state had denounced the use of their funding for the grants.

EQUAL EDUCATIONAL OPPORTUNITY
AND ECONOMIC GROWTH

As promised, Governor Sanders appointed the Commission to Improve Education early in the session. The creation of the commission was without controversy; however, the political appointments caused a reaction in the Senate because Governor Sanders followed the state tradition of giving more seats to members of the House of Representatives than to the Senate on joint legislative committees. When the proposal creating the commission came before the upper house, Carter spoke out against the use of the traditional ratio, and the Senate amended the language of the bill to give itself equal representation. The amended proposal was passed unanimously.[21]

Historically, members of both the Georgia Senate and the House of Representatives had represented specific geographic areas of the state rather than the population of the state as a whole, and the rotation that governed the election of senators had kept the upper house politically weak. Thus, membership on joint legislative committees had always favored the House by a ratio of three representatives to two senators. After the Senate attempted to change the ratio to one of equality, the House of Representatives demanded the continuation of the tradition of numerical superiority. Although Sanders had served three terms as a senator, he sided with the House and announced that the commission would have three members from the Senate and five members from the House, sustaining the tradition of House dominance.[22]

Sanders's support for the House disappointed Carter. His decision to run for the Senate had been based on its reorganization and potential for enhanced political influence as well as Sanders's reputation as a progressive. The House districts were still based on geographic representation and, as lampooned by Charles Pou at the *Atlanta Journal*, members from rural areas generally represented as many livestock as they did people. After the reapportionment, Senate seats represented the people of Georgia—not trees and cows.[23] Maintaining the traditional ratio of representatives to senators diminished the potential power of the upper house.

Despite Carter's disappointment about the Senate's lack of equal representation on the Commission, he accepted an appointment when Sanders offered it.[24] This experience had a significant effect on the young senator, serving to solidify his beliefs about education and the improvements required to facilitate economic growth in Georgia. By studying the information gathered by the commission and its consultants, he connected the chronic economic needs of Georgians to the issue of equal educational opportunity, concluding that improving access to educational opportunity was the key to providing more economic opportunity to the people of Georgia.[25] Through this process, Carter strengthened his belief that equal educational opportunity and the efficient use of resources for economic growth were intertwined.

The twenty-five member Commission to Improve Education consisted of Governor Sanders as chair, three senators, five representatives, and seventeen members representing business and education. At the first commission meeting, Sanders stated, "education is the single most important factor in determining the economic and social well-being of the state."[26] After emphasizing the importance of their findings, Sanders gave the commission only six months to develop a "broad outline" that included the costs of the program and suggestions for financing it. Although he realized that the short time frame limited the range of ideas commission members could identify and evaluate, he wanted the report in hand prior to the 1964 legislative session.[27] Ultimately, the commission report became the master plan for education in Georgia, guiding educational policy until Carter became governor in 1971.

The commission adopted a report by the Southern Regional Educational Board's Commission on Goals for Higher Education in the South to guide its work. The goals set forth for colleges and universities in the report included equal educational opportunity, socialization of citizens, excellence in teaching and scholarship, support of economic progress in the South, and leadership in solving "social problems created by population changes, racial difference, urbanization, and technological growth."[28] To explain their use of the report for education in general, the commission members stated, "Although developed with specific reference to higher education, these goals are equally applicable to education at all levels."[29]

Governor Sanders added specific goals, which focused more sharply on the particular educational needs of Georgians. His list included the establishment of minimum standards for school size and curriculum so that all Georgia schools could become accredited, a balance between academic and vocational curricula, higher standards and compensation for teachers and university faculty, development of public television, equitable distribution of the educational funding burden, and assurance of more support for the University System of Georgia.[30] Combining these sets of goals, the commission developed a plan for Georgia's educational system, elementary through graduate level and made suggestions about how to finance it. It did not, however, address how to desegregate it.

The commission published its report, *Educating Georgia's People: Investment in the Future*, in December 1963. After discussing the goals and purposes of the commission, the report explained that change was necessary or the state would "find it increasingly difficult to attract industry," while individual Georgians would "find it difficult or impossible to secure desirable employment either within or outside the state."[31] The foundation of the commission members' declaration that change in education was necessary was the median educational attainment level of the adult population in Georgia—a mere nine years of schooling. Beyond the obvious loss of human potential, the commission members found this low level of education detrimental to the state's industrial development, particularly given the predicted changes in the job market. They believed that the jobs that Georgians would be called to undertake in the future would "more likely be professional, technical, or clerical than semi-skilled operative or laboring."[32] The commission believed that education at all levels needed improvement and that the state needed "new types of education to equip its citizens for the specialized jobs which are essential in assuring economic growth."[33] The changes demanded were so great that "only the highest type of educational and political leadership will be able to cope with them."[34]

Throughout the 1950s, the legislature had used the educational budget largely to equalize public school facilities and personnel to avoid desegregation. School funding, teacher allotment, and support for curricular materials were all based on students' Average Daily Attendance from the prior year; thus, "equal" in Georgia meant offering the same funding per child. In the course of its investigation, the commission found that the teacher allotment in this formula also included noninstructional personnel such as administrators and secretaries. Because teachers, administrators, and other personnel were grouped together, teachers actually taught more students than developers of the funding formula had intended. The commission recommended creating specific categories for administrative and instructional support personnel to allow a reduction in the pupil–teacher ratio to maintain the intended level of funding.[35]

The next recommendations acknowledged the discrimination in the dual educational system and went farther than the state government had gone before in accepting desegregated schools. The commission members made the benign statement, "Equal educational opportunities should be provided to all of the children and youth within each local school district."[36] The supporting materials for the recommendation admitted that discrimination existed within districts based on "racial groups . . . geographic sections of the district, and sometimes . . . groups of children" and that some districts "by policy" gave only white teachers supplemental pay.[37] Black teachers and administrators received only their state salary. This discrimination against black teachers and administrators was illegal, and the commission members understood that they were pushing districts to admit that school boards treated black and white teachers as well as students differently. Finally, the members of the commission took the political risk of stating in their report, "This Commission goes on record as respecting the law of Georgia and of the nation."[38] This vague declaration came very close to supporting the United States Supreme Court decisions to desegregate the schools while remaining in the legalistic realm of being law-abiding citizens.

After addressing the principle of equal educational opportunity, the commission focused on the efficient use of resources for the future of the students and the economy of Georgia. They agreed that the single most important step toward improving education in Georgia was the consolidation of small schools. For the year 1962, "almost 10% of Georgia's schools still operated with 5 or fewer teachers."[39] For the same reason that Carter had campaigned to consolidate his home district with that of the city of Americus, the commission supported the consolidation of smaller high schools with limited course offerings into larger countywide high schools, which could offer broader curricula to students in the districts. Whether the state would mandate that the districts offer the same curriculum to the black students segregated into different schools remained unstated, but the earlier section on equal opportunity implied that such an action would be necessary.

Because Georgia ranked first in the nation in the number of school dropouts and only two out every ten high school graduates went to college, the commission supported the expansion of vocational education in the consolidated schools. Traditionally, Georgia's vocational education focused on agriculture. Current employment trends, however, demonstrated movement away from agriculture to technical and service industries. The commission recommended that vocational programs become diversified and that the General Assembly fund cooperative programs that placed students in businesses for on-the-job training. They hoped that the changes in vocational education would make schooling relevant for teenagers and encourage them to finish high school. This emphasis on high school graduation and increasing college attendance would bring Georgians into the modern "space age" economy.[40]

In higher education, the commission made recommendations to increase both enrollment in undergraduate education and support for graduate studies in the state. The Board of Regents—a constitutionally independent body appointed by the governor—was responsible for overseeing the University System of Georgia. Although the Board of Regents submitted their budget through the governor's office, they were independent in issues of governance. Therefore, the board, rather than the legislature or the governor, would decide if the commission's higher education recommendations would be accepted. Aware of their limited influence on the Board of Regents, the commission members focused on the significance of higher education for the growth of the state not only educationally but economically and socially as well. Their report contained five recommendations for undergraduate education: expanding current facilities to accommodate growth, maintaining low tuition and fees, developing more regional campuses or community institutions, increasing financial support for students (both undergraduate and graduate), and adding alternative admissions requirements to expand opportunity. The commission members believed that these changes in higher education would encourage Georgians to attend traditional and community colleges in greater numbers. By increasing the educational level of the adult population, they hoped to make Georgia more attractive to businesses.[41] These recommendations also fell in line with Carter's pledge to support the elevation of Georgia Southwestern College to four-year status.

Commission members acknowledged that their concerns about the number of college graduates in Georgia might eventually resolve themselves because college enrollments were expected to double by 1975. However, this increase was less substantial than it seemed. Only 21.7 percent of college-age Georgians attended college compared with the national rate of 39.2 percent. Thus, even if enrollments doubled, only 43.4 percent of college-age students would attend institutions of higher education as the national average increased as well. The commission believed that this lag in college attendance resulted in an unfavorable competitive environment for Georgians. The growing mobility in the United States increased Georgia's problem because the small number of technically trained people in the state forced local companies to import their technical and managerial personnel.[42] For Georgians to be competitive, the educational system had to address college preparation as well as technical skills.

The same economic concerns dominated the commission's discussion of graduate studies in Georgia. Because graduate studies provided "professional leaders and faculty members for our schools and the high level specialists needed to serve agriculture, government, business, and industry," they argued that the state should give graduate education a high priority in funding and support.[43] During the 1961–1962 academic year, the University of Georgia and the Georgia Institute of Technology, the only doctoral degree–granting institutions in Georgia, awarded only thirty-six doctoral degrees. In 1963, the University of Georgia offered doctoral degrees in twenty-three fields and the Georgia Institute of Technology offered them in twelve. Because the commission members believed that university research could offer solutions to many of the major problems facing the state, their report recommended more funding for the university system as a whole with special attention to the needs of research applied to the problems in the state. As with the elementary and secondary education, the commission member's explicitly stated their belief that unless the legislature increased funding for the university system, Georgians would not be able to compete for highly skilled and professional jobs in their own state.[44]

As Governor Sanders intended, the commission's report significantly affected the 1964 legislative session. All levels of education received increased funding, but the legislature gave special attention to higher education. From the late 1950s through 1963, state appropriations had increased by approximately 12 percent per year. In 1964, the General Assembly increased appropriations to higher education by 20 percent. Within that budget, expenditures on research increased by a million dollars per fiscal year.[45] The commission's report had effectively exposed the limitations of Georgia's educational system and provided a blueprint for the future.

EXPANSION OF OPPORTUNITY AND MAINTENANCE OF THE STATUS QUO

Despite his position as chair of the Subcommittee on Higher Education, the independence of the Board of Regents limited Carter's ability to influence policy. His key objective with respect to higher education was the elevation of Georgia Southwestern College to four-year status, which was consistent with the Commission to Improve Education's recommendation to extend access to higher education. Furthermore, because Carter supported increased funding for education, Governor Sanders also supported his proposal. The only real obstacle was Howard "Bo" Callaway, a member of the Board of Regents, who had for several years opposed the elevation of Georgia Southwestern. Callaway was a Republican from Columbus, Georgia, which also had a two-year college. Because Columbus was less than 100 miles from Americus, Callaway may have been more inclined to elevate the status of his local two-year college. Despite Callaway's opposition and because of Governor Sanders's support, Carter succeeded in gaining approval for the conversion of Georgia Southwestern to a four-year institution during his first term in the Georgia state senate. Callaway's opposition, however, became a personal issue for Carter—one that drew him into the governor's race in 1966.[46]

While Carter worked for the expansion of higher education in his region, he was silent on the continued segregation of the majority of the colleges in Georgia. During his first term, the Board of Regents, through the Southern Regional Education Board (SREB), continued to offer scholarships to black graduate students who wished to study medicine and veterinary medicine. In 1962 and 1963, the Board of Regents provided $65,000 to the SREB as part of an exchange program for black students from Georgia to attend Meharry Medical College in Nashville, Tennessee, and veterinary school at Tuskegee Institute in Alabama. The SREB exchanges also enabled white students from South Carolina, North Carolina, Virginia, and Maryland to attend veterinary school at the University of Georgia, which would not accept black students. The regional exchange of students was advantageous to the states, reducing the need to fund expensive programs such as veterinary medicine, but in states like Georgia that had both medical and veterinary schools, it also effectively slowed the speed of desegregation in higher education.[47]

Carter knew that the Board of Regents was a constitutional body that wielded significantly more political power than the newly formed Subcommittee on Higher Education. He also wished to gain approval for Southwestern College's expansion to a four-year institution. Given these circumstances and the conservative nature of his district, there was little chance that as the chair of the Subcommittee on Higher Education he would propose a move as radical and politically costly as the complete desegregation of the university system. Not only would such a suggestion endanger his ambitions for the elevation of the local campus, but also he and his new subcommittee could suffer the humiliation of being ignored or denounced by the Board of Regents. An example of the board's independence was its ability to disregard the subcommittee's publicly expressed opinion that one million dollars budgeted for a new coliseum at the University of Georgia would be better spent on the construction of needed academic buildings.[48] Although the subcommittee's suggestion was consistent with the recently published recommendations of the Commission to Improve Education for capital improvements, the Board of Regents ignored the subcommittee's input and continued planning the coliseum. Thus, while the Board of Regents may have acknowledged the existence of the new subcommittee, especially during the legislative session when the Senate approved their budget, they felt no need to act on the subcommittee's or its chair's recommendations. The political risks involved in suggesting the extension of access for all students to all institutions in the state were not worth taking.

THE DEMAND FOR EQUALITY

In the summer of 1964, Sanders called a special session of the General Assembly to revise the constitution and to consider the federal Fair Elections Act. During that session, Carter made his first public statement concerning racial discrimination. In his maiden speech before the state senate, he urged his fellow senators to abolish the "thirty questions" test used to prevent African Americans and whites whose politics were suspicious from voting. The questions consisted of technical constitutional issues or silly ones that no one could answer like "How long is a piece of string?" that county and state officials intended to humiliate and intimidate the potential voter.[49] The impact of his speech was probably negligible because it was not recorded and Sanders had called the special session to address voting rights.

Carter, however, believed that he was taking a risk, although the Senate only recorded speeches in the register at the request of the senator. He remembered that he "spoke in that chamber, fearful of the news media reporting it back home, but overwhelmed with the commitment to the abolition of that artificial barrier to the rights of an American citizen."[50] At the time, Carter knew that he was running for reelection in one of the most conservative districts in Georgia, but he was also aware that he and Rosalynn were living a dual existence. While in Atlanta, they saw the beginning of social desegregation—black and white people beginning to eat in the same restaurants and share public spaces. When they returned to Sumter County, however, the social and political separation continued with black men and women denied their voting rights and access to "whites only" areas.

Despite his fears, Carter was reelected to the state senate and served on the education and appropriations committees. On the latter committee, he learned how state money was allocated and witnessed firsthand the difficulties associated with removing a program from state government; once a program was funded, no one actually reviewed its effectiveness. So-called reforms often led to the creation of new agencies and programs rather than revision of the older ones. This practice ran counter to the goal of efficiency, which Carter believed should guide the operations of business and government alike. Another practice that troubled him was the submission of "sweetheart" bills favoring special interest groups. Carter saw himself as a champion of the rural citizens against the powerful special interest of wealthy organizations.

He firmly believed that the purpose of government was social justice, which he defined as addressing the needs of the citizens, and that efficiency objectives should guide priorities in state spending.[51] The problem with this belief emerged when the majority denied a minority their rights as had happened in the southern states or when a powerful minority, like the white population in Sumter County, used its power to prevent the majority from exercising their rights. All of the people involved, those with power and those without, were citizens of Georgia. In these situations, the efficient use of funds and resources offered little to guide Carter in his decisions.

Carter's belief in social justice was tried the following year when racial violence erupted in Americus. The Student Nonviolent Coordinating Committee (SNCC) registered voters, picketed stores that refused to hire black clerks, and led a sit-in to integrate the movie theatre. On August 8, violence began after a mass meeting of the black activists. Some of those who attended wanted to march in the area of town designated for black residents, but were told by police to disperse. The marchers refused to obey and the police attempted to force them to disperse. By the end of the night, seventy-five demonstrators had been arrested, twenty-eight demonstrators and seven police officers were wounded, and one black man had been killed—shot in the back by a police officer.[52] Warren Fortson, the Sumter County Commission's attorney and a close friend of Jimmy Carter, attempted to create a biracial committee to negotiate between the county government and the black community. For his effort, Fortson became ostracized at the county commission offices and his law practice was boycotted. When the Sumter County Commission received a petition demanding his dismissal, he closed his law practice and moved his family to Atlanta, where he became the attorney for the public school district.[53]

Fortson knew that Carter had decided to run for Congress in 1966 and that he had begun his campaign in his local district, which included Americus. Because defending Fortson could have endangered his plans, Fortson asked Carter not to speak on his behalf to the Sumter County Commission. Carter spoke up anyway and, in the words of Fortson, "caught hell for it."[54] His most public stance, however, occurred in his own church the week after the violence in Americus.

On August 1, when a biracial group attempted to attend services at the Americus Baptist Church, an armed minister denied them entry. The following week, the same group went to the Methodist church that Warren Fortson attended only to have the church elders block their way. Fortson left in disgust, and later representatives of the congregation asked him not to return to church. Some members of the Plains Baptist Church, where Carter was a deacon, feared that the churches in Plains would be next; they planned a meeting to decide whether to bar "Negroes and other agitators" from attending services. The morning of the vote, Carter and his family plus one elderly gentleman were the only members who voted against the restrictive resolution. Others who held many of the same beliefs as the Carters simply abstained from voting.[55] For those who supported the resolution, his defense of Warren Fortson and his opposition to restricting church attendance to nonagitating whites confirmed for them what they already suspected—that he was a liberal who supported desegregation.

As if to contradict his liberal reputation at home, when Carter returned to Atlanta for the next session, he focused his energy on the work of the Appropriations Committee. Demonstrating his belief that the state had a responsibility to spend taxpayer monies carefully and to administer its agencies and programs as efficiently as possible, he combed through bills to find unnecessary expenditures. He also stressed that the rural school districts needed relief from their property tax burdens and more support from the state because of their poverty.[56] This side of his political personality brought him praise from the voters in his district without betraying his belief in social and political equity. These often-conflicting perspectives—social liberal and fiscal conservative—would shape his campaign for governor in the fall of 1966.

CONCLUSION

In his decision to run for the Georgia state senate, Carter focused almost exclusively on education. He believed that the tuition grants for parents who wished to pull their children out of desegregated public schools threatened the integrity of public education in the state. Rather than abandon the public education system, he wished to see the state better finance and support it. If the small public high schools in Sumter County could not afford to provide a challenging and diverse curriculum, neither could the small private schools that were created to skirt the Supreme Court's desegregation orders. Therefore, it was a waste of public tax money to fund the grants. In addition, as Carter became more familiar with the needs of the state, he accepted that quality public education was vital for the economic and social growth of Georgia. From his perspective, the lack of adequate funding and the segregated system had cost the state economically and wasted the potential of many students.[57]

By connecting education and the economy, he also began to separate the process of education from the local community that supported it and to associate it with the state system that supported the statewide economy. As the state's responsibility increased, the focus of schooling for Carter became increasingly a function of the state for the state. This view of school systems as a part of the state government rather than as part of the community where the schools existed prevented local groups from blocking necessary reforms that would allow more efficient use of tax dollars in education. It also isolated the children attending schools from their communities from the perspective of reform. This symbolic removal of children from their communities was prevalent in school reform not just for Carter, but also for most people proposing and making educational policies.

His second goal, the elevation of Georgia Southwestern College to four-year status, was a political aim that also addressed equal educational opportunity, at least for white students, in his region. Students who were financially able and academically qualified to attend one of the four-year colleges or the University of Georgia did not attend local two-year colleges. However, those who could not afford to leave the area only had access to a two-year degree, regardless of their academic qualifications. If students could live at home or commute short distances, more of them would be prepared to participate in the future economic growth of Georgia.

His belief in political equality and the racial tension in his district drove Carter to make his first speech on the state senate floor. He believed that circumventing the political process through voter intimidation was immoral, and he wished to stop it on the state as well as the local level. His stance against the exclusion of black worshippers from the Plains Baptist Church followed the same logic—everyone had the right to worship where they wished. This socially liberal position probably cost him votes in his district, but he believed that he could weather the storm and win the next election, as he had after the school district consolidation defeat.

Carter's experiences on the Sumter County Board of Education had taught him many lessons regarding the needs of his local school district and the obstacles associated with meeting them; his activities in the state senate and his participation on Governor Sanders's Commission to Improve Education extended these lessons, shifting their context to the state level. In his subsequent political campaigns and offices, Carter would continue to attempt to balance his beliefs in equal access and opportunity with fiscal efficiency in administration and funding. In educational policy, his successes and failures in this endeavor would have national consequences.

THREE

The Compromise of
Equal Educational Opportunity

THE CIVIL RIGHTS ACT, which Congress passed in 1964, prohibited discrimination based on race, religion, or national origins in all federally funded
programs. The following year, President Lyndon Johnson announced his War
on Poverty and pushed through the Elementary and Secondary Education
Act and the Head Start program, both emphasizing educational programs for
children from low-income families. Because the Civil Rights Act disqualified
segregated schools from these programs, the southern states, with their high
levels of poverty and segregation, felt increasing pressure to desegregate
schools and public facilities in order to participate. Nevertheless, political
and social resistance to desegregation continued across the South.

In Georgia, the 1966 Democratic primary became a referendum on segregation and the federal government. The main contenders were Ellis Arnall,
Lester Maddox, and Jimmy Carter. Arnall was a former governor with a liberal reputation for educational reform. Maddox had gained national attention when he stood in front of his Atlanta restaurant with an ax handle to
stop African American protesters from entering it; he eventually closed the
restaurant rather than serve black customers. Although Carter originally
planned to run against Republican Bo Callaway for the Third District congressional seat, when Callaway switched to the governor's race, Carter
switched races as well with only three months to campaign for the primary.[1]

Carter's campaign centered on a theme that he would use repeatedly in
his later political races: "We need in the state a competent, compassionate,
caring government that is as good as its people."[2] Within a month of
announcing his candidacy, he released his platform to the press, emphasizing
three main issues: education, mental health, and crime prevention. In education, he promised that "every Georgia child" would receive "an excellent

49

education regardless of his station in life." To achieve this level of excellence, he intended to encourage school consolidation across county lines, expand two-year colleges and area vocational schools, and work with the counties to develop an "equal and adequate tax digest for the local support of education."[3] These educational reforms were drawn directly from the Commission to Improve Education's report and built on Sanders's education initiatives.

In a speech at the Rotary Club in Dalton, a town in northern Georgia, Carter expressed his belief that education was the key to economic growth and social reform in the state. Echoing the emphasis on education of President Johnson's War on Poverty, he argued that crime prevention, industrial development, and poverty reduction all depended on "educational excellence." Citing demographic data from the report of the Commission to Improve Education, Carter pointed out that Georgia had the highest dropout rate in the United States. He believed, however, that Georgians wanted their children "to have quality education, to have the right to go to college—without regard to economic considerations—if they had the ability and motivation."[4]

Carter continued this theme of educational excellence, connecting it to economic growth and social progress throughout his campaign. He carefully avoided the topic of segregation and other controversial issues, while attacking Ellis Arnall, who led in the polls, as too old and too liberal. Calling him "bald, squat, and old" and saying the he was "wild with promises and money," Carter attempted to appeal to voters only attached to Arnall through name recognition. From July to September, support for Carter increased steadily and by election day, a runoff with Arnall appeared likely.[5]

In the end, however, it was rural Georgians and Republicans who pushed Carter out of the anticipated runoff election with Arnall. When the rural vote came in on the night of the Democratic primary, it went to Maddox. Furthermore, because the Republican candidate was selected through a state convention, Republicans who were registered as Democrats were able to cross over and vote for the candidate they believed too weak to beat Callaway. As a result, Lester Maddox edged Carter out of the runoff by less than three percentage points.[6]

Maddox won the runoff with Arnall; however, in the November election, Arnall supporters organized a write-in campaign that denied either Maddox or Callaway a clear majority. The decision of whom would be the governor of Georgia fell to the state legislature. The Democrat-dominated legislature gave the election to Maddox, who responded to the news of his victory by shouting, "Thank the Lord and pass the ammunition."[7]

During the year following his election loss, Carter's political career reached its lowest point. He was in debt and out of public office, and a blatant segregationist governed the state of Georgia.[8] By 1967, however, he began to unofficially campaign through speaking engagements at civic organizations and coordinating multicounty regional planning boards.[9] Through these activities, he increased his visibility and his understanding of Georgia voters. Under his direction, his volunteers prepared a study of elections over the last twenty years for all 139 counties in Georgia. By analyzing this data, he found that most Georgians were more conservative than he was on the majority of issues. In order to win, he was going to have to appear to reflect the views of the typical Georgia voter.[10]

By 1970, white working-class voters throughout the United States had reacted strongly against the federal programs on behalf of the poor and minorities, and George Wallace, the governor of Alabama, had attempted to capitalize on this sentiment in two presidential elections. When Carter's analysis of voters in Georgia indicated that most were more conservative than he was, he adjusted his campaign themes to reflect their concerns rather than his vision. Thus, in his 1970 gubernatorial campaign, he sounded more like a traditional Georgia politician than he had four years earlier.[11]

In his speeches and pamphlets, Carter focused on components of public education programs rather than sweeping policy statements. His loss in 1966 taught him to be vague on controversial issues and stronger in his attacks on his opponents.[12] Therefore, he based his race against Carl Sanders, the former governor who had given him many opportunities to learn about educational policy, on personal wealth and personality rather than the issues. Carter intended his campaign to appeal to voters who felt alienated from their government. Although he accepted financial support from J. Paul Austin, chairman of Coca-Cola Company, and Ann Cox Chambers, chairman of the board of Cox Broadcasting Company, he still claimed to represent "ordinary working people." In his campaign against Sanders, Carter painted the former governor as a wealthy lawyer who had used his office for personal financial gain. Sanders, on the other hand, focused mainly on his own record as governor to appeal to voters interested in continued educational reform and economic growth.[13]

When both men were invited to speak to the Georgia Education Coordinating Committee, a group comprised of representatives of the State Department of Education, the Georgia School Board Association, and other major education associations, Carter focused on the proliferation of private schools. Although he rejected "putting one single dime of taxpayers' money in private schools," he acknowledged that the private schools established by affluent parents were "doing a good job for the wealthy children." The problem, he argued, was the "fly-by-night schools out in the woods" that would only last three or four years. In contrast, Sanders spoke about increasing teachers' salaries and larger policy initiatives such as the creation of state-supported kindergartens.[14] The contrast between the two men, with Carter focusing on a topic rather than an issue and Sanders presenting a policy package, was evident in their speeches for this audience.

Carter's campaign had progressive messages as well, but he often wrapped them in conservative rhetoric. For example, in March 1969, he told the Atlanta Lion's Club that the major problems in Georgia were "a low level of educational performance and race relations" and that race relations in the state were, in his opinion, "almost insoluble." If a solution could be found, he believed it would be at the local, not the federal level because most of the difficulties in Georgia, including "inadequate education, lack of job opportunities, and insufficient health care," cut across racial lines. He believed that because everyone faced these problems, the solution would be at the state level through fiscally responsible programs. Appealing to his audience of mostly white businessmen, he told them, "Make no mistake about it, Georgia is a conservative state" and local problems needed local solutions, not ones from the federal courts or congress. Answering the liberal charge that southern conservatives lacked compassion, he asserted, "We resent the equalization of conservative with racist, or with hard-heartedness, or with an unawareness of problems that prevail in our state."[15] For Carter, the state government did have responsibility for poor and disadvantaged citizens, but it also had to answer to the taxpayers.

In July, Carter released his platform, which included strict enforcement of laws during civil unrest, judicial reform, environmental reform, and the return of "control of our schools to local people, within the framework of the law."[16] The last area brought the issue of local control or "freedom of choice" into his campaign. When Carter was a state senator, freedom of choice plans had offered segregationists in Georgia, and other states, an avenue for avoiding the integration of public schools through social pressure. Most of the black population worked for white people and feared retaliation if they requested that their children attend an all-white school. Thus, white students and their parents continued to select all-white schools, and through social and economic pressure, black students and their parents were discouraged from applying for transfers.[17] In 1968, the United States Supreme Court rejected freedom of choice plans in *Green v. County School Board of New Kent County* and demanded the integration of public schools. Although illegal, Atlanta and other cities continued to use versions of the plans unofficially, and most politicians aspiring to higher office in Georgia denounced the *Green* decision either directly or indirectly and supported local control.[18] Thus, Carter's references to local control implied opposition to the *Green* decision while maintaining the safety of claiming to remain "within the framework of the law."

The rest of Carter's educational proposals were more moderate, if not actually liberal—the creation of state-supported kindergartens, the expansion of vocational education, and increased funding for higher education. His interest in the creation of statewide kindergartens overlapped with Sanders's platform and reflected Carter's interest in equal educational opportunity. In urban areas, the school districts used local funds to offer kindergartens and public and private organizations utilized federal funds for Head Start programs. In rural areas, there were few Head Start programs and middle-class children attended private kindergartens, whose tuition was too high for most impoverished families. Because of the lack of local funding, the majority of black children and white children from low-income families began their schooling in first grade. Carter was well aware of this disparity from his years on the Sumter County Board of Education and as a father.[19]

In Carter's plan, public kindergartens would be introduced over a period of four years and would begin by serving the "most deprived children . . . so they can go into the first grade . . . without being embarrassed." In his presentation of the needs of children from impoverished families, he pointed to the advantages this program offered middle-class children. Children denied access to reading materials and educational facilities in their early years forced classes to move more slowly through material. Providing early childhood education for disadvantaged children would, he argued, "prevent the holding back of the more fortunate children in the same grade with them."[20]

The strong connection Carter saw between education and economic growth was apparent in his support of high school vocational education programs. From his service on the Commission to Improve Education, Carter knew that only a small percentage of Georgia's college-age students attended college. He also knew that the majority of high schools in the state focused their curricula on college preparation. Increasing the enrollment in vocational programs would accomplish two objectives: graduating seniors would be better prepared to join the workforce and more students would stay in high school because of the economic relevancy of their course work. He also wished to modify vocational curricula to include more academic subjects throughout high school, thereby, removing the stigma associated with vocational tracks.[21]

Through his explanations of his programs and his description of himself as conservative, Carter effectively placed himself to the right of Carl Sanders. This political positioning won him the Democratic nomination for governor. In November, he defeated Republican Hal Suit, and on January 12, 1971, Jimmy Carter took the oath of office as governor of Georgia.

EQUAL EDUCATIONAL OPPORTUNITY

In Carter's inaugural speech, he surprised many with his statement that "the time for racial discrimination is over." He followed this dramatic statement with "No poor, rural, weak, or black person should ever have to bear the additional burden of being deprived of the opportunity of an education, a job, or simple justice." Given the tone of his campaign, many perceived these statements as a reversal of his position. His focus, however, remained on the people of Georgia, the state government's responsibility to them, and the removal of outside control. The wisdom of Georgians, he argued, would keep his administration on track because the people, not the politicians, controlled the government. Returning to the theme of his 1966 campaign, he told his audience that "in a democracy, no government can be stronger, or wiser, or more just than its people," and the vision of the people would drive the "destiny" of Georgia.[22] Carter changed his tone and message to include equality and opportunities for all, but his emphasis on local decision making belied the fact that local school boards and government officials had discriminated against many people in the past.

Carter was not alone in his message of opportunity and social justice. In other southern states, voters elected men to the governor's office who supported equal opportunity and believed that education was the foundation of economic growth. These leaders of the "New South" represented modernization and moderation in politics.[23] During his administration, Carter hired more African Americans for state government positions than any predecessor and he hung portraits of African American Georgians who had made significant contributions to society, including Martin Luther King Jr., in the capitol.[24] Just as significant as these very visible, but mostly symbolic, gestures was his attitude toward the poor in Georgia, most of whom were African Americans. In a candid statement reminiscent of Michael Harrington's critique of poverty in the United States, *The Other America*, Carter had told a group of businessmen, "The only thing that you have in common with a resident of the ghetto is getting stuck in a traffic jam every morning—highways."[25] He believed that the archaic structure of the state government, with its profusion of departments with overlapping responsibilities and services, placed a burden on residents who looked "to the state for welfare, for unemployment compensation, for public health services."[26] To address the barriers faced by the people who needed the services of the state the most, Carter pushed for increased efficiency through the reorganization of the executive departments to increase access. For Carter, social policy meant administrative reform and the appointment of qualified individuals.

Through a public survey, Goals for Georgia, he found that Georgians believed education was the most pressing problem in the state.[27] Thus, in 1971, as he concentrated on the reorganization of state government to make it more efficient and accessible to the public, his staff began laying the groundwork for his Early Childhood Development Program, a precursor to his educational reform package, Adequate Program for Education in Georgia. Through these educational initiatives, he planned to coordinate educational services throughout the state to provide equal access for all students to a quality education.

Simultaneous with Carter's administrative and educational reforms, the Supreme Court issued its ruling in *Swann v. Charlotte-Mecklenburg*, which allowed the busing of students as a means of desegregating the public schools. The emotional reaction of the press, politicians, and some southerners turned the spotlight on this issue, causing it to overshadow all other educational programs. In the firestorm that ensued, Carter faced boycotts and white, middle-class flight from the public schools. In response, he publicly protested court-ordered busing in Richmond County (Augusta) because he believed that it interfered with the state's ability to pursue long-term planning and alienated the middle class from the public schools. Conversely, he supported and praised the agreement between the Atlanta chapter of the National Association for the Advancement of Colored People (NAACP) and the Atlanta Board of Education, which in essence accepted segregation within the Atlanta school district. Local control, which had been a theme in the 1970 gubernatorial election, became the paramount political issue in the country.

EQUAL OPPORTUNITY FOR SOME

In 1964, while Carter was still a member of the Georgia state senate, *Acree v. County Board of Education of Richmond County* was filed on behalf of Richard Acree, a student who had graduated from the all-black Lucy C. Laney High School. In the original decision, the district court ordered the county to develop a desegregation plan. The county responded by submitting a freedom of choice plan that applied to grades 4, 5, 6, and 12. But, by 1968, only one white student had requested admission to an all-black school and only 5.5 percent of African American students had requested admission to an all-white school.[28] (In the 1967–1968 school year, there were 12,250 black children in the Richmond County School District, 670 of whom attended predominantly white schools. Although the district recorded 336 white students attending predominantly black schools, the number was actually closer to 40.) In July of that year, lawyers representing the plaintiffs returned to court to request a new plan for the desegregation of Richmond County. District Judge Alexander Lawrence agreed and ordered the Richmond board to develop a plan using attendance zones for the 1969 school year.[29]

For the next three years, the Richmond board continued to present freedom of choice plans to the court. After the *Swann* decision, Judge Lawrence brought in experts from the federal Department of Health, Education, and Welfare to design a plan and decreed that the only remedy for the desegregation of Richmond County was one that clustered grades within attendance zones and used busing to transport students to the schools. In his comments on the resistance of the Richmond School Board to his order to dismantle the dual school system, he accused the board and the superintendent of abdicating their responsibilities and behaving in a "contemptuous and intransigent" fashion. Judge Lawrence further charged that the board had "chosen to ignore the Constitution and the courts" because "apparently, they, together with a segment of the population of Richmond County, deem themselves above and beyond the law."[30] Because it was the middle of the school year, Lawrence ordered the movement of elementary students to begin by February 15. Secondary schools, according to the plan, could be desegregated the next fall.

The response was immediate. Citizens for Neighborhood Schools and Save Our Children, two anti-busing groups in Augusta, Georgia, declared that they would boycott the local schools on the first day of busing and called for a statewide boycott on February 28. On the first day of busing, nearly half of the county's students stayed out of school.[31] This response encouraged the opponents of busing and alarmed officials at the state department of education.

Dr. Jack Nix, the state school superintendent, referred to the boycott as illegal and encouraged concerned Georgians to write to President Richard Nixon in support of a constitutional amendment that prevented students from being assigned to schools based on race, religion, or national origins.[32] Joseph Edwards, deputy state superintendent, contacted Larry Gess, Governor Carter's education policy specialist, and explained the ramifications of the parents' plan. If the majority of the students stayed away from school for three days, the Average Daily Attendance (ADA) would drop substantially and both state and federal funding for the school system would decline the next year. Edwards knew that the governor planned to have a news conference and expressed his concerned about the governor's reaction to the parents' threat of a statewide boycott. When Gess informed Carter of the fiscal consequences of the impending boycott, the governor indicated that he would consider the situation that night.[33]

As the political leader of Georgia, Carter faced a dilemma. In the past, he had praised the good people of Georgia for accepting the principles of desegregation and their desire to move on to the education of all children "including the rural, the poor and the black."[34] He had also spoken out against busing many times; he believed individual settlements with local systems prevented the establishment of desegregation standards throughout the state. The absence of uniformity negated Carter's efforts to make the state school system more efficient. While he did believe that only efficiency and planning could bring the equality that he professed the good people of Georgia wanted in their schools, he also understood that a boycott would devastate school funding because the basis of the state funding formula was student attendance.

In his press conference, Carter sympathized with the parents' desires for their children to attend school in their own neighborhoods, but stated that he preferred an amendment to the U.S. Constitution prohibiting the assignment of students based on race, religion, or national origins above a boycott. Because a resolution for such an amendment had already passed the Senate and was now in the Georgia House of Representatives, he supported a boycott only as a last resort. Carter also rejected the idea that those against busing were actually segregationists, reemphasizing his belief that "all Georgians have accepted in good faith the proposition that schools are going to be integrated" and proclaiming his continued dedication "to education and to the treatment of all citizens without discrimination." He then called Judge Lawrence's decision "the most serious threat to education that I can remember."[35]

Carter held a second press conference two days before the threatened statewide boycott. While he maintained his stance against busing for racial integration, he told reporters that he felt that the resolution for the constitutional amendment, which had passed both the Georgia Senate and House of Representatives, was sufficient to express "Georgia's feelings on the subject." Acknowledging the different quality of public schools, he added, "parents who would voluntarily allow their child to be bused to a 'sorry' school would be 'abrogating their responsibility as parents.'" Referring to the resolution to amend the U.S. Constitution to prohibit busing for racial integration, he stated that busing violated the Civil Rights Act and would be abandoned one day.[36]

During this tense situation in Georgia, Carter remained consistent in his response to busing, and actually worked to extract promises from the Democratic presidential candidates that they would oppose busing if elected president.[37] His assertions that (white) Georgians accepted the inevitability of desegregation seemed optimistic in light of statements to the *New York Times* by the superintendent of Richmond County schools, Roy E. Rollins, who readily admitted that he was a segregationist with "serious doubts about the intelligence of black people."[38] The day after the scheduled statewide boycott, the *Atlanta Daily World*, an African American newspaper, described a meeting between parents and their U.S. representative, Robert G. Stephens. At a meeting of close to 100 black and white citizens, the most vocal white parents protested more than just the transportation of their children. In what was referred to as an "angry exchange" between black and white parents, a white parent said, "If Blacks would get half as interested in quality education as they are in hauling their kids out to the white neighborhood and having half-white grandkids, they'd get a good education." The *Atlanta Daily World* reported that black parents shouted back, "That's what it's all about. It always comes out."[39] Clearly, these public statements did not reflect acceptance of desegregation. Instead, they reinforced the idea that many white parents would oppose desegregation to the bitter end.

FLIGHT FROM EQUAL OPPORTUNITY

The situation in Atlanta differed significantly from what occurred in Richmond County. Since 1960, the Atlanta Public School District had operated under court orders to desegregate. The first plan desegregated one grade per year beginning with twelfth and used pupil placement evaluations to decide which black students would be allowed to attend the white schools.[40] This arrangement, which was part of "tokenism," was designed to keep the number of black students in the white schools to a minimum. One historian referred to the use of pupil placement evaluations as the "ideal delaying device" for segregationists because the burden of desegregation rested on the black students, who were evaluated on an individual basis for entry into the white schools.[41]

Desegregation in Atlanta followed the model of other southern cities; only ten students were admitted through the pupil placement procedures, although 268 had applied. The important aspect of desegregation for the city leaders was that there was no violence. The police kept white protesters away from the schools while the black students arrived, and the city government gave the press access to police radio communications from city hall; no one but students, parents, and staff were allowed near schools. Mayor William Hartsfield expressed his pride in the lack of violence in the city, and acted as if the city schools had desegregated with the admission of ten students.[42]

After the *Green* decision in 1968, the Atlanta board replaced the pupil placement procedures with a Majority to Minority program (M-M plan), in which students could transfer from a school where they were a majority to one where they would be a minority. This plan was similar to the original freedom of choice plan, but it allowed students to transfer without meeting the pupil placement requirements. Only the racial population in the school could prohibit student choice. Even under this plan, however, most schools in the district remained segregated. When the Supreme Court supported busing in the 1951 *Swann* decision, the local NAACP returned to court to ask for metropolitan desegregation.[43]

Between 1961 and 1971, the student body of the Atlanta public schools had become 70 percent African American. In order to desegregate the schools, the NAACP sued for a metropolitan plan that included the suburban districts, which would reduce the African American population in the Atlanta Public School District to 55.9 percent.[44] The local NAACP chapter in Detroit, Michigan, also filed a suit for a similar solution. If either of these metropolitan areas were to desegregate, white students from surrounding districts would have to be bused into the city districts and black students would have to be bused out to the suburbs. Within a year, however, the Atlanta chapter of the NAACP decided to accept a settlement that involved mandatory busing of roughly 3 percent of the students. The rest of the students would continue to participate in the M-M plan. The agreement also included more black administrators and a black superintendent to reflect the race of the majority of the students in the schools.[45]

The local NAACP asked Carter for half the funding for the implementation of the proposed compromise. In a memo to the governor, Larry Gess suggested that Carter support the agreement between the NAACP and the Atlanta Board of Education because "the program they envision could be used in all busing situations,"[46] an appeal to the governor's desire for statewide planning. Carter supported the plan, stating that he wanted to see Congress accept the Atlanta plan as a model for a uniform desegregation law.[47]

Carter's comments about uniform desegregation legislation spoke to the difference between the Richmond County and the Atlanta decisions. While the court decision in Richmond County followed the precedent set in *Swann*, the Atlanta case was more in line with Carter's idea of local control and statewide planning. However, Carter's public statements supporting the NAACP's compromise ignored the political reasons for the settlement between the local NAACP and the Atlanta school board.

When the idea of trading a court settlement for African American control of the school system first arose, Lonnie King, the president of the local NAACP chapter, rejected it; but the NAACP lawyer, Herman Moore, who had begun to embrace the separatism of the Black Power movement, was ready to accept it. By the time the agreement was reached, King acknowledged that the Atlanta district was already 78 percent African American.[48] From his perspective, the "compromise" was not designed to desegregate; it was to stop white flight to the suburbs and create an administrative structure that reflected the population using the public schools. As policy analyst Gary Orfield explained, "[the district court] simply pronounced the city desegregated and said that further busing would lead to rapid flight from the city by the remaining whites."[49] Preventing white flight from the urban schools did not meet the mission of the NAACP. Thus, while the governor and others greeted the compromise with enthusiasm, the national NAACP office denounced the agreement as abandoning metropolitan desegregation and suspended the local chapter's leadership.[50]

Carter consistently opposed busing solely for the purposes of integration because it lacked "uniform, nationwide application," but he believed that "any child should be able to transfer from a poor school to a better school at public expense."[51] From his experiences on the Sumter County Board of Education and the Senate education committee, Carter knew that less funding and fewer materials were available in the schools built and designated for African American children. This practice violated his belief that all students deserved access to quality schooling. The movement from one school to another in most cases would involve busing and most of the children transferring for a higher quality education would be black or poor. The pupil placement and freedom of choice plans prevented such transfers, but the M-M plan of the Atlanta settlement allowed it. However, Carter's ideal desegregation plan did not necessarily encourage transfers either, as the Atlanta public schools were 78 percent

African American. Few black students could transfer to a school where they would be a minority, and those who did faced a long bus ride to the schools in the predominately white neighborhoods of north Atlanta.

DESEGREGATION IGNORED

Desegregation litigation also affected the University System of Georgia. In 1970, the NAACP filed *Adams v. Richardson* and included Georgia as one of ten states charged with violation of Title VI of the Civil Rights Act because of its segregated system of higher education.[52] The objective of the case was to press the Nixon administration to enforce Title VI of the Civil Rights Act by withholding federal funding from states already found to have segregated colleges and universities. The case also demanded monitoring the progress of those state systems that had already submitted desegregation plans and conducting additional investigations in other states.[53]

The NAACP won the *Adams* case, and, in 1973, the Board of Regents received two court orders concerning the desegregation of the university system. The first one came from the *Adams* case with the U.S. District Court for the District of Columbia ordering Georgia's Board of Regents (and the other nine states' higher educational governing bodies) to submit a desegregation plan for the university system to HEW.[54] The second court order demanded the desegregation of Fort Valley State College, a predominately black college with land grant status. In response to these orders, the Board of Regents developed two desegregation plans during the 1973 academic year that called for programs to increase minority enrollment and employment of minority faculty members at all institutions within the system and for Fort Valley State College in particular.[55]

In the university system plan submitted to HEW, the Board of Regents outlined their "long-established program, implemented and conducted—on a largely informal, but nonetheless effective, basis—to eliminate discrimination based on race, sex, or any other indefensible basis."[56] This plan contained voluntary faculty exchanges between predominately white and predominately black campuses, finding private sources for financial aid, expanding remedial (developmental) programs, and implementing campus improvements. The Board of Regents supported this plan with the construction of new classrooms at Fort Valley State, Albany State, and Savannah State colleges (all predominately black colleges) and encouraged minority enrollment on all campuses (white students on predominately black campuses and black students on predominately white campuses).

The Board of Regents claimed that the voluntary efforts addressed desegregation effectively: in 1965, only 454 students (.6 percent) attended institutions where they were a minority and in 1972, the number had increased to 6,692 students (6.3 percent). Minority faculty members in the university system had grown slower, but still were significant. In 1965, minority faculty members numbered 15 (.6 percent), and in 1972 that number had increased to 319 faculty members (5.1 percent).[57] The Board of Regents believed that these increases demonstrated that steady progress had been made in desegregating the university system.

The Civil Rights Division of HEW asked the Board of Regents to revise the university system plan twice in 1974. The first revision concentrated on specific steps within the university system for full desegregation of the system. The second one asked for timetables and specific projections for individual institutions. In the 1973–1974 *Annual Report*, the Board of Regents claimed that HEW rejected none of the information; however, the university system remained part of the *Adams* suit.[58]

The Fort Valley State College plan submitted to Judge Wilbur Owens Jr. of the U.S. District Court for the Middle District of Georgia mirrored the voluntary character of the university system plan but addressed Judge Owens's specific instructions for the institution. In March 1974, Owens had issued an order for "a plan of affirmative action directed towards elimination of the racial identity of the faculty and students" on the campus.[59] The elimination of the racial identity of any campus could not be achieved through voluntary means. Nevertheless, the Board of Regents resubmitted the same plan with specific steps for Fort Valley State College.[60]

The specific programs outlined in the plan included Special Studies programs, or remedial classes, for all but two of the university system institutions—only Georgia Institute of Technology and Georgia Medical College were exempt from providing remedial classes, although both institutions were mandated to offer tutoring and extra laboratory classes for students who needed academic assistance. During the first semester of the Special Studies programs, 6,134 students took the classes. Of these students, .1 percent were Native American, 39 percent were African American, .8 percent were "Spanish surnamed" and 59 percent were "Other," who were mostly Caucasian.[61] The program that the Board of Regents intended for the remediation of black students served more white students and reflected the predominately white enrollment of the university system.

Another equity problem in the university system was the lower number of faculty holding doctorates at predominantly black institutions. The Board of Regents addressed the needs of these and other faculty members by developing a policy of academic leave to allow the pursuit of doctoral degrees.[62] Ninety-four faculty members went on academic leave during the 1974–1975 academic year, including forty-seven from the predominately black colleges, forty-five with pay, and forty-seven from the predominately white colleges, twenty-five with pay. While the number of faculty members from each type of institution was the same, the cost to the university system varied greatly. The salaries for the forty-five from the predominately black institutions on

paid leave totaled $216,253 and the salaries for the twenty-five from pre-
dominately white institutions on paid leave came to $56,395.[63] This differ-
ence implied that senior faculty members on the predominately black campuses participated in the program, while the predominately white institutions
focused their development dollars on junior faculty members. In the
1974–1975 *Annual Report*, the Board of Regents hailed the program for
increasing "the number of doctorates held by faculty members at the three
predominately black senior colleges."[64] With only four new faculty members
at predominately black colleges, but an increase of seven faculty members
with doctorates, the faculty leave program was slowly equalizing the credentials of the faculty in the system.[65]

The $272,648 in funding for the academic leaves came from federal and
state sources. Title III of the Higher Education Act of 1965, part of Lyndon
Johnson's Great Society legislation, contained funding for developing institutions. Because predominately black colleges and universities traditionally
and currently served students denied equal access to the predominately white
higher educational institutions during segregation, the Board of Regents
could use the Title III funds to support academic leave for faculty members at
Georgia's predominately black institutions. For the academic year
1974–1975, the Board of Regents received $113, 230 in Title III funding. The
state of Georgia provided $159,418, which covered the $56,395 for faculty at
the predominately white institutions and additional funds for faculty at predominately black institutions.[66]

Carter was aware of the efforts of the Board of Regents to address the
mandates of the desegregation cases and the federal government, and he
knew that they lacked public support. In a 1973 speech to the Georgia Association of Colleges, he informed his audience that Georgia's higher education system was still segregated. He knew that segregation was wrong, but
was reluctant to agitate for desegregation because of public resistance. He
also knew that HEW's demands were serious and that the university system
needed the research grants and student financial aid that came from the federal government. Despite these pressures, or perhaps because of them, he
told his audience of college administrators, "We haven't yet in the higher
education system successfully assimilated, or in my frank opinion, attempted
successfully to assimilate the integration of our black and white students."
He believed that in Georgia, "we will predicate our present and future plans
basically on a separate black and white college system." Rather than lay
blame for the situation on the Board of Regents, he placed responsibility on
the "black and white educators, black and white parents, black and white
students," who he believed wanted racial separation in higher education.
Despite the seemingly intractable nature of the segregated system, he
believed that it was not permanent, but rather "a reversible process" and that
with time more integration would occur through higher education's

responses to the individual needs of the students.[67] Beyond these encouraging words, Carter left the desegregation of the university system in the hands of the Board of Regents.

CONCLUSION

After losing the 1966 gubernatorial election, Carter presented himself to white voters as a more conservative and sympathetic candidate than his Democratic opponent. While he did not abandon equal educational opportunity or his desire for efficiency in educational administration, he implied that local districts understood the problems of their students better than the federal government, despite the fact that the local districts were responsible for past acts of discrimination.

Busing presented Carter with a dilemma. While he consistently stated that Georgians had accepted the principles of desegregated schools and equality between the races, he was equally consistent in his rejection of busing to mix students who lived in racially segregated neighborhoods. His support for the Atlanta settlement and Nixon's constitutional amendment prohibiting busing for reasons of race, religion, or national origin was condemned by organizations that supported desegregation. Eventually, his opposition to busing would compromise his reputation as a racial moderate with journalists such as James Wooten of the *Atlanta Constitution*.[68]

His support for equal opportunity and his rejection of systemwide busing was also somewhat contradictory. From his statements to the press, Carter seemed to believe that all that was necessary to offer all students equal access to education was to allow students who lived in the same neighborhood to attend the same neighborhood schools and to allow any child who went to a substandard school to transfer to a better one. This position may have been moderate in the early 1960s, but by the early 1970s, it clearly supported the status quo.

As governor, Carter may have also privately acknowledged that the majority of white adults in Georgia could not accept the idea of black children sitting beside their own children in school. His comments to the Georgia Association of Colleges on the desegregation of institutions of higher education implied a belief that, court orders aside, changes in attitudes and culture were going to come slowly. While this is a compelling argument, it does not fit Carter's personality or leadership style, though it does fit his campaign style. Carter expected competence and loyalty from those who worked for him but, in his second campaign for governor, he did not trust the voters to elect a moderate. He presented himself as a much more socially conservative candidate than he was at heart. This knowledge of the public appeared again when he referred to the resistance of "both black and white educators, black and white parents, and black and white students" to the integration of institutions of higher education.[69]

Carter's attention to the mood of the voters was an important aspect of his public appeal, but he knew that in Georgia the governor only had one term. While his stanch opposition to busing appealed to many whom his inaugural speech had alienated, his push for kindergartens and his educational reform package, Adequate Program for Education in Georgia, would resurrect the emphasis on equal opportunity from his 1966 candidacy and give him a national audience.

FOUR

Equal Educational Opportunity through System Reform

ALTHOUGH JIMMY CARTER opposed court ordered busing, he did support the back to basics movement and the state accountability reforms that swept through the South while he was governor of Georgia. Like Dale Bumpers of Arkansas and Reubin Askew of Florida, Carter believed that state government could address many economic and social problems by attracting business and industry from other states and countries. His plan for developing Georgia's industrial base included increasing educational standards and creating a solid educational system that offered equal opportunity to all students through the most efficient means possible.[1] To achieve his equity and efficiency goals, in 1972 and 1974, he championed programs similar to those that he had supported as chair of the Sumter County Board of Education and as a member of Governor Carl Sanders's Commission to Improve Education. These programs included statewide public kindergartens, consolidation of rural school districts, expansion of special education services, equalization of funding between rich and poor districts, and consolidation of state financial aid programs for college students.[2]

As the governor of Georgia, Carter had many successes—environmental protection, prison reform, and reorganization of executive departments, but the shining success of his administration in education was the Adequate Program for Education in Georgia (APEG).[3] This legislative package replaced the Minimum Foundation Program for Education (MFPE) originally passed in 1949 and updated in 1964 by the commission on which Carter had served. Through APEG, Carter achieved many of his educational goals; however, the political road to these reforms proved to be steep.

Although Carter saw himself as the leader in educational policy for Georgia, in issues pertaining to the governance of public education, the office of the State Superintendent of Schools and the Board of Regents of the University System had legal independence as well as specific powers and responsibilities outlined in the state constitution. As an elected officer, the State Superintendent of Schools held even more power than the appointed chancellor of the university system. Both officials had constitutional responsibilities that limited what Carter or any governor could achieve. The constitutional circumstances were further complicated by State School Superintendent Jack Nix's belief that the governor should play a supporting role to professional educators. These different interpretations of the role of the governor caused conflict in the implementation of educational policy during Carter's administration. What he accomplished occurred largely through public pressure.[4]

As noted earlier, during his gubernatorial campaign in 1970, Carter focused on specific components of public education programs rather than sweeping policy statements.[5] When he took office in 1971, educational funding and services were distributed unequally throughout the state. An example was the use of intellectual enrichment funds, supplemental local funding that independent school districts used to support kindergartens and other programs. The poorer, rural districts could not offer kindergarten unless the state allocated funding for it, which it did not. Because Carter believed that early childhood education was an important component of equalizing educational opportunity, addressing differences in the availability of these enrichment funds or the services they provided became a priority and played an important role in the school finance reform he initiated.

Carter also wanted to increase the number of high school vocational education programs and remove the stigma attached to vocational curriculum.[6] From his service on the Commission to Improve Education, Carter knew that the curricula in the majority of high schools in the state traditionally focused on college preparation. Increasing the enrollment in vocational programs would accomplish two objectives: (1) graduating seniors would be better prepared to join the workforce and (2) more students would stay in high school because of the economic relevancy of their coursework. These two goals followed the policies of earlier gubernatorial administrations and direction of national trends in vocational education. Carter's ideas differed from traditional vocational education advocates in his desire for vocational students to continue academic coursework, which allowed them to stay within the academic arena even if they chose to pursue a trade.[7] This educational plan followed his overall campaign strategy, which focused on increasing access to services for the poor and lower middle classes and economic development; however, it involved the cooperation of both the Board of Regents and the department of education in postsecondary vocational education.

GOVERNMENT EFFICIENCY

In his 1971 State of the State Address, Carter listed his priorities for his first year. Although education was high on his list, the reorganization of state government was his first priority.[8] His arguments for restructuring focused on his belief that "many functions of government are performed inefficiently and are difficult to understand or control." By streamlining departments and eliminating agencies, he promised that state government would be "more responsive to the needs of [the] people" and would operate more economically.[9]

In line with his desire to increase efficiency by reorganizing state government was his goal to improve education in Georgia. Explaining educational achievement in terms of efficiency, he stated, "It is certainly false economy to perpetuate ignorance and thus to encourage continued economic, medical and social dependence of deprived citizens upon the rest of society." To help the disadvantaged, he pledged to address the dropout problem, begin public kindergartens, hire more teachers for exceptional students, and fund remedial reading programs. Other areas mentioned in his speech were vocational education, standardized testing, state curriculum standards, consolidation of services, and increased salaries for teachers and college faculty.[10]

For Carter, higher education offered special opportunities for the state. The growth in student enrollment across the University System of Georgia was astounding. From 1960 to 1970, the student population had grown from 30,000 to 92,000. The increasing enrollments meant that the university system needed substantially more funding. In addition to providing the state with future teachers and professionals, Carter believed that the colleges and universities should apply their "intellectual and instructional resources . . . in a forthright and practical way to help in solving the many chronic problems faced by our Georgia people."[11] Following the model of the agricultural experiment station where he had learned modern farming techniques, Carter viewed research as a means of finding solutions for problems facing the state rather than as an end in itself. By linking research to the solution of economic and social problems, he justified increasing the higher education budget by 19 percent during the economic recession of the early 1970s.[12]

Implementation of his educational proposals and the promised extension of educational opportunity, however, waited until he completed the reorganization of the state government. During the 1971 legislative session, Carter and his legislative supporters submitted House Bill 1 (HB 1) to authorize the governor to consolidate functions, establish new departments, abolish departments (except those constitutionally mandated), and transfer responsibilities among agencies.[13] The bill became a litmus test of whether the governor or the lieutenant governor, Lester Maddox, would hold the power of the state government.[14] Despite Maddox's claims that Carter was usurping the power of the legislature, Carter managed to get HB 1 through both houses and begin the task of assembling the executive committee and study groups for the Reorganization and Management Improvement Study. The purpose of the study was to evaluate the functions of the departments in state government to improve services to the public and reduce duplication of services.[15]

The composition of the study groups reflected Carter's technocratic approach to reform. After consulting with other governors who had reorganized their governments, Carter and his staff decided to use a management company, volunteers from business (who remained on their companies' payrolls), educators, nonprofit leaders, and state employees. A total of 117 people worked to reorganize the functions of state government in "seven functional areas: education, human resources, natural resources, transportation, protection of persons and property, economic development, and general government activities." When they completed their work, the study groups had generated 2,500 pages of recommendations and 300 proposals for reform.[16]

As the groups compiled materials to support their reports, Carter met with most of them, listened and discussed the merits of their findings, and encouraged them to ignore the political ramifications of their recommendations. If he was familiar with the area, as in education, he usually pressed his own opinions and assessments of the necessary reforms. On issues where he was less familiar, as in mental health, he often deferred to the recommendations of the study group.[17] By accepting that the study groups could master the details involved in the reorganization of an administrative area, he demonstrated his belief that committed people working together could make positive changes in state government.

When the reorganization plan was completed, Carter's office disseminated the results, and the political battles in the General Assembly resumed with the support of the department heads and the lieutenant governor. Because he sought sweeping changes in departments under his control and those controlled by other elected officials, communication with department heads was vital for the success of the reorganization. To smooth the way for the passage of the reorganization legislation, Carter agreed to meet with the department heads when they wished to discuss the proposed changes in their departments and indicated that they could veto proposed statutory changes involving their areas.[18] Unfortunately, communication between the reorganization leadership and these officials often failed. In one instance, Carter announced the removal of licensing and regulatory responsibilities from Secretary of State Ben Fortson's office. Fortson, a popular political figure, publicly denounced Carter's intended changes in his responsibilities because the governor had neglected to inform him of them. When asked whether Fortson had been consulted, Carter admitted that no one had contacted him.[19] A similar problem occurred with State Superintendent Jack Nix, who protested the public release of reorganization information concerning the department of education before the administration had consulted him. In a public letter, he reminded Carter of their agreement that Nix could review any changes in the educational bureaucracy before a public announcement.[20]

This incident was representative of the sorts of exchanges and misunderstandings that frequently occurred between Carter and department heads, including State Superintendent Nix. Although the governor was the head of the executive branch of the state government, Nix had been appointed by Governor Sanders and elected as an incumbent in the 1966 election—the one that Carter lost and Lester Maddox received from the House of Representatives. Because Maddox owed his office to the representatives and believed strongly in the separation of powers, the General Assembly had acquired more power and independence than it had enjoyed in previous years.[21] Heads of departments had maintained their traditional independence and had continued their strong relationships with legislators and other agency heads. As the state superintendent, Nix had set his own legislative agenda and educational policy priorities. Guided by Nix and the chancellor of the university system, Maddox had focused his energy on maintaining the racially segregated education system, giving teachers raises, and increasing funding to the university system.[22]

Unlike his predecessor, Carter intended to exercise centralized control over departmental legislation. In the fall of 1971, he sent a memo to all department heads requesting that they submit their legislation through his office "in order that we will have no duplication of effort."[23] At the bottom of his copy of the memo, Nix wrote, "take no action—get individual sponsors during session."[24] Their conflicting views of jurisdiction caused considerable tension between the two men, and the reorganization study exacerbated the friction in their relationship.

The reorganization study produced several recommendations for the department of education: the addition of a supervisory board for all state and federal educational programs, the removal of the Division of Rehabilitative Services (vocational), the coordination of programs in vocational-technical schools and junior colleges, the development of long-term planning within the department, and an appointed state superintendent.[25] All of these measures directly encroached on the state superintendent's constitutional powers, and Nix exercised all of his political influence to prevent the majority of them from occurring.

To coordinate educational efforts in Georgia, the Reorganization Study committee recommended that the legislature create an Educational, Planning, Evaluation and Coordination Board, whose purpose was to unify and strengthen "all the components of education in Georgia."[26] The duties of the board would entail "integration of short and long range plans from all sectors of education, review of budgets in relation to plans, research and analysis into Georgia's educational needs . . . allocation of funds under state-administered federal programs, and administration of student financial aid."[27] Centralized control over planning and system development from early childhood through graduate education in a single board encouraged coordination of reform efforts with the growing federal educational programs.

Despite the benefits of having a single board oversee the entire system, the study also listed three serious disadvantages to the creation of such a board: the addition of another layer of bureaucracy in education, the potential weakness of the board itself, and the likelihood that the State Board of Education and the Board of Regents of the University System would object to its creation. The proposed board would be dependent on the governor and the General Assembly for strength and would have very limited control over the State Board of Education and the Board of Regents.[28] Without the cooperation of the constitutional bodies, the new board would face the same limitations Carter had when he served as the chair of the Subcommittee on Higher Education in the state senate.

Creation of the Educational, Planning, Evaluation and Coordination Board also involved changing the constitutional status of the state superintendent's position by making it an appointed rather than an elected office and giving the State Board of Education, which the governor appointed, the power to select the state superintendent. This change was designed to reduce the role of political influence in the state superintendent's office and to streamline and improve the public schools. The study authors explained,

> Aside from this resulting in a position similar to that of the Chancellor's (of the Board of Regents) it will also eliminate the necessity of campaigning for office and being politically oriented, thus providing the opportunity of dedicating full professional effort toward the huge task of directing the public school system.[29]

A change of this magnitude required a constitutional amendment.

After the Reorganization and Management Improvement Study became public in December 1971, Carter endorsed a constitutional amendment to make the state superintendent an appointed official. He had long supported such a measure; in 1964, he had voted in favor of a bill to change the method of selecting the state board of education and the state superintendent. Although the bill failed, the next year he sponsored a constitutional amendment giving the Georgia Board of Education the power to appoint the state superintendent. Carter believed the pressure of elections often forced the leader of the Georgia school system to focus on the demands of educational professionals represented by the unions and professional organizations rather than on the needs of students.[30] He neglected to point out that an appointed superintendent would be politically dependent on the governor and on the appointed state board of education.

At the beginning of the 1972 legislative session, Nix criticized the governor's position, saying that the public had the right to elect either the state board or the state superintendent. He believed that people in these positions made important decisions that affected Georgians, young and old, and that the public had the right to hold an elected official or board accountable.[31] While this argument added to the tension between the state superintendent and the governor, it was politically effective. By the end of the session, Carter dropped many of the recommendations for the reorganization of the department of education, including changing the constitutional status of the state superintendent. He continued, however, to push for the coordination of the vocational-technical schools and junior colleges.

An important organizational obstacle to Carter's belief that students in vocational programs should continue their academic classes, even on the postsecondary level, was the division between the supervision of the junior colleges and oversight of the state's vocational-technical schools. The junior colleges were under the jurisdiction of the Board of Regents, while the Georgia Department of Education supervised the vocational-technical schools. Coordination between the two agencies had been a problem in the past. The Department of Education reorganization study group described the situation as "one of the most difficult problems considered by the Governor's Commission to Improve Education in 1963." The authors continued, "this situation exists in even a worse form today, although the two boards are in the process of creating a joint agreement in what appears to be a move to ameliorate outside influence."[32]

Ignoring the desire of the boards to avoid "outside influence," Carter appointed and chaired a seven-member Education Coordinating Committee to facilitate the development of joint programs between junior colleges and vocational-technical schools. The past resistance to program coordination by both the Board of Regents and the Georgia Board of Education prompted Carter to push for the "mandatory cooperation" that "was suggested [in the reorganization study] between vocational-technical schools and junior colleges," while assuring the public and the two governing boards that the institutions under their separate supervision "would remain separate."[33] In keeping with his reorganization of state government, Carter wanted to expand the programs and end duplication of effort between the two adult education systems. Under pressure from the governor, the two boards reached an agreement and began to offer joint programs at two junior colleges by the end of the 1972 academic year.[34]

Carter's efforts to improve the efficiency of the Georgia Department of Education stemmed directly from his belief that "many functions of government are performed inefficiently and are difficult to understand or control."[35] He was committed to a reform plan that would make all state departments, including the department of education, accessible to the public and responsive to the executive. Nix had a different view of the most efficient way to administer the educational system in Georgia. He believed that his role as the constitutional officer for education included setting educational policies and priorities that would address the needs of both the public at large and the state's educational establishment. These opposing interpretations would appear again when the state legislature funded Carter's Early Childhood Development Program.

EQUAL OPPORTUNITY FOR THE YOUNG

Concurrent with the Reorganization Study, Carter directed his staff to gather information about how to fund the implementation of a statewide kindergarten program without increasing taxes. They identified federal monies available through the Social Security Act, the Elementary and Secondary Education Act, and the Head Start program to fund preschool and kindergarten education for children from impoverished families and those with special needs.[36] Through these federal programs, the state could begin a state-supported kindergarten program for a mere $1.4 million while receiving $4.2 million in federal matching funds.[37]

The Early Childhood Development Program Carter sent to the legislature for the 1972 session mirrored the federal programs by creating kindergartens and early intervention services for poor children and those with special needs. The legislation included measures for state agencies to coordinate health and social services with educational services. To achieve this level of cooperation, departments that had never worked together had to organize services for delivery in the areas of the state with the new preschool and kindergarten programs. The difficulties involved in the establishment of such a broad program were enormous in the best of circumstances; unfortunately, Carter proposed this program the same year he requested $55 million in budget cuts from state agencies. Many of the agencies he sought to involve in the Early Childhood Development Program, including the department of education, wanted to use their scarce resources to maintain existing programs and services.[38] New programs needed new funding.

Public support for statewide kindergartens and early childhood programs for children with special needs came from groups as diverse as the Georgia Congress of Colored Parents and Teachers, which passed a resolution that the State Board of Education consider establishing "adequate kindergartens" in "every school system in Georgia,"[39] and the Georgia Educational Improvement Council (GEIC), an advisory committee of business, political, and educational leaders, which recommended establishing public kindergartens in phases. From within the education community, both the state superintendent and the Georgia Association of Educators (GAE) supported the development of statewide kindergartens. Nix had supported statewide kindergartens since his election to the office of state superintendent. In 1969, he told the audience at the Governor's Conference on Education, "We must not delay longer to provide opportunity for kindergarten experience for every Georgia child."[40] Nix went on to explain, "the fact that kindergarten training helps to close the gap between disadvantaged youngsters and their peers from higher socioeconomic backgrounds is another reason we should move now if we ever expect to fulfill our commitment to education for ALL Georgia children."[41]

By 1972, competing demands on the education budget complicated the GAE's and Nix's support for Carter's Early Childhood Development Program. While the GAE included statewide kindergartens on their legislative agenda, their first priority was a $1,000 pay raise for teachers. Teacher salaries in Georgia averaged $6,760, which was $2,810 below the national average. Carter suggested a $507 average salary increase, but the GAE rejected this figure and continued to agitate for the $1,000 increase. Nix and a majority of state legislators also supported the raise. Eventually, the governor accepted the General Assembly's support of the teachers, but he branded the GAE as a special interest group that ignored the needs of children.[42]

Superintendent Nix also supported the pay raises for both teachers and administrators, demonstrating his different financial priorities. In a speech, he articulated his support for the governor's kindergarten program as he expressed his concern about starting a new program without increasing revenues. To an audience of educators, Nix announced that he favored state-supported kindergartens, but given current resource limitations, he preferred to maintain existing programs rather than start a new one.[43] Although Carter had not asked the state superintendent to cut any programs, with the looming budget cuts, Nix knew that starting kindergartens without additional funding would cost the state either in existing programs or personnel.

To increase pressure on the General Assembly to pass the Early Childhood Development Program, Carter turned to the public. In several press releases, he explained that kindergartens for children from low income families or with special needs would help to solve many of Georgia's social and economic problems. He provided three benefits to illustrate the need for his program. First, he pointed out that early childhood education would reduce welfare payments because unemployed parents would have childcare, enabling them to work outside of the home. Second, he argued that the number of juvenile delinquents and students dropping out of school would decline. Finally, the costs of special education would decrease because of early intervention.[44] Like many inside and outside the political establishment, Carter believed that the schools as social institutions could solve the economic and social problems of the poor and the earlier that the schools started addressing their needs, the better.[45]

Another reason he gave for the creation of statewide kindergartens was the federal government's threat to intervene. In a speech to the National Association of State Boards of Education, Carter explained that "[Senator] Walter F. Mondale . . . is planning to establish an early childhood program (nationally) that would completely bypass the states."[46] Carter claimed that the federal government could do this by going directly to the cities and counties, as it had with the Head Start programs, and that these individual agreements prevented long-term planning by the state government. Another problem he saw with federal intervention was the loss of local control as had occurred with busing. Carter's plan for state kindergartens offered the public an alternative to federal control of preschools.[47] Whether he persuaded the public that federal government threatened state and local control of education or the support for kindergarten and early childhood education had simply grown strong enough to convince the members of the General Assembly that the public supported it, the House and Senate passed Carter's Early Childhood Development Program with $1 million in funding.

When the Early Childhood Development Program became law, it appeared that Carter had triumphed over Nix and legislative opponents. The conference committee, however, had added a sentence prohibiting the use of state funds "'directly or indirectly' for day-care and social services." Because of this addition, the State Board of Education refused to administer the federal daycare programs, which had been part of the federal funding package developed by the governor's staff to gain public and legislative support.[48] Carter accused the state board members of "blocking educational opportunities for the poor, the black, and the handicapped by stalling action on the Early Childhood Development (ECD) program." He also noted that the board's rejection of daycare and social services forced the creation of "two state departments of education" because the federal programs could exist without the approval or cooperation of the state board with the Department of Family and Children Services administering them.[49] With one sentence, the General Assembly had maintained the fragmented structure of state services and destroyed the integrated structure of Carter's first educational reform.

As Carter garnered support for the Early Childhood Development Program, Richmond County, Atlanta, and the University System of Georgia all faced desegregation suits and decisions. His efforts to provide equal educational opportunity for children through the Early Childhood Development Program stood in contrast to his opposition to busing. It was as if the public schools could equalize education through the development of programs that addressed the educational needs of all children without challenging the continued segregation in Georgia's schools. In higher education, he supported the Board of Regents' desegregation plans through the centralization of the financial aid network and increased funding for faculty development and research. Although motivated by court orders, he aided the Board of Regents because their efforts included programmatic approaches that expanded access for poor as well as minority students.

EQUAL OPPORTUNITY IN HIGHER EDUCATION

The majority of financial aid for colleges and universities in Georgia came from the federal government through the National Direct Student Loan and Guaranteed Student Loan Programs, Basic Educational Opportunity Grants, and college work-study programs. Most of this funding was distributed through institutions of higher education. Funding for job training and vocational rehabilitation also came from the federal government, but the state had to provide matching funds for some of the programs and supplemental funds for others.[50]

Carter wished to increase the state's role in the financial support of college students and rationalize its distribution. The authors of the Reorganization Study found that six departments, including the Board of Regents and the Department of Education, offered students financial aid for postsecondary education. All of the programs based their selection process on the financial needs of the students, and each department determined the particulars of the application process, the method for setting monetary awards, and the repayment conditions. Recipients of student loans and scholarships had to show scholastic achievement, but each department applied different standards to assess their performance. Potential applicants had to go to each of the six departments to inquire about financial aid because of the decentralized structure.[51] The lack of coordination among the departments created barriers that prevented many high school students and adults seeking new skills from finding out about the scholarships and loans offered by the state of Georgia.

The changes outlined in the Reorganization Study report included creating uniform application processes through the coordination of award announcements and deadlines, equivalent awards from the different departments, and equal interest rates on loans. The Reorganization Study Group for Education recommended the consolidation of services into one department as the best means for achieving consistency in the student financial aid system.[52]

Although the structure outlined in the Reorganization Study seemed simple to implement, the results of Carter's consolidation efforts were limited. In its 1972–1973 *Annual Report*, the Board of Regents listed four other agencies supplying students financial aid: the Veterans Administration, the Social Security Administration, the Georgia State Scholarship Commission, and the Georgia Higher Education Assistance Authority.[53] While the federal agencies offering aid for veterans and Social Security benefits had to maintain their independence from the state government, the state agencies offering financial aid also remained separated.[54] Despite this limited success in the consolidation of financial aid, more and more students enrolled in postsecondary institutions turned to federal student loans, which continued to flow into Georgia at an increasing rate.

From 1971 to 1975, while Carter was in office, student financial aid in Georgia increased dramatically, although the state contributed little. During this period, state expenditures for student aid fluctuated by more than $1 million in any given year. In 1975, however, the legislature authorized an increase of $2.7 million for "fellowships, scholarships, Educational Opportunity Grants" (state's matching funds).[55] The huge increases in student financial aid came from the federal programs, which, in 1971, amounted to $16 million and was distributed through state institutions. By 1975, awards to students through "scholarships, grants, loans, and work-study programs" totaled $40 million.[56] While this number included the $8 million expended by the university system, in aggregate, the percentage of state funding for college and university students financial aid fell from 35 percent to 20 percent during Carter's years in office.

In contrast, state-sponsored funding for applied research increased substantially while he was in office. In his 1971 State of the State Address, Carter called for colleges and universities to apply their "intellectual and instructional resources . . . to help in solving the many chronic problems" in Georgia.[57] The federal agencies with research dollars also wished to fund research on social and economic problems. This shift in research emphasis from theoretical to applied studies cost the university system $5.4 million in federal research dollars in 1970. The state, however, increased its funding by 11.8 percent that year, partially offsetting the decline in federal monies.[58] To help attract more state dollars and answer the new federal requirements, the Board of Regents began to highlight the efforts of the colleges and universities to collaborate with state agencies for staff development and public service.[59] It continued this practice throughout Carter's administration.

Although the percentage of the university system's budget for research remained stable from 1971 through 1975, allocations to the university system increased 31 percent during that period.[60] Because of the decline in student financial aid, total state funding for research increased overall during Carter's administration. How these funds were allocated between and within the different institutions was not clear in the Board of Regent's *Annual Reports*, but it was apparent that the Board of Regents prioritized funding for projects that involved public service and applied research. This emphasis on the application of research to current problems became a hallmark of Carter's public policies and his later private actions.

TENSIONS WITHIN THE ADMINISTRATION

In 1973, the tensions between Carter and Nix exploded. In his budget for Fiscal Year (FY) 1974, Carter had requested an $111 million increase in state funding for education, but the House Appropriations Committee cut his request to $88 million. After reviewing the modified budget, Carter wrote Nix a heated letter charging, "what has been done to the school children of Georgia in the FY 74 budget is a shame and disgrace."[61] In his examination of the budget, Carter found that "almost every portion of the increased funds which would have gone directly for the benefit of the school child has been eliminated." Furthermore, he noted, "This has been an annual occurrence during the last seven or eight years, except when initiative has been taken by the General Assembly or the Governor's Office."[62]

One of the main issues that bothered Carter was the kindergarten program. Accusing Nix of undermining it, he wrote,

> As you know, last year even the very restrictive kindergarten program approved by the Legislature was substantially eliminated because of quiet but adamant departmental objections to it. Now the remaining $1,438,000 to continue the existing 44 local programs has been deleted from the 1974 budget. In addition, the five-year-old children with mental or physical afflictions are being robbed of $5,380,000 to begin a minimum kindergarten program for them.[63]

He continued to list the losses from other programs: $21 million for facility renovation and maintenance, $3 million for instructional media, and $15 million for local enrichment in systems with low property values per child. Finally, he asked,

> Where has the money gone? It has been diverted to salary and retirement benefits for teachers, administrators, and other employees of your department. It has been frittered away in fragmented State takeover of local educational effort, which we all know is unlikely to benefit local taxpayers and which is above and beyond the 50 million in mandatory property tax relief which will become effective this year.[64]

Carter closed by informing Nix that he had sent a copy of the letter to the legislative leadership.

While Nix acknowledged the governor's letter, he refused to answer the specific allegations. The day he received it, he wrote, "I am extremely disappointed by your letter. . . . The assumptions which you made are based on such gross misinformation that it seems inappropriate to attempt to respond."[65] Nix defended his actions as the state superintendent by telling Carter that "the record of my administration as State Superintendent of Schools in Georgia since 1966 is an open record and speaks for itself." He followed his defense with a veiled insult to Carter. "I would not want to be placed in the position of debating the merits of the record with the chief executive of the state, a position for which I have the highest regard."[66]

This disagreement between the two men highlighted Carter's frustration with educational governance in Georgia. As the state superintendent, Nix had the ability to stop education legislation or to thwart implementation of legislation that he disliked. Carter could turn to the public for support, but Nix had the support of the school boards and the superintendents in the state. The power of this constituency in the early 1970s was great. In most of the rural districts, the public elected the superintendent, who then became the largest employer in the area. These superintendents then looked to the state superintendent for leadership and, perhaps, a position if they lost the next election. This hierarchical structure informally, but effectively, limited the power of the governor in education.[67]

ADEQUATE PROGRAM FOR EDUCATION IN GEORGIA

A few months after the exchange between Carter and Nix, the Minimum Foundations Program of Education (MFPE) Study Committee began its meetings. In 1963, Governor Carl Sanders's Commission to Improve Education had updated MFPE and, in the same spirit, the General Assembly charged the committee with reexamining it "to bring about a more adequate program."[68] The problems with Georgia's educational policies resulted from unequal distribution of local educational funding because of varying property values, the numerous court decisions in the 1960s and early 1970s, and the increased role of the federal government in compensatory education. The southern states also had a reputation for low educational standards and few college graduates. By focusing on equalizing the distribution of funding and increasing standards as well as services, Carter and members of the legislature hoped to make Georgia more attractive to national and international businesses.

Robert Farrar, chair of the House Education Committee, and Terrell Starr, chair of the Senate Education Committee, cochaired the committee. Although Carter wished to appoint most of the committee's members, in a compromise with members of the General Assembly, he agreed that he would select one-third of the members of the committee and each cochair would select one-third. The committee divided its members into three teams to examine instruction, support, and finance. Carter served as the chair of the Instructional Program Committee, and from this position directed the recommendations for state curriculum changes.

The Instructional Program Committee appraised the condition of education in Georgia in both broad and specific terms. Examples of the general topics addressed included general education, special education, compensatory education, adult education, and preschool education. More specific topics ranged from drivers education to detailed suggestions for program improvements. In each of these areas, the committee looked at existing programs and assessed the future needs of Georgians in relation to the services offered.[69]

The recommended changes included allocation of funding by instructional units rather than by number of teachers, distribution of incentive funds to local boards for the development of comprehensive programs including both college preparatory and vocational curricula, and the retention of teenagers who were pregnant, married, or parents.[70] The committee's recommendation addressing the needs of these at-risk teens girls related to *Ordway v. Hargrave* (1971), a Massachusetts court case decided in favor of a teen expelled from school because she was pregnant, and Title IX of the Higher Education Act, new legislation that banned discrimination based on sex, martial status, or pregnancy.[71] Until the 1970s, school systems in Georgia, and most other places, expelled pregnant teenage girls and married teens. While the Instructional Program committee neglected to include any discussion of the educational needs of this population, it acknowledged the need to follow current court decisions and federal legislation.[72]

In special education, the committee advocated testing, individualized programs, mainstreaming, and a class ratio of one instructional unit per twelve exceptional students. Going beyond the curriculum, the members discussed testing services, teacher training, transportation of children with severe disabilities, and sufficient appropriations. To ensure adequate funding, the committee examined and listed the different categories of disabilities and recommended that "funds and services" for children with special needs should "be provided on the basis of accurately established needs of each subpopulation and comprehensive plans developed to meet those needs."[73] In addition, the committee recommended small class sizes for self-contained classrooms, but suggested that many students with special needs would benefit from placement in the regular classroom. The lack of trained teachers and funding for gifted students was a particular concern addressed in the report. In small rural districts, the committee believed that cooperative programs among districts through student transportation or itinerate teachers would meet the needs of students until districts could be consolidated. The progressive nature of these recommendations anticipated the federal mandates in Public Law 94–142, Education for All Handicapped Children's Act (1975), by two years.

The committee members proposed compensatory education as a supplement to federal programs in the Elementary and Secondary Education Act. Focusing on students who were behind their peers in basic skills (reading, math, and use of English), they recommended diagnostic testing to aid teachers in identifying "the specific skills that each student has not acquired within each subject matter area."[74] Teachers would then design individualized learning programs for the children who were behind in their basic skills. Although the committee recommended that teachers assume the responsibility for identification of individual student's needs, the evaluation process included an achievement test and a "comprehensive evaluation, which includes physical, psychological and educational components."[75] The members of the committee differentiated between compensatory and special education; compensatory education was a temporary program to aid students in catching up with their peers. They believed that this sort of intervention could increase students' interest in school, thereby, increasing graduation rates across Georgia.

The preschool education recommendations followed the Early Childhood Development Program that the General Assembly had already passed but not fully funded. The committee began its recommendations with the assertion that "kindergarten should be provided for all five-year-old children in Georgia who reach age five on or before September 1 of the school year."[76] Children with mental or physical disabilities were to receive state-supported preschool education by age three. Class size differed according to the needs of the children, with twenty students per teacher in the regular half-day kindergarten classes (two sessions) and twelve students per teacher in self-contained class for children with disabilities.[77] The recommendations of the committee omitted the social services that Carter's original legislation had included. The absence of those services reinforced the isolation of educational services from the health and welfare services needed by the poorest segments of Georgia's population. As president, Carter would accept this administrative isolation of education from the economic and social needs of poor children again during the creation of Department of Education.

Under program assessment, the committee explained, "Georgians . . . demand more than an equal educational opportunity for their children. They demand an equity of results."[78] To measure the performance of students and teachers, the Instructional Program Committee suggested the use of "a systematic process of program assessment . . . which includes the establishment of educational goals and objectives . . . measurement devices to assess how well the goals and objectives are being met, and the comprehensive utilization of assessment results."[79] Through this process, committee members believed that budget priorities and program decisions could be made to better serve students and teachers.

While the language in the summary of the Instructional Program Committee's discussions implied that Georgia had neither standards nor state assessments, the General Assembly had passed legislation in 1967 containing both. The committee recommended the continuation of the statewide testing program and the inclusion of readiness testing for children in first grade. The innovation that the committee proposed was that it also urged the General Assembly to appropriate funds to cover the costs of testing and analysis, which had burdened the budgets of the local boards in the past.[80]

The other two committees also made many recommendations. The Supportive Services Committee examined state and local services necessary to facilitate the instructional program. Among this committee's recommendations were long-term planning for facility needs, transportation of all students living more than one and a half miles from school, and mandatory state standards.[81] The suggestion that school systems supply transportation for all students living more than a mile and a half from the school was politically dangerous because of community fears about court-ordered busing. The Supportive Services Committee's intended the state to furnish buses to the independent city districts, which only received state transportation funds for students in special education programs.[82] Because of the limitation of state funding for busing, the independent city districts under federal court orders to bus students for desegregation purposes had to fund the increase transportation costs from local funds. This recommendation allowed the state to assume these costs as well.

The Supportive Services Committee went farther than the Instruction Program Committee's recommendation for standardization; its members suggested moving to qualitative measures for the standards and implementing sanctions against schools found deficient. In an early attempt to align what was taught to what was tested, the committee suggested that the state, along with local school personnel and citizens, establish "performance based criteria" for instructional programs. Schools that failed to meet the standards would receive additional assistance from the state until they met the standards.[83] This move toward accountability through statewide testing and standards followed the national trend where thirty-three states required minimum competency testing during the 1970s.[84]

The Financial Foundations Committee described the different roles federal, state, and local funding played in Georgia's educational system and suggested ways to make the flow of funds to schools more efficient. Local funding for schools accounted for 28 percent of Georgia's total education budget in 1971–1972, but the local contribution per child varied from $23 in the Jefferson City district to $182 in Putnam County. This local funding came from property taxes, which had become increasingly unpopular. To abolish property taxes, the state would have to assume the entire burden of financing education for all districts, a $1.2 billion responsibility. The committee recommended maintaining the current method of taxation.[85]

Changes in funding also appeared under the section entitled "enrichment funds," referring to monies that came from local taxes above the mandatory level. In theory, these funds permitted the addition of new courses and services to the basic curriculum; in practice, the funding provided a necessary supplement to the state education budget for individual schools. Although MFPE (as reformed in 1964) offered "equality of educational opportunity for Georgia's children and youth regardless of where they may live or what their station in life may be," statewide assessed property values varied from $3,922 to $37,188 per student.[86] The committee recommended retaining the present MFPE formula and setting a guaranteed minimum enrichment level, with the state providing the difference between local enrichment funds and the minimum level. This method, the committee believed, would equalize educational opportunity in Georgia by offering all students an adequate education no matter where in the state they lived.[87]

The recommendations by the three study committees contained most of Carter's wish list for education in Georgia. After the MFPE study committee published its report, the battle over legislation began. The problems in the legislature were political. Because the proposed bills supporting the study committees' recommendations came from the governor's office, superintendents claimed that the governor's office had left them out of the process.[88] The House Education Committee responded to the complaints of the state's educational leaders, making changes in the allocation of funds and the categories to be funded in FY 1975. Among the affected budget categories were instructional media and early childhood education. In prelegislative meetings, the House Education Committee gave the kindergarten expansion bill a "do pass," but no one put the bill on the Rules Committee calendar.[89] Lacking specific information on the costs involved, the House Education Committee sent the bill for early childhood education for children with mental and physical disabilities to a subcommittee for further study. In response to the actions in the House of Representatives, Carter's educational advisor, Larry Gess, sent the governor a memo admitting that early childhood programs had become unpopular nationally and that the Education Committee was reluctant "to deal with tough issues this year."[90] The negative evaluations that the federal Head Start program had received in the early 1970s made early childhood programs look inefficient and a poor use of political capital.[91]

Carter took his support for early childhood education to the public and to educators in the state. In February, he spoke on early education and its low priority at the Tristate Winter Conference, a meeting of educators from Alabama, Florida, and Georgia. Expressing his disappointment, he said,

> My own experience has been one of some frustration, because we have never been able so far to escalate or to elevate the priority for early child-hood education to get a unanimous commitment from the state board of educators, the state school boards association and the General Assembly. . . . The consequences of placing in the same first grade classroom children of widely diverse backgrounds are bad enough, but to put children in the same classroom with these diverse backgrounds plus a very wide disparity of educational development hurts the fortunate and the unfortunate child.[92]

Carter also wanted funding for the purchase of audiovisual materials, books, and other classrooms resources specifically designated in the budget. The House Education Committee wanted to combine that funding with other programs to allow school districts more flexibility in their use of state funds. Based on his own personal experience with the department of education and the advice of his staff, Carter disagreed with the House Education Committee on the need for this flexibility because he doubted that the funds would remain in the educational media budget.[93]

The House Education Committee also challenged the MFPE funding formula. The basis for estimating Average Daily Attendance (ADA) numbers had changed from an average of annual attendance to an average based on student attendance during the first four months of the school year. When the number of students declined in a school system, the district received less funding the next year. Nix supported changing the funding formula to use the first three months instead of the first four. Because the fourth month had a greater potential for enrollment decline, basing ADA numbers on the first three months would increase the computed average. For the state budget, this change meant areas with declining populations would receive more funding than the current MFPE formula allowed. The difference in funding ranged from $12 to $15 per student; in a district the size of Atlanta, such a difference had significant impact.[94]

Despite the disagreements, on March 26, 1974, Governor Carter signed the Adequate Program for Education in Georgia bill to replace the MFPE legislation. The new law consolidated many of the programs Carter had initiated during the first three years of his administration and most of the recommendations of the study committee. The section of APEG outlining instructional services included preschool education (and kindergartens), special education, and education for teenagers who were pregnant, married, or parents. The system for the distribution of state funds changed from allocation by number of teachers per school to instructional units. Almost everything assigned to the schools involved this form of measurement, including number of teachers, administrators, and funding for intellectual enrichment.[95] This shift in the allocation of funding, personnel, and materials placed an emphasis on the function of schooling rather than on the personnel in the schools. This change along with the added emphasis on testing moved the Georgia school systems closer to a technocratic model centered on accountability.

CONCLUSION

Carter signed APEG at the end of his administration and believed that he had moved Georgia's educational system closer to equity. While the programs and the expansion of educational access mandated by the legislation did indeed offer more materials and funding to students in urban and rural areas, his opposition to busing in Richmond County and his support of the Atlanta settlement reinforced the inequalities within the schools districts. The necessity for federal courts to make desegregation decisions on a case-by-case basis denied him and succeeding governors the ability to formulate a statewide plan for the desegregation of Georgia's schools. However, his preference for local decisions made the federal courts the best alternative for desegregation policy. There was also the dilemma of the concentration of urban poverty in the Atlanta School District. Middle-class families increasingly looked to the suburbs or private schools rather than to the public schools for the education of their children. Carter and his advisors hoped to stop the flight of white students through their support of the Majority to Minority (M-M) plan. In the end, however, both the M-M plan and APEG left the distribution of students and funding at the local level, where whether students had access to instructional technology or gifted programs still depended on the generosity of the school board governing their district.

After the passage of APEG, Carter seldom gave a speech on educational policy unless he was speaking to a group of educators or county officials.[96]

Because a governor could not run for reelection at that time in Georgia, the funding battles for APEG were left to his successor, George Busbee. Foreign policy, judicial reform, and national politics became the dominant themes of his speeches. Once his educational reform package passed in 1974, Jimmy Carter began his campaign for the presidency.

FIVE

An Opportunity Missed

WHEN JIMMY CARTER campaigned for president in 1976, distrust permeated the political atmosphere in the United States. President Richard Nixon had resigned in the wake of the political scandal caused by the connection of his administration to the burglary at the Democratic National Committee Headquarters at the Watergate Hotel. In an attempt to end the scandal, the newly sworn in President Gerald Ford pardoned his predecessor, creating public outrage and greater distrust of government in general. Continuing inflation and growing unemployment plagued the American economy, and the public was divided in their reactions to federal social policies in support of equal educational opportunity and affirmative action; civil rights activists protested that the federal government was moving too slowly to equalize opportunity and opponents of these equalization programs claimed that the federal government was engaged in a social revolution.[1]

In his presidential campaign, Carter employed the same themes that had brought him success in the governor's race in Georgia: efficiency and equal opportunity. Capitalizing on the scandal that had shaken their faith in the Republican Party, he promised the American public that he would listen to them and never lie to them. In his speech announcing his candidacy, he praised the integrity of the people of the United States and condemned the political establishment in Washington. Identifying himself as an ordinary citizen, he told his audience, "We have dared to dream great dreams for our Nation. We have taken quite literally the promise of decency, equality, and freedom—of an honest and responsible government." He believed that the American people still held those same dreams, but acknowledged that their "commitment . . . [had] been sapped by debilitating compromise, acceptance of mediocrity, subservience to special interest, and an absence of executive vision and direction."[2]

Separating himself from the political establishment, Carter accused beltway politicians of making "decisions from an ivory tower" and distancing themselves from the American people. While politicians made decisions in Washington, he argued, "few [had] ever seen personally the direct impact of government programs involving welfare, prisons, mental institutions, unemployment, school busing, or public housing." For the public, the solution to their feelings of alienation was a reaffirmation of "our ethical and spiritual and political beliefs." As part of the renewal process, he proposed making the federal government "understandable, efficient, and economical," calling for wholesale changes ranging from "a drastic and thorough revision of the federal bureaucracy, to its budgeting system and to the procedures for analyzing the effectiveness of its many varied services."[3]

Carter also promised to restore the public's faith in the federal government, emphasizing the need for all citizens to "know that they will be treated fairly." Echoing his gubernatorial inaugural speech, he stated emphatically, "the time for racial discrimination is over."[4] Equal opportunity could only be realized through judicial fairness, tax reform, and the restructuring of government services. These emotion-laden promises became the crux of his campaign. Issues peppered his speeches, but the main thrust of his message rested on his personal integrity and argument that the federal bureaucracy should be reorganized to ensure a more equitable distribution of services.[5] As with his gubernatorial campaign, his promises of greater fairness in and access to government services appealed to white, blue-collar voters and African American voters, who supported Carter in record numbers,[6] although for different reasons. The same message and his attack on the beltway politicians brought opposition from his own party, which viewed him as too socially conservative.[7]

In the months and weeks preceding the election, speculation about Carter's educational priorities centered on his policies as the governor of Georgia and his responses to a survey sent to all potential candidates by the National Education Association (NEA). Based on Carter's political biography, *Why Not the Best?* and his professed admiration for public school critic Admiral Hyman Rickover, curriculum specialist William Van Til predicted that a Carter administration would be a "hybrid administration, tending to be liberal-progressive as to equal opportunity . . . [and] financially supportive of public education while tending to be conservative-traditional as to curriculum and instruction."[8] Because of Carter's push for reorganization of Georgia's state government, Van Til concluded that Carter's approach to any educational reform would be comprehensive in scope.

In his written response to the series of questions posed by the NEA, Carter agreed with the teachers organization's goal for a separate cabinet level department of education, explaining, "Generally, I am opposed to the proliferation of federal agencies. . . . But the Department of Education would consolidate the grant programs, job training, early childhood education, literacy training and many other functions scattered throughout the government. The result would be a stronger voice for education at the federal level."[9] This department, as Carter described it, would both dispense federal funding and act as an advocate for education with direct access to the president. The creation of this department was also consistent with Carter's pledge to make the federal government less cumbersome by reorganizing departments. In 1976, the Department of Health, Education and Welfare (HEW) was immense— only the total budgets of the United States and the Soviet Union exceeded that of HEW.[10] Moving the Office of Education out of this enormous bureaucratic structure appeared to be more feasible than making health programs independent of welfare programs.

Jimmy Carter won the presidential election, and, in proclaiming his victory, told his supporters in Plains, Georgia, "I think the sun's rising on a beautiful new day, a beautiful new spirit in this country, a beautiful new commitment to the future."[11] To prepare for his presidency, Carter met with experts in energy, health care, economics, domestic policy, civil rights, foreign affairs, defense, environmental protection, and labor to plan his policies. His inaugural speech referred to his immediate priorities in domestic policies, defense, and environmental policy and to the limits of the federal government's ability to solve all problems. It was a short speech that he hoped would prepare the nation for his administration.

However, when he became the forty-eighth president of the United States, the nation faced escalating inflation and growing unemployment, an economic situation eventually labeled stagflation. These economic conditions both constrained and helped focus Carter's educational policy initiatives. Even though he believed that the federal government had to limit its actions, the economic problems facing the country were its responsibility, and balancing the federal budget was his answer. To pull spending in line with available funding, Carter instructed his administration to eliminate outdated programs and boost funding for programs that more equitably addressed the needs of the middle and lower socioeconomic classes. Many who doubted his social agenda welcomed his emphasis on programs that served the middle and lower socioeconomic classes, but members of his staff quickly ran afoul of congressional leaders and department heads once they began to request budget cuts.

EQUAL OPPORTUNITY THROUGH EFFICIENCY

According to Carter, the federal government needed to focus its resources on those groups that had historically been neglected by their federal, state, and local governments.[12] As part of addressing the needs of these groups, he wished to increase funding levels for programs that aided disadvantaged students. Through this influx of funds, he intended to stimulate educational opportunities in impoverished school districts and increase access to higher education. Carter's administration, however, had a lean budget, and his own vision of government demanded austerity. One biographer explained, "Contrary to most

Democrats, he believed that while there was a vital role government could play in alleviating human suffering, there was a real limit to what it could do for people without going bankrupt."[13] In his effort to pull these two ideas together, he became "preoccupied with cost efficiency and improved management."[14]

Carter expressed his understanding of the tension between public spending on social programs and fiscal conservatism in a statement about southern populism:

> Among the most important goals in the Southern brand of populism was to help the poor and aged, to improve education, and to provide jobs. At the same time the populists tried not to waste money, having almost an obsession about the burden of excessive debt. These same political beliefs—some of them creating inherent conflicts—were to guide me in the Oval Office.[15]

The competing priorities of liberal social policy and conservative fiscal policy shaped the Carter administration's educational polices throughout his term as president. He supported programs such as Title I of the Elementary and Secondary Education Act, Basic Educational Opportunity Grants for postsecondary education, and state grants for the Education for All Handicapped Children's Act (PL 94–142), all of which concentrated federal efforts on disadvantaged groups. He also wanted to refocus or eliminate legacies such as Impact Aid Grants, which supported school districts with military bases, federal facilities, and federal public housing.

The justification for Impact Aid funding was that military and federal personnel often moved from area to area, making use of locally funded public schools without contributing their fair share of taxes. Impact Aid Grants compensated the district for the services provided to those families. Carter objected to the program because it compensated wealthy and impoverished districts without regard to their actual needs. Through the reduction or elimination of Impact Aid, he planned to focus federal dollars on those programs that directly aided poor and minority students. School districts with enough local and state funding to support the additional federal and military employees' children would contribute to controlling the federal budget. Unfortunately, the proposed cuts to Impact Aid included federal aid for schools serving children from public housing. In these areas, the federal compensation offered an important supplement to local and state funding.

Another of Carter's plans involved his campaign promise to streamline the management of education programs by consolidating them under a cabinet-level department of education. The creation of this department was, however, a low priority during the first two years of his administration. Instead education was part of his larger domestic policy agenda, with the reauthorization of the Elementary and Secondary Education Act (ESEA) taking center stage. Under the Nixon and Ford administrations, education had suffered from neglect. Through his reauthorization of ESEA, Carter wished to make education a priority. Until education became a cabinet level department, it remained subsumed within the Department of Health, Education, and Welfare (HEW) and the secretary had to promote the president's changes to ESEA in Congress.

Because of the importance of this position, Carter followed Vice President Walter Mondale's advice to appoint Joseph Califano as the secretary of HEW. While not a specialist in education, as Lyndon Johnson's assistant for domestic affairs, Califano played a central role in the creation of the Great Society education legislation, which focused on equal educational opportunity.[16] He agreed with Carter that it was the responsibility of the federal government to equalize opportunity for disadvantaged groups, and he shared Carter's belief that federal government had shirked its duty in this area during the Nixon and Ford years. As secretary of HEW, Califano hoped to restore funding to programs that advanced this objective and to reemphasize equal opportunity programs through sizable funding increases for both ESEA programs and financial aid for college students.[17] Thus, both Carter and Califano believed that the way to increase funding for equity programs was to redistribute funding from general programs to those with a compensatory purpose.

EQUAL EDUCATIONAL OPPORTUNITY OR EXCELLENCE?

Despite Carter's and Califano's agreement on the primary role and responsibilities of the federal government supporting education at all levels, Carter's educational policies lacked direction and a clear sense of purpose his first year. Instead of offering a clear agenda for educational reform, he reacted to court orders, the Ford administration's budget, and pressures from his former mentor, Admiral Hyman Rickover. This lack of direction created confusion about his ultimate objectives. Although busing was still an emotional topic on the state level, the major federal court action involving desegregation of his administration was *Adams v. Richardson* (1973), an unresolved higher education case. The plaintiffs initially charged ten states with deliberately slowing the desegregation of both historically black colleges and predominately white colleges. By 1977, the case involved just six states, Arkansas, Georgia, Florida, North Carolina, Oklahoma, and Virginia, and the plaintiffs returned to court in hopes of compelling HEW to enforce Title VI of the Civil Rights Act in those states.[18] As governor of Georgia, Carter had left the resolution of the suit to the Board of Regents of the University System. When the plaintiffs returned to court, responsibility for resolving it fell to Joseph Califano who became the defendant in this action.

Under Califano, HEW promulgated desegregation guidelines for state colleges and universities in accordance with the demands of the district court. The guidelines stipulated four elements for compliance with Title VI of the Civil Rights Act: restructuring of the dual system, increasing black enrollment in predominately white schools and increasing white enrollment in predominantly black institutions, increasing faculty and staff of other races, and improving reporting and monitoring systems.[19] To comply with these guidelines, the state systems needed to strengthen predominately black institutions by offering high-demand programs on their campuses, eliminating duplicate programs at black and white institutions, developing shared or interinstitutional programs, and merging institutions or branches of predominately black and white colleges and universities. For predominately white campuses, state systems also had to develop numerical goals for recruitment of black students, and, once met, enhance the curriculum at historically black schools to attract white students. The guidelines advanced by Secretary Califano were designed to reduce the racial identity of the public colleges and universities in the states named in the case.[20]

Early in 1978, Secretary Califano released a statement indicating that three of the states named in *Adams*—Arkansas, Oklahoma, and Florida—had submitted acceptable desegregation plans. After congratulating the governors of those states, Califano explained that the remaining states had forty-five days to enter into negotiations with HEW. If no agreement were reached in that time frame, HEW would begin Title VI enforcement procedures to terminate all HEW funding, including student aid, for educational institutions within those state. By the end of the year, only North Carolina remained a part of the lawsuit.[21]

Califano's actions in the *Adams* case reflected his commitment to equal educational opportunity as well as his beliefs about the purpose of federal intervention in state educational policies. By establishing the guidelines and enforcing them, he confirmed the Carter administration's commitment to equal educational opportunity in higher education. Carter, however, remained outside of the decision-making process, focusing instead on modifying Ford's budget. Because of the fiscal calendar, the Ford administration submitted its budget for FY 77 before Carter took office. The only choice for Carter was to amend his predecessor's numbers or accept them.

With respect to education, Carter's adjustments included increasing the budgets for Title I of the Elementary and Secondary Education Act (ESEA) as well as Basic Educational Opportunity Grants for impoverished postsecondary students. He had supported both programs while governor of Georgia and both fell within his definition of what the federal government could do to increase educational opportunity. During the 1960s and early 1970s, states received federal aid and distributed it to colleges and universities, who in turn accepted students based on the level of funding. The Education Amendments of 1972 changed the focus of financial aid from the institutions of higher education to the students, and the Basic Educational Opportunity Grants (BEOG) went directly to students based on their financial need. The Carnegie Council on Policy Studies in Higher Education referred to this type of financial aid as "primarily [designed] to encourage equality of opportunity."[22] Unfortunately, from the program's establishment in 1972 through the Ford administration, Congress had underfunded the BEOG program and restricted access to it by strictly limiting eligibility to students whose family income fell below the poverty line. With Carter's support, Califano sought to expand the program by raising eligible family income from $17,000 to $25,000 and to increase the grants themselves from $1,600 to the congressionally mandated $1,800.[23]

Consequent to the decision to support these equal educational opportunity programs, Califano's budget for HEW accepted the Ford administration's cuts in two programs: Impact Aid Grants and National Direct Student Loans. The Senate Subcommittee on Labor-Health, Education and Welfare, however, increased funding for these programs as well as close to 100 others. In a letter to Warren Magnuson, the chair of the subcommittee, Califano explained that to begin the "steps that must be taken to hold down Federal spending . . . to balance the [federal] budget by FY 1981" the increases to these programs, as well as others, had to be eliminated from the budget.[24]

Because of its wide distribution, Impact Aid was popular with Congress. Califano and others in the administration believed that this scattering of federal dollars was its biggest fault. In a memo to the Office of Management and Budget (OMB), Califano explained that Impact Aid funds gave federal assistance to "both the educationally disadvantaged and advantaged." To realize the federal purpose of encouraging equal access for disadvantaged children, Title I offered the most effective use of federal dollars. By eliminating Impact Aid funds for children "whose parents worked, but [did] not live on federal property," the Carter administration signaled its intentions to concentrate federal dollars on compensatory educational programs.[25] In budgetary terms, this meant a $398 million reduction in Impact Aid and a $350 million increase in Title I.

In higher education, Califano continued to support programs that were consistent with the administration's emphasis on addressing the needs of the poor and minority groups. Following the example of the BEOGs, Califano wished to phase out the National Direct Student Loans, which went to postsecondary institutions, and increase Guaranteed Student Loans, which went directly to the students and focused on middle-class families. To phase out National Direct Student Loans, Califano proposed no additional funding in his budgets for 1978 and 1979. In his letter explaining the budget, Califano justified the lack of funding for the National Direct Student Loans, noting that the $275 million available from the repayments of past loans would generate sufficient funding for this program in the future. He preferred that any increases in funding focus on the BEOGs and the Guaranteed Student Loans. He did, however, admit that increased funding for the BEOGs did not greatly increase the population receiving the grants.[26] Although the 94th Congress had voted to increase the maximum payment to $1,800, HEW had restricted payments to only the $1,600 given in the past in an attempt to stretch its budget and reach more students with economic needs.[27]

A new program in the funding equation was the 1975 Education for All Handicapped Children's Act (PL 94–142). This legislation forced states to provide individualized education for each special education student. Representative John Brademas (D, IN), one of the bill's authors, explained that Congress intended to give "states and local school systems additional resources to do what by their own laws they should have been doing."[28] Carter understood the expense and necessity of the legislation. As a member of the Sumter County Board of Education, he had supported the creation of a special education classroom to address the needs of white children with special needs and, as the governor of Georgia, his educational legislative package, Adequate Program for Education in Georgia, had included providing appropriate services for students with special needs.

The expenses that the states faced to implement PL 94–142 were enormous—most needed more facilities, teachers, and specialists. Califano requested $60 million in HEW's budget to assist state and local educational systems. Magnuson's subcommittee increased the HEW budget for this item to $100 million. Because Califano had promised to "aggressively seek new federal monies . . . to help elementary and secondary schools meet their obligations" he acknowledged the subcommittee's addition to HEW's budget in this area with appreciation. Carter, however, questioned this item. On a memo listing budget changes, he noted that he and Califano discussed $60 million rather than $100 million.[29] Although Carter supported PL 94–142, the plan for increasing funding through reductions in less efficient programs meant that the additional $40 million would have to come from another area.

While Califano focused on funding for equal opportunity programs, Carter pursued a goal of improving academic achievement through efficiency. As governor, Carter had pushed for achievement testing as a means of attaining accountability in the schools. After he became president, Admiral Hyman Rickover, his former mentor in the navy, approached him about instituting national achievement testing through the Office of Education in HEW. Beginning in the late 1950s, Rickover had urged Congress and the American public to create national standards for education and to demand that schools concentrate on academics rather than "life adjustment" courses, which focused on socializing American youths for a productive life in their communities rather than college preparation. Like many critics of the public schools following the launch of Sputnik by the Soviet Union, Rickover cited the adoption of life adjustment theories by the educational community as the main source of the reputed deterioration of American education.[30]

In August 1977, Carter asked Califano to meet with Rickover to discuss the topic of voluntary national standardized testing. Califano recorded that in the meeting Rickover "lashed out at HEW's 'incompetent and counter-productive' Office of Education . . . teachers who do not teach, and schools that 'are so pleased to achieve mediocrity they mistake it for excellence.'" Although Secretary Califano met with Rickover and listened to his arguments supporting national standards, he believed that state and local officials were closer to the students and that communities understood their problems better than the federal government could. For him, the appropriate role of the Office of Education was to support state and local initiatives for raising student achievement.[31]

In November 1977, the president received a letter from Senator S. I. Hayakawa (R, CA) about a speech Califano made at the College Entrance Examination Board's Annual Meeting in October. Hayakawa, an advocate of standardized testing and national standards, was "puzzled and disappointed" by Califano's public resistance to "even voluntary national scholastic standards and tests of competency in reading, writing, and mathematics."[32] Senator Hayakawa summarized Califano's expressed opposition to national competency testing: first, Califano believed that "if a test is given largely because someone in Washington seems to think it is a good idea. . . . The tests may end up as little more than a distracting waste of time and money, rather than part of an enthusiastic effort to spur individual educational achievement." Second, the secretary pointed out the differences between localities and stated, "There is no single test that is right for every school." Citing the cultural differences among students, Califano asked, "What kind of test best measures early basic competency in a bilingual educational situation?" To answer this question, he called for further studies of the tests and of testing in general. Finally, Califano warned, "any set of test questions that the Federal Government prescribed should surely be suspect as a first step toward a national curriculum."[33]

Hayakawa found Califano's remarks "specious" and believed that the secretary was "paying only lip service to the concept" of national standards and testing. He also accused the secretary of attempting to prevent the development of standards and tests by calling for more studies on the tests. The senator concluded his letter by suggesting to the president that "the most constructive and immediate measure you could take would be the development of a set of voluntary standards and tests which states and localities could use as they see fit."[34]

Hayakawa's assessment of Califano's opposition was accurate. In his memoir, Califano explained that he opposed voluntary national standards and testing because state departments of education could feel coerced to use them, they ignored the diversity in the local school populations, and they increased the pressure national political groups could bring to bear on local school districts. As with programs for equal opportunity, Califano saw the federal government's function as filling gaps left by the states. Establishing national tests or standards, whether voluntary or not, would place the federal government in the primary educational role that, in his opinion, rightfully belonged to the states.[35]

Around the same time that Carter received the senator's letter, Rickover met with members of the White House staff and repeated his suggestion that the federal government "develop a voluntary testing program which parents can use to assess their children's progress." In these meetings, Rickover stressed that "the federal function would be simply to develop the (linguistically appropriate) tests in the basic skills" (reading, writing, and arithmetic), not to usurp the functions of the states.[36]

Based on these meetings and the belief that such a policy had congressional support, the White House staff initiated a push for test development. On principle, Califano continued to oppose federal involvement in standardized testing. Carter continued to support the idea and saw Califano's opposition as an obstruction to development of a more efficient method to promote achievement. In a letter to Califano, Carter clearly stated his desire for a national standardized test but agreed that the tests should "be used only *optionally* when states and/or local school systems want them." He ended the letter with the question "How do you suggest we do this—through HEW, or National Science Foundation?"[37] HEW's Office of Education could be involved in the process or be excluded from it.

Califano was probably aware that members of the White House staff supported placing responsibility for test development with the National Science Foundation.[38] In his answer to the president, Califano pointed out that while in the United States "there [was] no shortage of achievement tests," he believed HEW better equipped than the National Science Foundation to develop a testing program.[39] The National Institute of Education, a research unit under the jurisdiction of HEW, had already begun to develop assessment tests for state and local curricula, and HEW had the expertise to provide "assistance and information" to educators.[40] By focusing on the states' or local districts' requests, Califano continued to resist the idea of even voluntary national testing. In their next exchange, Carter expressed his frustration with Califano, "Your memo on testing does not answer the question, What can we do (without deliberate evasion or delay) to provide local and state governments with funds & satisfactory tests, and to encourage—not require—their use?"[41]

This time Califano responded that HEW would develop a bank of achievement tests, offer workshops to encourage testing, provide funds for testing programs, move quickly to develop tests in needed areas, and "convene a conference of state education officials to inform them of all the ways that HEW can assist states and localities in conducting testing programs."[42] This specific list of actions still did not address the creation of a national standardized test.

On December 28, 1977, Califano announced the promised conference, stating that the underlying premise of this meeting would be "that testing, like many other educational matters, is primarily a State and local concern."[43] Reiterating his statements before the College Entrance Examination Board, he once again provided the assurance that "HEW will not mandate testing, nor will it develop a single national test or set of national standards." As in his memos to Carter, he offered the assistance of the federal government to the state and local educators in hopes "that this Conference will lay the groundwork for a new partnership between the Department and State and local educators."[44] Califano had taken his opposition to national voluntary standardized testing to the educational public, and the issue remained a point of contention between him and Carter.

Another area of contention between the secretary and the president was the creation of the cabinet-level department of education, a plan that was vigorously promoted by the National Education Association (NEA) and supported by both Carter and Mondale during their campaign.[45] The department, as Carter and other proponents within his administration saw it, would act as both the dispenser of federal funding and as an advocate for education with direct access to the president. The creation of this department also fulfilled his campaign pledge to efficiently reorganize the executive departments in the federal government.

Beyond the Carter–Mondale campaign promises, the administration also felt pressured by Congress because Senator Abraham Ribicoff (D, CT) had already submitted a bill creating a separate department of education. Ribicoff, chair of the Senate Governmental Affairs Committee and former secretary of HEW, believed that HEW was too large to manage and that its enormous size and structure swallowed up education. The Senate Committee began holding hearings in the spring of 1977. The proposed department outlined in Ribicoff's bill included the education function of HEW and education programs from other departments including Head Start from the Office of Welfare in HEW, the school lunch program in the Department of Agriculture, the schools for military dependents in the Department of Defense, and Native American Education under the Bureau of Indian Affairs in the Department of the Interior.[46] The large department in the Senate bill (S. 991) fulfilled Carter's campaign promise and the political goals of the NEA.

During the Senate deliberations, the creation of a department of education became a politically charged issue inside the executive branch. Throughout the first year of the administration, Stuart Eizenstat, Carter's domestic policy specialist, met with Mondale and Califano to decide the best means for pulling together the various educational programs scattered throughout the executive branch. The choices were either to reorganize the Office of Education within HEW to include more of the educational programs or to create a cabinet-level department similar to the one outlined in the Ribicoff bill.

Although he agreed that the reorganization of the Office of Education com-
plied with the administration's push for efficiency in the executive branch,
Eizenstat agreed with Mondale that the administration would alienate the
NEA unless it advocated the creation of the department. Califano opposed
the creation of a department. He asserted that a strengthened Office of Education, headed by an under secretary, along with a supportive legislation
package for the reauthorization of ESEA and other programs would answer
the desires of both opponents and supporters.[47] He also believed that politically popular programs like Head Start would be staunchly defended and prevented from moving to the new department. As a result of these differences,
Mondale recommended a six-month study that would include constituent
groups, like the NEA and representatives from higher education, and representatives from departments likely to be affected, such as Labor, Agriculture,
Interior, and HEW.[48] Carter agreed, and the decision whether to create a separate department of education was postponed until the end of the year.

Hamilton Jordan, Carter's chief of staff and political advisor, strongly disagreed with the need for the study. In two memoranda, he reminded Carter
that the creation of the department was an "explicit campaign promise made
repeatedly by you" and that the nature of the commitment to the NEA was
"complete and unequivocal." Jordan listed other political considerations, but
only one concerned the tight federal budget: the department was the only
thing the administration could offer the NEA since balancing the budget prevented any substantial increase in educational funding. According to Jordan,
the burden of proof rested on those who opposed the creation of the new
department, not on those who supported it.[49]

James McIntyre, the director of OMB, also favored the creation of the
new department because it promised to bring the majority of the federal education programs into a neat administrative structure.[50] His support was con-
tingent on whether the new department included most of the federal education programs and social services programs related to education rather than
only the educational programs housed in HEW.[51] The OMB study reinforced
McIntyre's arguments for the broad-based department, but both Califano
and Eizenstat disagreed with the inclusion of social services in a department
of education.

Califano continued to support the consolidation of services and administrative reorganization within the Office of Education. Eizenstat agreed with
Califano, but as he told Carter, "no commitment we made was clearer."[52] The
president and the vice president had persuaded him that education needed an
advocate on the cabinet level; however, he opposed OMB's proposal to add
social services to the new department because it "divorced social services from
welfare, Social Security, Medicare, and Medicaid." Although it was a worthy
goal for education and social services to be tied together, he did not believe
that "we could defend, as a policy matter, separating social services from these

[health and welfare] programs." He also argued that education groups would see such a broad-based department as "subsuming the education function."[53]

These arguments reflected different approaches to the delivery of services to students living in poverty. If the department of education's purpose were to administer compensatory programs, the inclusion of the social welfare programs that addressed the needs of children and their parents would address the needs in the children's lives, not merely their schooling. If the new department followed the tradition of gathering data and administering preexisting programs, then it needed only to house the various educational programs supported by federal funding. The former structure would introduce a new inclusive approach to educational policy that accepted the child as a member of a community and family, while the latter reflected the technocratic model of state departments of education. The choice of the structure became a fundamental decision for the direction of educational policy during and after his administration. In January 1978, Carter made his decision.

A PLAN FOR EQUAL OPPORTUNITY AND EFFICIENCY

Concurrent with the internal controversies over voluntary standardized testing and the creation of a department of education was the planning for the reauthorization of the ESEA. From this process, Carter's educational policies began to coalesce. He summarized his administration's educational policy in his 1978 State of the Union Address, where he explained that his administration would focus on increasing the federal government's financial commitment to disadvantaged students, supporting financial aid for postsecondary education, strengthening the coordination between the federal, state, and local efforts in education, and cooperating with Congress on the creation of a cabinet-level department of education. This message clarified the programs and policies his administration would support for the next three years.[54]

Within a month, his staff and the staff of HEW presented Congress with the budget for FY 1979, which contained increases and reorganization proposals from his State of the Union Address. For HEW, he proposed a budget of $12.9 billion—a $3.7 billion increase over his own 1978 budget request. He planned for more than half of the requested appropriations to go to ESEA programs. The administration's budget designated the rest of the funds for financial aid programs that served college students from both economically disadvantaged families and middle income families hard-pressed by escalating tuition costs.[55]

In his proposals for elementary and secondary education, Carter described the role of the federal government as supporting "improvements in educational quality for all children and [improving] the educational opportunities and achievement of the disadvantaged, the handicapped, those with limited English language skills, Native Americans and other minorities."[56] To support such a broad reaching approach in compensatory programs, he requested a $644 million increase in funding for Title I of ESEA from its FY 1978 level. He also planned to restructure services by concentrating funding in areas with either high numbers or a large proportion of low income families.[57] By distributing funding in this manner, Carter believed that more children in both urban and rural districts could benefit. He also supported the addition of "programs with a strong emphasis in basic skills" because, as he explained to Califano, he wished for "every child in the third grade in America . . . to read at a third grade level."[58] To achieve this goal, he wanted to create a Basic Skills and Educational Quality title in ESEA to "encourage local and state demonstration efforts to improve basic skills in reading, writing, and mathematics."[59]

The creation of voluntary national standardized tests was part of the aid offered to state and local educators. In his December 1977 prelegislative memo to the president, Califano suggested the creation of an Education Quality Act to consolidate programs offered by the federal government into four clusters: Basic Skills, Special Skills, School Reform, and Teacher Development. The one concerning basic skills contained the federally funded Right to Read program. Although the secretary omitted national standardized testing, Eizenstat included testing in his memo to Carter describing Califano's proposed changes to ESEA.[60]

In financial aid for college students, Carter's proposal included the initiative from the House of Representatives to focus on Guaranteed Student Loans. Unlike the Basic Educational Opportunity Grants modified the year before, students from middle-class families could apply for the Guaranteed Student Loans. With inflation increasing the cost of higher education annually, middle-class parents struggled to pay college tuition. To answer their needs, Carter requested a $45,000 ceiling on family income for this program. These federally backed loans became the center of the Middle Income Student Assistance Act of 1978.[61]

While the extension of student loans served to expand educational opportunity in higher education, Carter and his administration also pushed this program to undermine the movement in Congress for college tuition tax credits. Congressmen Brademas had warned Califano "of a political vacuum in the absence of a White House alternative to tax credits that would help families with college-bound students."[62] Brademas feared that within the federal budget the funds lost to tuition tax credits would become "expenditures" for education. He and other members of the House Education and Labor Committee wanted to block the use of tuition tax credits as college student financial aid. They informed Carter through Califano that they would submit legislation with or without his support. In his educational message, Carter explained that he opposed college tuition tax credits because "they would cost too much, would provide benefits to those without need, [and] would provide less benefit to genuinely hard-pressed families."[63] Because Carter believed that equalizing educational opportunity was the purpose of federal programs in education, a tax credit failed to meet his standard for federal action, and he refused to support it. Shortly after this message, he announced the Middle Income Student Assistance bill to help lower and middle income families with college tuition.[64]

The administration offset the increases for ESEA and student loans with reductions in Impact Aid Grants in three categories. The first two consisted of areas where school districts listed federal employees who lived out of the country and where the children of federal employees made up less than 3 percent of the school population. The third proposed cut was the gradual phase-out of payments to school districts with students in public housing. This reduction hit impoverished areas already suffering from low tax support for education. Particularly vulnerable were urban districts that depended on the grants to replace local property taxes. Patricia Harris, the secretary of Housing and Urban Development, protested the reduction in payments for districts with public housing "because it significantly [endangered] the public housing program."[65] Even though this decision seemed contradictory to Carter's fundamental purpose of serving disadvantaged students, he may have sought the reduction because of the proposed focus of Title I funds in areas of concentrated poverty, which would include school districts with public housing. This kind of trade-off reflected the isolation of schooling from the daily lives of children in policy. Without the Impact Aid Grants, cities would suffered greater economic stress in their attempts to provide housing and schooling for the poor.

Although Carter had included national voluntary standardized testing in his description of his educational policy, by the end of April, the administration dropped the concept as an educational policy initiative because of expert opposition and dwindling interest in Congress. In March, Califano convened the promised National Conference on Achievement Testing and Basic Skills. At the conference, the National Academy of Education (NAE), a prestigious association of researchers who often prepared reports for HEW, released its report on basic skills and testing. The NAE stated that it sympathized with national standardized achievement testing, but found such a testing system "basically unworkable" because it exceeded "the current measurement arts of the testing profession, and [would] create more social problems than it [could] conceivably solve." During the conference, Senator Claiborne Pell (D, RI), a supporter of national testing, asked the audience of several hundred state education officials, congressional staff members, teachers, and parents if they supported a national standardized test. Only two individuals indicated that they did.[66]

In April, Admiral Rickover sent Carter a copy of a speech he had delivered at the National School Boards Association Convention. In it, Rickover called again for voluntary national standards in language arts and math, competency standards in reading, writing, and math, and a reduction in electives. In a memo accompanying the speech, Eizenstat informed the president that the House had dropped its bill to create a national commission to develop voluntary standards because of a lack of cosponsors.[67] As much as Carter and his staff might have agreed with Rickover, they knew that a policy with little political support in Congress or from the state educational bureaucracies would fail. The administration separated basic skills from testing and proposed support for state tests under a different title in the reauthorization of ESEA.[68]

A SOURCE OF EQUALIZATION AND ADMINISTRATION

The creation of the United States Department of Education became the central component of Carter's educational policy in his 1978 State of the Union Address. Mondale, McIntyre, Eizenstat, and Jordan all supported it. In the administration, Secretary Califano stood alone in his opposition to it. Because he saw the function of the federal government in education as coordinating compensatory services, he believed that the department was a mistake. By isolating the federal educational bureaucracy from other areas affecting poor children, the federal government could change from supplemental and regulatory to dominant and directive, a constitutionally inappropriate function in the field of education. Califano also believed that Carter's support for the new department originated with the NEA endorsement of his candidacy for president. For him, the creation of a new bureaucracy required more justification than mere political debt.[69] Despite his opposition, Califano said that if he had to support a change, he favored the OMB plan, which included all the executive branch educational programs. The broad structure of the OMB plan encompassed multiple programs with strong constituents who could have potentially brought opposition from Congress.[70]

Carter viewed the creation of the department as affirming his administration's emphasis on "the federal government's role in compensatory education—helping to remove inherent inequalities among student opportunities that remained even after the best efforts of state and local authorities."[71] The achievement of this goal seemed unlikely as long as Washington treated education as an "afterthought or nuisance" to be discussed in cabinet meetings only when "lawsuits concerning equal rights for black, Hispanic, handicapped, or female students" arose.[72] A new department that concentrated on education and advocated for the rights of students appeared to be the answer.

In April 1978, the administration submitted its proposal for the creation of the department to Congress. Compromises to facilitate passage included the removal of Head Start, the school lunch program, veteran's education, and the National Foundation for the Arts and Humanities from the department. On September 28, the Senate approved the creation of the department in a vote of seventy-two to eleven. The bill, however, died in the House of Representatives where roughly one hundred amendments, including one to prevent busing and one to allow voluntary school prayer, killed it.[73]

The problems this bill faced in the House reflected reservations about the role of the federal government in American education. In several dissenting statements, members of the House expressed the belief that "Cabinet-level departments should only be established where there is a major national policy to carry out."[74] If the creation of the department signaled the development of a major federal policy initiative in education, then the department compromised the fundamental relationship between the federal, state, and local governments. Those dissenting accused the administration of attempting to establish a "ministry of education."[75]

In his 1979 Message to Congress, Carter made a personal commitment to the creation of a department of education. To answer his critics in the House, he outlined the role of the department as ensuring educational opportunity in elementary and secondary schools, increasing access to postsecondary institutions for low and middle income students, preparing students for employment through training programs, encouraging improvement in the quality of education, and generating research and supplying information to state and local districts.[76] These were traditional objectives of federal education policy that maintained the principle of state and local control of education and would follow the bureaucratic model established by state departments of education. The new department merely offered a more efficient organization of the affected educational programs in an effort to improve coordination, not a "ministry of education" complete with national policy and objectives.

As in the previous year, the Senate passed the bill creating the department of education (seventy-two to twenty-one) and the House again resisted. The arguments given on the House floor resembled those of 1978. Dissenters claimed that the reorganization of educational programs meant changes in federal educational policy, which could intrude on the state's prerogatives and, if the new cabinet department had no intention of increasing supervision, then there was an absence of any real need for a separate department of education. Opponents also asserted that the new department would not facilitate the coordination of services; by adding another layer of bureaucracy, the process would become more difficult.[77]

The most damaging accusation was that the creation of the department was "vested interest" legislation. Congressman Eldon Rudd (R, AZ) argued that the bureaucratic habit of submitting regulatory guidelines to interested parties already gave the NEA considerable power among middle-level bureaucrats in the Office of Education. The same bureaucrats would staff the new department, and the NEA would have a cozy relationship already established with them. Rudd charged that the NEA now sought to dominate the education bureaucracy from the top level, which they had not been able to accomplish in the past. The creation of the department would give the NEA control of education from the top down.[78]

Some of the most influential newspaper editors also opposed the creation of the new department. The *Washington Post*, the *New York Times*, and the *Chicago Tribune* all ran editorials against congressional approval. *Change*, a publication focused on higher education, summarized the position of the print media:

> Stagnation will not be removed by reshuffling organizational charts. What it takes are imaginative people with a charter plan beyond the bounds of overseeing programs now on the books. More social imagination, not more federal agencies, will accomplish that. A new Department of Education is an attractive placebo, but it may just be that and no more.[79]

Critics of education in the United States wanted to see more commitment to student learning, not another layer of bureaucracy.

The department of education eventually passed the House by a narrow margin, 210 to 206. The final version of the legislation confirmed Califano's predictions that the new department would fail to consolidate the education programs in the executive branch. Head Start remained in the Office of Welfare, the school lunch program stayed in the Department of Agriculture, and Native American education continued to be part of the Bureau of Indian Affairs in the Department of the Interior. Because of the limitations imposed by the compromises made by the Carter administration to get the legislation passed, the new department received the responsibilities Carter had outlined in his State of the Union Address, but few more.[80]

After Carter signed the bill creating the new cabinet department, the question of leadership became paramount in reassuring the political opposition that the NEA would not dominate its activities. Through his selection of the secretary, Carter had the opportunity to prove his independence from the NEA and his genuine interest in equal educational opportunity. In a memo, two members of his staff described the characteristics of the perfect secretary as "a leader with vision, intellectual power and imagination." The duties of this individual included "determining education's future direction" based on social needs; "formulat[ing] short term objectives and strategies to achieve those objectives . . . motivat[ing] the nation's state, local, and private institutions to act accordingly," and re-instilling public confidence in education.[81]

Public speculation concerning the president's choice for the first secretary began shortly after the bill was signed. Names discussed by the press included Jerry Apodaca, former governor of New Mexico, Alan Campbell, head of the Office of Personnel Management, and Dr. Mary Francis Berry, assistant secretary of education in HEW. Carter's first choice was Bill Moyers, a member of Lyndon Johnson's staff and public television commentator. On October 9, Vice President Mondale informed the president that he had spoken to Moyers and did not believe that Moyers would accept the position. Mondale suggested that "we . . . throw a much wider net out to review other possibilities as well."[82]

A few days later, staff members sent another memo listing several names, including Bill Moyers and Shirley Hufstedler, a federal judge in California, as possible candidates. The text of this memo discussed the issue of identifying more women and minorities as possible candidates, but claimed that none met the criteria as well as Moyers. The Carter staff favored Moyers because he had a national reputation and political experience, "was no one's captive," and had "an appreciation for the limits of Federal authority but [understood] how to lead."[83]

Shirley Hufstedler's qualifications centered as much on what she represented as who she was. As a woman, she helped satisfy Carter's policy of hiring women and minorities for high-ranking positions. As a judge, she was respected and rumored to be a candidate for the United States Supreme Court. Early in 1978, she expressed her views on the role of the federal government in the life of Americans. In an article for the *Washington Post*, she wrote, "we now expect courts to end racial tensions, sweep contaminants from the globe and bring about an armistice in the battle of the sexes."[84] She concluded, "Courts are primary deciders, not supervisors or social problem solvers."[85] Although Hufstedler had been the appellant judge in the *Lau v. Nichols* case, a bilingual education case that eventually went to the United States Supreme Court, her evaluation of the responsibilities of the courts corresponded to Carter's idea that the federal government had limits in the services that it could provide.

Probably as important as her prominent legal position and beliefs about the limits of federal intervention was her lack of association with the education community. Although she had served on many boards connected to education, she had law credentials and had remained aloof from the educational community as an appellate judge. She stressed this distance in her confirmation hearing before the Senate Committee on Labor and Human Resources. During her testimony, Hufstedler clearly stated that she perceived the role of the Department of Education as focusing on the individual child:

> I believe in the individual. Every policy of the Department of Education should be examined for its impact on the individual child in the classroom, and the individual student at all levels of education, which is, of course, a lifelong experience. It is far too easy for insensitive bureaucracies to see children in categories or as statistics, and even easier for children to become pawns in adult chess games.[86]

Her statement assured the committee that, under her leadership, the department would view students, rather than educators as its primary constituents. On October 30, 1979, Carter announced that Hufstedler would serve as the first secretary of education.

EQUAL OPPORTUNITY IN HIGHER EDUCATION

At the same time that Congress created the United States Department of Education, it held hearings on the reauthorization of ESEA. In the final bill, the administration gained many of its proposed changes in compensatory education, basic skills, and school desegregation. In a memo to the president outlining the reauthorization bill, Eizenstat pointed out that Congress had agreed to authorize "supplemental [Title I] payments to districts with concentrations of low income children" and to improve "access of private school children to the Title I program."[87] In the area of basic skills, the new federal literacy program added writing and math skills to reading. Title IV—Educational Improvement, Resources and Support included support for testing, and the creation of planning grants "to implement court-ordered desegregation plans" to assist desegregation efforts.[88] The administration did not, however, achieve the reduction in Impact Aid Grants to help defer the costs of the increased funding for Title I. Instead the reauthorization bill contained increased funding for Impact Aid and included the children of federal employees as well as those in public housing. Although this part of the bill violated Carter's beliefs about the use of federal dollars, Eizenstat suggested the president sign the bill because the administration had achieved most of its policy objectives for ESEA.[89]

At the same time that Congress reauthorized ESEA, it also addressed another program from Johnson's Great Society legislation, the Higher Education Act of 1965. The titles within it funded community education, college libraries, developing institutions, and student financial aid programs.[90] Title III specifically focused on providing financial support for developing institutions as they moved toward becoming financially independent. When Congress passed the bill in 1965, the definition of a developing institution was vague, but, by 1979, it meant predominately black colleges that served disadvantaged students.[91] Many of these colleges lacked funding, offered only limited programs, and employed fewer faculty members holding doctorates than predominately white institutions.

In the fall of 1979, the Senate began hearings to reauthorize the Higher Education Act. Dr. Mary Francis Berry, the assistant secretary of education, testified that the administration proposed changing the wording of the title to agree with the practices of the federal government. The president wanted clear language that stated plainly that Title III "focus[ed] on institutions that provide higher education opportunities for low income students . . . and that have few resources to spend on educating these students."[92] This clarity was important because Congress had raised the budget for the program by $200 million, increasing access to federal monies for underfunded institutions serving disadvantaged students.[93]

While one of the administration's general goals was to aid disadvantaged students in their pursuit of higher education, Carter wanted to aid the predominately black colleges in particular. He knew that the Board of Regents of the University System of Georgia had taken steps to improve the credentials of faculty at predominately black public colleges and was familiar with the private colleges in the city of Atlanta (Clark Atlanta University, Morehouse, Spelman, and Morris Brown colleges); thus, he was well acquainted with the financial problems these institutions faced. In February 1978, he met with the presidents of several predominately black colleges and pledged his support. A year later, he sent a memorandum to all departments and agencies requesting a review of all programs to "eliminate unintended exclusion of historically black colleges and universities" and to increase communication with representatives of those institutions.[94]

The Office of Education responded by creating a special unit to evaluate and make recommendations to the other departments concerning the federal government's relationship with these institutions. Their findings indicated that the majority of the federal support for predominately black colleges consisted of "student financial assistance and the developing institutions program" in Title III. They also pointed out that federal support to these institutions had declined from 5.2 percent of their funding in FY 1978 to 4.4 percent in FY 1979.[95] The administration sought changes to Title III to remedy the funding shortfall.

In response to the instructions from the president and its own recommendations, the Office of Education revised the eligibility criteria for Title III funding to focus greater attention on low expenditures per students and the number of Basic Educational Opportunity Grants (BEOGs) in relation to the number of full-time students. Institutions with more students receiving BEOGs and with low per student expenditures received priority in the distribution of Title III funding for institutional development. These criteria described many of the predominately black public and private colleges.[96]

Carter's commitment to these institutions demonstrated his desire to increase poor students' access to higher education and his belief that these institutions fulfilled a community need. As the governor of Georgia, he had expressed his belief that "black and white educators, black and white parents, and black and white students" all sought to keep higher education segregated.[97] If, in the minds of the parents and the students, colleges devoted to the education of black students best served their needs, he believed it was his duty to maintain those institutions. His support for these colleges may have also reflected the overwhelming support that African American voters had shown him the 1976 election.

CONCLUSION

Carter's administration suffered from many economic and political pressures. Although he wished to emphasize excellence through testing, the opposition of HEW Secretary Joseph Califano, the collapse of congressional support, and the creation of the Department of Education kept the focus of the federal government on the equal opportunity programs from Lyndon Johnson's Great Society. Carter's interest in curriculum and desire for students to perform on grade level gave basic skills an important place in compensatory education programs. The loss of interest in and opposition to national voluntary standardized testing kept Carter's educational policies squarely in the context of budgetary efficiency and equal educational opportunity. Testing, while increasingly important in educational reform movements, remained a state issue.

The creation of the United States Department of Education disappointed those who believed that Carter would make comprehensive changes in the federal educational structure. Congress passed the legislation too late in his administration for him to do more than appoint the secretary and for her to begin the organization of the department. Also, the resistance in the House successfully limited the bureaucratic restructuring of federal education programs. Finally, six days after Carter signed the legislation, Iranian students seized the American Embassy in Tehran and took employees hostage. While Carter fulfilled his campaign promise to the NEA, the operational development of the Department of Education became a low priority.

Beyond his campaign promise, the establishment of the Department of Education may have resulted as much from Carter's own preference for administrative reorganization as the political pressures from the Senate and the NEA. During his presidential campaign, he had pledged to reduce the number of departments in the federal government and to rationalize those that were left. The size of HEW made it a target for reorganization. The removal of education from the huge department appealed more to administrative logic and had more political justification than removing health from welfare programs. It was the same administrative logic that resulted in the loss of the opportunity to follow the revolutionary approach to compensatory educational programs suggested by OMB director James McIntyre and supported by Califano. The economic stress of the late 1970s, however, may have hampered the coordination of educational and social services even if the department had included them.

By the end of Carter's administration, the rate of inflation exceeded 20 percent. As a result, the federal budget declined in real dollars and the projected budgets for 1980 and 1981 could not keep pace with increased prices. What looked like budget increases on paper were actually decreases. In December 1979, secretary-designate Hufstedler appealed to OMB for enough funds to prevent cuts in services to disadvantaged students. Proposed budgetary cuts included "flagship" programs, such as Title I of ESEA, the Handicapped State Grant Program, and Basic Educational Opportunity Grants. In her appeal, she stressed that

The Carter administration has demonstrated its strong commitment to education by a series of legislative achievements and large budgetary increases over the past several years. . . . If we do not at least offset the effects of inflation on these flagship programs, the upward trend will be replaced . . . by a substantial decline in the general level of services to the neediest segment of our population. We cannot permit that to occur.[98]

Despite her request, the director of OMB and Carter approved the budget cuts. While Carter believed that the federal government had a responsibility "to alleviate affliction and to enhance the development . . . of our most needy citizens," programs that addressed the needs of these citizens were expensive. Double-digit inflation effectively destroyed his administration's ability to commit additional funding to compensatory educational programs. As inflation soared, the only way that educational spending could increase was by raising the national debt or making painful budget cuts in other areas. Carter had committed to balancing the budget to control inflation, necessitating budget cuts in every area possible. Reduction in educational spending proved inevitable.[99]

SIX

Return to Local Leadership

The Carter Center and Atlanta Project

DURING THE LAST YEAR of his presidency, Jimmy Carter faced many challenges that diverted his attention from educational policy and the development of the new Department of Education. On November 4, 1979, Iranian students stormed the U.S. Embassy in Tehran and took the sixty-six employees hostage. This event began a year of negotiations for the release of the hostages with daily news coverage counting the number of days of the "Hostage Crisis."[1] In addition, the Soviet Union invaded Afghanistan,[2] and Carter and his secretary of state, Cyrus Vance, continued the efforts started the year before to solidify the Camp David Accords between Egypt and Israel.[3] In domestic policy, inflation and unemployment demanded his attention. Finally, from within his own party, Senator Ted Kennedy (D, MA) threatened Carter's candidacy for reelection.[4] Collectively, these events overwhelmed Carter's second bid for the presidency.

Ronald Reagan, his Republican opponent, pledged to downsize the federal government, dismantle the newly created Department of Education, and cut taxes. While these campaign promises may have appealed to many voters, Carter was actually defeated by inflation and the hostage crisis. Election day marked the one-year anniversary of the hostage taking in Iran. The print media and television networks focused special issues and broadcasts on the events of the preceding year the night before the election. Pat Caddell, Carter's pollster since his gubernatorial administration in Georgia, found that most of the undecided voters shifted to Reagan after these broadcasts. On election day, 51 percent of the vote went to Reagan while Carter received 41 percent, and Senator John Anderson, who ran as an Independent, received most of the remaining 7 percent.[5] The Iranian government released the hostages immediately after Reagan's inauguration, and, on January 21, Carter left for Wiesbaden, West Germany, to welcome home the hostages.

Traditionally, former presidents have little influence on policy in the United States.[6] Most go quietly into retirement, lending their names to special causes and serving on various boards. Carter, however, decided to take the advice of his favorite poet, Dylan Thomas, and "not go gentle into that night."[7] Both Jimmy and Rosalyn Carter wished to continue to work, and the former president knew that he had the daunting task of raising money for the construction of his presidential library. Neither of the Carters wanted a "mausoleum for his presidency."[8] They wanted a place to continue the work for human rights that they had begun during their White House years.

THE FOUNDING OF THE
CARTER CENTER OF EMORY UNIVERSITY

In 1982, Carter accepted an appointment at Emory University as a University Distinguished Professor. He did so for several reasons. First, he wanted to connect his library to an institution of higher education. Emory University was a logical choice because of the diversity of its colleges and schools, and its strong connection to donors in the Atlanta metropolitan area. Second, Hamilton Jordan spent a year on the campus writing his memoirs and sang the praises of its president, James Laney, to Carter during that year. Finally, Carter knew Laney and had invited him to the White House twice in 1980. Carter and Laney shared many experiences. Both grew up in small towns— Carter in Georgia and Laney in Arkansas; both sought to apply their Christian belief to modern life, and both had served in the military.[9]

After he accepted the position at Emory, Carter's role consisted of more than simply occupying an office in the library. During his first decade on the campus, he lectured in classes on ethics, theology, international relations, and politics and conducted forums—filled to capacity—on these topics. His faculty position also provided the basis for the relationship between the Carter Center and Emory. When he and his advisors began planning the mission of the Carter Center, Carter invited Laney and selected members of the faculty to voice their opinions.[10]

According to Rosalynn Carter, the idea for making the presidential library more than a repository of documents came to Carter in the middle of the night. He sat up in bed and told Rosalynn, "I know what we can do with the library. . . . We can develop a place to help people resolve disputes."[11] While this story may well be true as to the eventual focus of the Carter Center, Jimmy and Rosalynn had visited many foundations and university institutes looking for a model for what they wanted to create.[12] Carter's epiphany concerned the focus of the center and its connection to the presidential library.

Historian Douglas Brinkley describes the Carters' vision as duplicating "Camp David in Atlanta, creating a center that would serve as a neutral forum within which hostile groups could meet to explore common approaches to problems."[13] The Carters wished their institute to be "action-oriented" rather than academic, mirroring the efforts of a University of Georgia agricultural experiment station rather than a think tank.[14] Laney understood their vision and organized a working group to help formalize a plan for the center. It was through this group that the Carters ironed out the idea that their policy center would not have a degree program, but that members of the Emory faculty would work there on specific issues.

Carter liked the efficiency and accessibility of an experiment station, which directly addressed the agricultural problems faced by local farmers and offered classes on husbandry, planting, insecticides, and farm management. When he returned to Plains from the navy, he had attended classes offered by the Southwest Branch Agricultural Experiment Station. Through the applied research shared by the faculty in these classes, he learned the modern management and farming skills that helped him and other farmers in the area become more prosperous.[15] This model of direct intervention for the welfare of local farmers and villagers in health and agriculture appealed to him as the optimum use of his status as a past president.

After the Carters and their faculty advisors decided on the policy center's structure, they worked on its purpose. In July, they met with a group of their most trusted friends, including Cyrus Vance, Warren Christopher, Hamilton Jordan, as well as Laney and selected members of the Emory faculty. One of those invited was Kenneth Stein, an assistant professor whose specialty was the Middle East. Those who knew the Carters well understood that they wanted to continue their efforts to kindle peace between warring factions and address the agricultural and health needs of the poor throughout the world. Jordan cautioned the Carters about trying to do too many things, but others in the group encouraged them.[16]

Carter wished to begin the process of negotiating peace in the Middle East immediately. When he asked Stein what could be quickly accomplished, the assistant professor suggested an event to evaluate the progress of the Camp David Accords. As a first step, he suggested that Carter plan a tour of different countries in the region and speak with their leaders about the peace process. Then, when the leaders or their representatives came together in Atlanta, the delegates would have a foundation for their discussions. Carter agreed with Stein, and he and Rosalynn began planning the preliminary trip to the Middle East almost immediately.[17]

Upon their return and a year before the groundbreaking ceremony for the building that would house the Carter Center of Emory University (CCEU), Carter hosted "Middle East Consultation: Five Years After Camp David" to launch its peacemaking work. For this event, Carter invited diplomats and dignitaries from the United States, Middle Eastern countries, and the Soviet Union. In the *New York Times*, William Schmidt credited Carter with giving his policy center an "auspicious beginning" by bringing together "high-ranking officials from the Governments of Syria, Lebanon, Saudi Arabia, Jordan and Egypt" along with "a roster of former United States officials that reads like a Who's Who in foreign affairs"[18] Although the representation was incomplete because of Israel's refusal to send a delegate, the "Atlanta Initiative," as it was called in the media, brought Carter credibility as a mediator in his postpresidency and established the developing CCEU as a place for adversaries to meet outside the realm of official negotiations.[19]

While the first conference was lauded by the media and regarded as a personal success for Carter, the construction of the CCEU and presidential library soon became mired in controversy. The public debate centered on the construction of the Freedom Parkway, referred to as the "Exprezway" by detractors. The residents of the neighborhoods immediately surrounding the proposed CCEU and presidential library protested this 2.4 mile access to the major freeways as destructive of an historic neighborhood and park. The ground had been cleared of houses when Carter was governor of Georgia, and he had vetoed the bill to build an expressway on it then. Yet, in 1982, he and Andrew Young, mayor of Atlanta and former ambassador to the United Nations under Carter, both supported the construction of the parkway.[20] Although Carter managed to get the parkway built, his reputation in the city was tainted by this reversal.

A MISSION OF EDUCATION

The CCEU was dedicated on October 1, 1986, Carter's sixty-second birthday. Its mission statement was simple. The work of the center was "guided by a fundamental commitment to human rights and the alleviation of human suffering." To achieve this broad purpose "it seeks to prevent and resolve conflicts, enhance freedom and democracy, and improve health."[21] Five principles directed the work of the center: timely action, unique interventions, nonpartisan status, acknowledgment of the risk of failure, and the belief "that people can improve their lives when provided with the necessary skills, knowledge, and access to resources."[22] Delivering the information for the development of the skills and knowledge would entail an educational focus for the work at the CCEU. Thus, while education was not an overt mission of the center, it was one of the means used in the CCEU's programs for people to improve their lives.

This use of education was vastly different from the institutionalized schooling that Carter addressed through state and federal policies. Rather, it incorporated the social, economic, and political institutions of a society in the process of education.[23] Although the work of the CCEU often began at the highest levels of government, its ultimate intention was to improve the quality of life of local populations through culturally acceptable methods.

From its beginning, the work of the CCEU focused on arms control, election monitoring, mental health, health care in remote areas, and peace negotiations in the Middle East. In arms control, Carter worked closely with his predecessor Gerald Ford. While the two former presidents seldom agreed on domestic policy issues, they shared similar views regarding U.S. foreign policy, particularly the need for arms control, which included what they considered the insanity of the Strategic Defense Initiative (SDI), dubbed Star Wars by the press. In the area of mental health, Rosalynn Carter organized and led seminars to increase awareness of the lack of insurance coverage available for mental illness and dispel the stigma associated with it.[24]

The education initiatives associated with public and private schools began before the CCEU was officially opened in 1986. Most of these programs concentrated on curriculum development and college student internships. One of the first events planned for the new facility was the consultation, "Reinforcing Democracy in the Americas," with present and former elected heads of state from countries in the Caribbean and Central and South America. Robert Pastor, the center's specialist on Latin America, invited six Atlanta area teachers to participate in the planning process. After the CCEU hosted the event, he also worked with them to develop a social studies curriculum on Latin American countries, which one of them taught the following school term. Another workshop for health and social studies teachers focused on international development and put the teachers in contact with representatives from the Task Force for Child Survival, UNICEF, and International Services for Health, Inc.[25]

The bicentennial celebration of the U. S. Constitution also contributed to curriculum development. To commemorate this anniversary, the center planned to host "Women and the Constitution: A Bicentennial Perspective." Rosalynn Carter, Betty Ford, Pat Nixon, and Lady Bird Johnson invited former Representative Barbara Jordan (D, TX), Supreme Court Justice Sandra Day O'Connor, and Coretta Scott King to deliver keynote speeches and 150 other scholars and female leaders to participate in panels on the place of women in constitutional history. Among those attending were John Patrick of Indiana University and thirty Atlanta area teachers. Patrick's job at the symposium was to develop a social studies curriculum that addressed the social and political activism of women in the United States. The center invited the thirty teachers to disseminate materials through workshops in their school districts.[26]

In 1988, the center continued its work in curriculum development by inviting secondary teachers to a five-day workshop on the Middle East. Organized by the Middle East program in response to requests for material by secondary teachers, Kenneth Stein, the program's director, visiting research fellows, and Emory faculty offered fifty-seven teachers information about the "geography, history, politics, religion, and culture of the region."[27] The organizers asked two teachers to demonstrate how the information could be used in classrooms. The final stage was for the teachers participating in the workshop to develop curriculum to share with their peers.[28] By inviting teachers, rather than curriculum directors, the center attempted to reach the "grassroots" level of the educational system with information that could eventually inform many of the people of Atlanta about the Middle East and the peace process there. It also involved teachers in real world events and gave them access to experts for authentic curriculum.

This process of distributing information through workshops and local associations was also part of the center's political, health, and agricultural educational initiatives in Latin American and African countries. The Global 2000 agricultural program consisted of a "series of demonstration projects designed to increase food production by teaching farmers new growing techniques."[29] Following the model of the agricultural extension agency where Carter had learned modern farming techniques, the Carter Center began projects in Ghana, Sudan, and Zambia with Norman Borlaug, a Nobel Peace Prize recipient for his research on hybrid grains and his leadership of the "Green Revolution" in India and Pakistan, serving as the senior consultant.[30]

In a question-and-answer session for the Fall 1988 CCEU newsletter, Borlaug explained that past efforts to increase farm production in African countries had overwhelmed extension workers and village farmers with sophisticated technology. The approach he advocated was quite different. Using the traditional tools of the local farmers, Borlaug and his team planted one-acre demonstration plots alongside ones where farmers used traditional planting techniques. The close proximity of the fields allowed the extension agents and farmers to see the difference in per acre yield. Through this simple presentation, they could actually judge for themselves how new seed, fertilizer, and weed control methods could benefit them. Not surprisingly, the Global 2000 team found extension workers and farmers willing to cooperate and learn the processes used in the demonstration plots. Borlaug measured the success of this program by the increase in demonstration plots—from 20 in 1986 to 16,000 in 1988. He hoped that through this educational process, Ghana, the country making the most progress, would begin to export grain in three to four years.[31]

In the area of world health, Global 2000 used similarly simple and direct tactics for education. Working with the ministry of health in each country affected by a target disease, the CCEU helped to develop flip charts and other visual aids for field workers to use. Careful to keep the focus of the message on the information rather than the visual aid, culturally appropriate illustrations, photos, and language were used to communicate with local villagers.[32]

Through these means, the CCEU and its partner organizations tackled the problem posed by the guinea worm (dracunculiasis), an organism that had devastating effects on many rural populations in Africa and Asia and was easily spread due to the practice of gathering drinking water from rain ponds.[33]

Beginning in 1986, Carter and the staff of the CCEU obtained funding for materials and pledged to work with other groups to eradicate the disease by 1995 in all seventeen affected countries. Following the fifth principle of educating local people so that they could help themselves, the Center sent one resident technical advisor to work with the health department or ministry in each country with high numbers of people suffering from the disease. Using local coordinators or supervisors trained by the CCEU and its partners, the governments arranged for villagers to receive health education on the various methods for removing the larvae from their drinking water. By teaching local villagers how to purify their drinking water, the reproductive cycle of this deadly organism could be disrupted and guinea worm could be eradicated from the area.[34]

The duplication of multiple organization collaboration and education as means of self-help for other health and agricultural initiatives spread the influence of the CCEU internationally. At home, the work of the center gained little attention. It was Carter's personal efforts in the charitable homebuilding organization—Habitat for Humanity—and his personal war on poverty in The Atlanta Project that gained the attention of his fellow Americans.

A MISSION OF CHARITY

Simultaneous with the development of the CCEU and its programs, the Carters became involved with Habitat for Humanity. Born at Koinonia Farm, a desegregated homestead outside of Americus, Georgia, Habitat began in 1968 as a fund to build forty-two homes for the working poor. The idea developed by Clarence Jordan, owner of Koinonia, consisted of gathering funds from wealthy people and donations of surplus materials from homebuilders and using them to construct homes for those without the means to qualify for financing from banks or other lending institutions. The new homeowners would pay for their homes through "sweat equity," labor invested in building their own homes and those of others like them, and noninterest-bearing loans. The money repaid by the homeowners went back into the Fund for Humanity to support future construction projects.[35]

In 1965, Millard Fuller closed his law practice in Alabama and moved his family to Koinonia. Using his skills as a lawyer, he helped Jordan plan the funding and construction of the original forty-two sites. In 1973, Fuller and his wife decided to move to Mdandaka, Zaire (Democratic Republic of Congo) to build 2,000 homes in the area. After beginning the project and working there for three years, he and his family returned to Koinonia and launched Habitat for Humanity International.[36]

Fuller's homebuilding activities captured the attention of the Carters when he invited them to a house dedication in Plains during Carter's final weeks in the White House in 1980. When the Carters declined the invitation, Fuller lashed out at them in the local paper for claiming to care about the poor, but being indifferent to the housing needs in their own community.[37] After the Carters returned to Plains, they continued to hear about Habitat from the volunteers who visited their church. Finally, on a visit to New York in 1984, Carter went by an abandoned apartment house on the Lower East Side that a group of Habitat volunteers planned to renovate or rebuild as the roof was missing and many of the floors had collapsed. On hearing Habitat's plans for this dilapidated structure, Carter responded spontaneously, offering to come back "and do some volunteer carpenter work."[38] His words traveled back to Georgia faster than he did and, on his return, Fuller called to thank him for his offer.

On Labor Day weekend, Carter rode for twenty-five hours on a bus with other volunteers from Americus to reach the site. When they arrived, the trash had been cleared from the building, but the local volunteers had accomplished little else. It looked worse than when Carter had originally seen it. The condition of the building and the lack of a coherent plan for its restoration discouraged the volunteers, many of whom had taken vacation time from their jobs. In an attempt to renew their enthusiasm, Carter met with the experienced builders in the group that night and asked what could be accomplished in a week; together, they began to plan what fifty people could accomplish in five days. By the end of the week, the volunteers from Georgia had repaired most of the flooring and the roof as well as removed the ruined plaster from the walls.[39] This week began what would become Jimmy Carter Work Weeks, high-profile building efforts that generated houses, publicity, and financial support for the organization.[40]

Habitat for Humanity was the kind of organization that appealed to Carter. Volunteers supplied the labor, suppliers donated or sold materials at cost to the organization, and Jordan and Fuller based its debt payment method on Exodus 22:25—"If you lend money to My people, to the poor among you, you are not to act as a creditor to him; you shall not charge him interest."[41] Following his return to Plains from the navy through his presidency, Carter had used volunteers and civic organizations to promote economic development and area planning. While Habitat focused on individual houses or the development of a single street rather than urban or community planning, its volunteer energy and structure reinforced his belief that individuals could make a difference in the lives of others. In this spirit of volunteerism, Carter turned his attention to the home of the Carter Center, Atlanta, Georgia, in 1991.

ATTEMPTED EMPOWERMENT

Atlanta was a city of contradictions in the early 1990s. It had won the bid to host the 1996 Olympics because of its mild climate, modern transportation system, and active business and civic leadership. The city seemed to be booming; the Department of Housing and Urban Development (HUD) deemed it one of the fastest growing economies in the nation from 1975 to 1995. In 1989, however, 43 percent of the children in the city lived in poverty.[42] In the Annie E. Casey Foundation's demographic data of fifty cities, 17 percent of children lived in distressed neighborhoods in 1990, but in Atlanta 33 percent lived in an environment of high unemployment and poverty.[43] Furthermore, in 27 percent of Atlanta families with children eighteen or younger, one or both parents were unemployed in 1990—significantly more than in other participating cities where the average was only 17 percent.[44] Additionally, in the middle of the 1990s, the highest dropout rates concentrated in the three counties that contained most of the distressed neighborhoods in the Atlanta metropolitan area.[45] Finally, 19 percent of all the births in Atlanta in 1994 were to unmarried teenagers.[46]

The presence of this level of poverty and its accompanying urban challenges in a booming metropolitan economy illustrated that there were two Atlantas—one rich and one poor that often reflected the white/black racial divide in the city as well as the north/south residential separation.[47] The economic plight and isolation of the southern neighborhoods began in the 1940s when city business and government leaders cut off the African American working-class neighborhoods from the downtown area with the north–south expressway. In the 1960s, further development in the area destroyed more traditionally African American neighborhoods, leaving vacant lots where planned commercial development failed to materialize.[48]

The situation worsened as middle-class African Americans left the neighborhoods for the suburbs. The people who remained had little political power or control over their environment. As the area became mired in poverty, crime, and drug addiction, the city leaders paid little attention to the residents of these decaying neighborhoods.[49] The Olympics, however, threatened to bring Atlanta's urban blight to the attention of the world; thus, city leaders felt compelled to address the problems of the inner city and the people who lived there.

Georgia's first citizen also felt compelled to address the conditions where the children in south Atlanta lived. In October 1991, Jimmy Carter announced the creation of a task force to address the needs of the families living in poverty in Atlanta. His ambitious plan consisted of setting goals in "every area: housing, unemployment, school dropouts, drug addiction, and so forth, the maximum conceivable goal that would be at all practical."[50] With the promised infusion of funds and new employment opportunities, the 1996

Olympic Games offered an opportune time to focus the energy of the metropolitan area on the people and neighborhoods abandoned in the past. However, to take advantage of the growing interest in the Atlanta metropolitan area, he argued, city leaders needed to face the "unpleasantness" of the distressed neighborhoods and the people who lived in them and act "with some hope that the unpleasantness can be resolved."[51]

Carter decided to address the poverty in Atlanta for several reasons. In his work at the CCEU, he found that problems such as guinea worm could be solved through the collaboration of many organizations and the commitment of the local areas. While the problems in Atlanta were many and complex, he knew that many organizations had tried to respond to a single problem—mentoring students, job training, or drug abuse—with limited results because of the intricacy of the problems. The first step, as he saw it, was to assess what was needed, what was available, and how to fill the gaps creating a "synergistic effect of bringing together existing programs that are working side by side" in government and the private sector. To bring the city together, volunteers from business and wealthier communities would fill the gaps found in the services offered by existing organizations.[52] The Atlanta Project (TAP) was an ambitious five-year plan to make Atlanta a united city.

He also had personal and emotional reasons for turning his attention to his home city. First, James Laney, members of the Emory Board of Trustees, and even Carter feared the university could not sustain the overseas commitments of the CCEU after the retirement or death of Carter. Laney believed that the CCEU method of coordinating existing services and donations to allow people to help themselves could be successful at home. Carter had convinced drug companies to donate desperately needed medicines to third world countries; Laney believed that Carter could motivate the heads of corporations and foundations to aid in the alleviation of the social and economic problems faced by the poor in the United States.[53]

Second, foundations and city governments were increasingly interested in restoring and reviving central cities and addressing the problems of the people left in those areas as the more affluent fled to the suburbs. In Baltimore, the South Bronx of New York, and other cities, residents of distressed neighborhoods formed community development corporations (CDCs) and, with the help of foundations, reclaimed abandoned areas and created economic centers in the midst of urban blight. When Atlanta won the opportunity to host the Olympics, the city government and local organizers began to plan the venues for the games near the impoverished southern neighborhoods. Some of the residents responded by forming CDCs to work with developers to protect what was left of their neighborhoods. Carter believed that coordinating the efforts of these organizations offered an opportunity for community participation in the process of addressing poverty in south Atlanta.[54]

The third reason was emotional. On a tour of the public hospital, Jimmy and Rosalynn met "Pumpkin," a child born four months prematurely to a mother addicted to crack and alcohol. Her mother did not know that she was pregnant and had smoked crack the night before the little girl was born. When the paramedics arrived at the house, which had no electricity or running water, the infant's temperature was so low that it did not register on the thermometer. She weighed less than a pound and was so small that she fit in the hand of the emergency worker. When Carter saw her, she was covered in tubes for feeding, medicine, and breathing. She had her first stroke when she was two weeks old. After he and Rosalynn held the child, he said, "I never knew about this before . . . God knows I should have. I've been Governor of this state. I've been President of the United States. I didn't even know about things like this."[55] One of the doctors pointed out that, while Pumpkin was an extreme example, she was "the direct result of the social chaos today."[56] He also informed the Carters that her chances for survival were slim.[57]

Carter was also aware of the shacks of homeless urban squatters in a vacant city lot within a hundred yards of the Carter Center facility. In his account of Carter's motivation for TAP, Brinkley describes how the "ex-president's Christian conscience had gnawed at him all the five years he sat in his plush Carter Center office."[58] About the same time that he met Pumpkin, he walked over to the shacks and spoke with the homeless people for a couple of hours. He found that many had skills and wished to work.[59] These encounters brought home to him the many social problems that plagued the city and their interconnectedness. He saw that "all the problems—crack babies, teenage mothers, juvenile delinquency, dropouts—[were] related."[60]

With the support of Laney, Carter decided to stop teaching at Emory and devote more of his time to the development of TAP. His plan was to "go to the people in charge, enlist their support, assemble a winning team and let them do the work."[61] In November 1991, he began to talk to city officials about the programs that were available and to poor people and school personnel about their needs. In the schools, he talked to teachers and students who "told him of overcrowded classes and poorly motivated pupils."[62] After he spent an hour listening to the residents of public housing projects concerns about health care, unemployment, education, crime, and drug trafficking in the area, he told the media that the problems were bigger than he anticipated and that the process could take longer than the five years planned.[63] In addition to learning about the actual conditions in the south Atlanta neighborhoods, he also began the task of recruiting specialists, corporate leaders, and local activists to help address the issues.

Pulling these three groups together with the residents in the area, Carter planned to draw on the civic capacity that had brought the Olympics to Atlanta.[64] To engage the Atlanta business community in TAP, he hired Dan Sweat as the executive coordinator. Sweat was well known by Atlanta area business leaders because of his fifteen-year leadership of Central Atlanta Progress, a nonprofit organization of business leaders and civic organizations that focused on the development of the downtown area.[65] Sweat's job was to manage the resources available from various agencies, groups, and volunteers to create an organization that could achieve the goals set by the task force and involve representatives of the poor in the decision-making process.

To involve the community in the schools, Carter turned to Neil Short-house, the executive director of Georgia Cities in Schools (CIS). Carter may have favored the CIS program because its structure was similar to the one he had intended to create in his Early Childhood Development Program when he was governor of Georgia. A national organization, CIS had local affiliates that coordinated services for students living in poverty because its founders believed that students who were in danger of dropping out of school faced more than academic problems; the needs of their families had to be addressed as well. Through partnerships with government agencies, civic organizations, businesses, and community groups, CIS coordinated the delivery of services at schools—from mentoring for students to substance abuse counseling for parents.[66] By providing for the social and economic needs of the students' families at the school site, CIS made the school the center of the community. This program surpassed Carter's most ambitious goals for the Early Childhood Development Program; TAP's structure within the neighborhoods reflected the strong influence of CIS.

By combining the CIS structure, the volunteerism of civic groups, and the spirit of Habitat for Humanity, Carter believed that TAP could bring together business executives, local government leaders, and the people living in the distressed neighborhoods. He thought that bringing the residents into the planning and management of the project was a better approach than the past practices of the liberal "Santa Claus," which often imposed fragmented programs from the top to help those at the bottom. In his opinion, the activities of charities and government agencies, including "soup kitchens, homeless shelters, food stamps, housing assistance, schools in juvenile detention centers, and emergency health care" while valuable, "[gave] little promise of permanent change in living conditions."[67] The only way to achieve meaningful change was to acknowledge the desire of people "to participate in the actual improvements of their own neighborhood" and "exert authority or influence over decisions that affect them."[68]

For funding, Carter sought corporate partnerships. The week after he announced TAP, John Akers, the chairman of IBM, sent Carter a letter offering anything he needed.[69] The list of corporations that signed up to support TAP through either funding, materials, or loaned executives read like the Who's Who of Atlanta business: Nations Bank, the Home Depot, United Parcel Service, Coca-Cola, Delta Airlines, Equifax, Turner Broadcasting, Marriott Corporation, Wachovia, Bank South, Cox Enterprises, and Kroger, to name a few.[70] Mark O'Connell, the head of the United Way of Metropolitan Atlanta, agreed to organize the volunteers, and the superintendents of the area schools announced their support through Atlanta Promise, an umbrella organization of the Atlanta Chamber of Commerce.[71]

As he had when he was governor, Carter turned to the institutions of higher education for help with planning. Using census data, Professor David Sawicki at Georgia Institute of Technology worked with graduate students to develop tracts or clusters of neighborhoods with the highest infant morality rates, school dropouts, crime, teenage mothers, and single-parent households.[72] Following the model of CIS, high schools became the organizational center of each cluster. Through these centers, services could be distributed, workshops could be organized, and events could be scheduled. This model placed the education of children at the center of TAP's activities and encouraged the involvement of the communities in the schools.

The use of census tracts for the organization of the clusters facilitated the analyses of the social and economic problems within them, but it also created artificial boundaries. The areas with the highest percentage of teenage mothers and single-parent households spanned three counties (Fulton, Dekalb, and Clayton) and included the southern neighborhoods of Atlanta as well as neighborhoods in several smaller cities south of Atlanta. This area contained 500,000 people of varying economic status and needs. The population within each cluster ranged from 8,000 to 60,000; the median income levels ranged from $8,000 to $31,000, and unemployment rates varied from 5.8 to 18.3 percent.[73] This demographic diversity made developing relationships among residents, TAP representatives (clusters coordinators), and corporate partners difficult in most clusters.

Because the geographical area included in TAP was so large and the problems were so complex, it was organized on three levels. Within the cluster, a coordinator and an assistant oversaw activities and worked with committees focusing on health, education, employment, and housing. An internal steering committee, consisting of chairs of these committees (who were residents of the neighborhood), representatives of agencies in the area, and corporate partners, gathered information to complete an inventory of available services, develop a needs assessment for the cluster, and devise a master plan to answer the needs of residents.[74]

Above this level was the central office called the Carter Collaboration Center. Located in City Hall East, it housed state-of-the art meeting rooms and computers donated by corporate partners. Here the administrative staff and the two oversight boards worked to plan initiatives that spanned all twenty clusters. The staff of forty-three consisted of people with expertise in health, education, urban planning, economic development loaned from businesses, universities, government agencies, and area organizations as well as administrative and support personnel.[75] The two boards that set TAP's policies also met at the Collaboration Center. The Advisory Board, which consisted of representatives from all the constituencies of TAP, was a policymaking body, and a smaller Executive Committee maintained the focus on the mission and managed operations.[76] Thus, Carter and his advisors planned the structure of TAP to include the opinions and ideas of residents, partners, and government officials, but the grassroots level program planning in the neighborhoods was the responsibility of the residents and the cluster coordinators.

Managing the hierarchical structure of TAP represented the major challenge of the endeavor. The coordination of such a complex structure to ensure that all levels had a voice in the operations of the organization required open communications between the Collaboration Center and the clusters. Training in communications was lacking and inconsistent communications between the different levels and among the participants within each group proved to be one of the major weaknesses of TAP. The history of tense race and class relations in Atlanta quickly complicated the task of coordinating services among groups, both within TAP and outside it.

An example of the lack of communication with groups outside of TAP was the resistance of the Clayton County Board of Education, supported by many of the middle-class residents of the county, to the idea of the decentralized programming that was vital to TAP's success. When the organizers for TAP asked the county Board of Education for space for a cluster office at a high school, the board declined to participate in TAP at first and then voted to give an area that was ninety square feet to the organization. One board member, who opposed teaching birth control methods to teens, rejected the presence of TAP because "they might have a goal of preventing school-age pregnancy that I don't agree with."[77] She and other board members wanted to see the specifics of the cluster plan before allotting space for TAP. While it was the responsibility of the school board to oversee the policies and programs within the schools, their demand to see the specifics of the programs reflected the lack of communication between TAP and its collaborators. Until the residents of Clayton County who lived in the clusters planned the programs, no programs would exist; however, the school board wished to see completed plans before allowing TAP into the county schools.

Many of the high schools in the southern neighborhoods welcomed TAP because they hoped that it would aid them in coping with the social problems that their students brought with them each day. Carver High School, one of the Atlanta public schools hosting a cluster office, had the lowest graduation rate in the city because many of the students had to choose between working to support their families and going to school. One graduate explained, "If they didn't stop [going to school] for a while and go to work, they would be on the street, or their brothers and sisters would end up sleeping in abandoned buildings with drug addicts."[78] As the vocational magnet, the high school already had partnerships with businesses to improve graduation rates and achievement. What TAP brought was attention to the problems that the teens faced and opportunities for Carver to increase parent and community involvement through activities at the school.

THE LOSS OF VISION

TAP's mission statement provides insights into both the organization's guiding vision and the problems that would plague the implementation effort:

> In the spirit of The Carter Center's problem-solving philosophy, The Atlanta Project seeks to empower citizens to develop solutions to the problems they identify in their neighborhoods and fosters collaboration among government agencies, other service providers, people who want to help, and those who need help throughout the area.[79]

What Carter proposed was systemic change in educational, health, and economic programs to give residents of distressed neighborhoods power over their lives. As governor of Georgia and president of the United States, he had focused reforms and funding on groups suffering economic and educational stress because he believed that the function of government and organizations was to facilitate access to services rather than to hinder citizens needing them. TAP was an opportunity to expand equal opportunity, educational and economic, without additional regulations because of the accountability from and to the community. This vision of personal power and community activism contrasted sharply with the tradition of bureaucratic centralization for the efficient delivery of services. The system that Carter had supported in the past, especially in education policy, he saw now as a barrier to citizen empowerment.

Beyond the barriers of bureaucratic traditions, which may have been surmountable, was the history of race and class tensions in Atlanta, which erupted during the first year of TAP's existence. When he began to select members for the Executive Board (called the Secretariat at the time), Carter included African American community leaders. Dr. James Young, a professor at Georgia State University who had worked with the schools in dropout prevention since 1979, was one of three African American professionals who had accepted positions on the board. By September 1992, all three had resigned, two because of workloads or transfers and Young because of "'racial arrogance' and 'racial insensitivity' within the organization."[80] Young carefully exempted Carter from the accusations of racism but, in his letter of resignation, he pointed out "that while you seem to understand the moral, societal, and historical imperatives, that understanding has not been translated into official Atlanta Project policy."[81] Without naming anyone or referring to any specific event, he charged, "the same racial insensitivity . . . that allowed the so-called Founding Fathers to mouth their freedom songs while enslaving my entire race . . . continues to allow racial insult after racial insult to circulate within the Project, immune to challenge or remedy."[82]

While Carter defended himself and Sweat, the executive coordinator, against the charge of racial insensitivity, he did not deny Young's charges about the culture of TAP. He explained to the press that he had met with the professor to resolve the problems and to prepare an educational program for the organization.[83] Young's resignation accomplished what he intended by forcing Carter and other leaders of TAP to examine the existing racial and class tensions within the leadership of TAP. As Douglas Dean, an African American member of the Advisory Board, explained, "This is not good for the Atlanta Project at all because it continues to divide the community on a racial level. . . . You can't talk about helping people if you can't get past race, especially when 70 percent of the people you are trying to help are black."[84] He might have added poor as well. At the neighborhood level, the cultural and economic distance between the business executives and the residents of the clusters also became a hindrance to the success of TAP.[85]

The tension between the African American residents and the mostly white corporate executives who worked with the clusters caused misunderstandings and accusations of racism. Also, because the clusters represented geographic areas, they often included prosperous historically black neighborhoods and ones mired in poverty, as was the case with the Therrell Cluster. In her study of urban renewal projects, Joan Walsh described the neighborhoods within the cluster as "boast[ing] million dollar mansions and grim, dangerous housing projects, both inhabited by African Americans."[86] Because the mission of TAP was to save poor people, many of the African American middle-class and upper middle-class residents of Therrell did not want to be included in a cluster. The cluster coordinator, Helen Catron, an experienced African American organizer, had to work through class friction as well as sporadic resident resentment of the white executive, Nick Snider, who had been assigned to the cluster by corporate partner United Parcel Service (UPS).[87] Her experience as an organizer and Snider's belief in the project brought them success. The leadership of TAP provided little in the way of guidance.

As the clusters organized in 1992 and 1993, the leaders looked to big events to engage the residents and to cement the commitment of corporate partners to TAP. One of the most successful was the Immunization/Children's Health Initiative (I/CHI), a TAP-wide health initiative designed in the spirit of the international work of the CCEU. The central administration designed the I/CHI to work in three phases. First, 5,200 volunteers, including the Carters, spent two days walking through the clusters meeting the residents, distributing health pamphlets, and recording information about their preschool children to develop a database for tracking immunizations and boosters for individual children. An eight-day immunization drive followed that resulted in the examination of 16,000 children, with 6,000 receiving vaccinations of some type. The final event was a concert featuring pop star Michael Jackson.[88]

The I/CHI followed the CCEU's method of working with government agencies to organize the distribution of medicines and vaccines and sending volunteers to educate cluster residents about the need for vaccinations. Through door-to-door contact and intense media coverage, many residents participated; however, the massive drive reached only 400 children who had not already begun their immunizations. Nevertheless, the goodwill and cooperation that it generated among residents and volunteers was a positive step after the publicity about racial tensions the previous year.[89]

By the end of 1993, the clusters were beginning to function effectively, but, like the leadership team, many of them focused on one-time events. These large programs brought residents together on a weekend for a neighborhood cleanup or a cultural celebration, but did little to improve the social and economic pressures on the families and children within the neighborhoods. The clusters that did develop programs that addressed the long-term needs of residents, in particular the educational ones, pulled diverse cluster residents together and built a foundation for sustained relationships after TAP's first five years. An example was the Therrell Cluster, which despite its tense beginnings developed into a neighborhood program that lasted until the late 1990s.

With the help of UPS, the Therrell Cluster developed the Family Tree Resource Center for after-school mentoring programs and families to learn about technology and entrepreneurship in workshops at the high school. Through its focus on education and employment at the school site, the Family Tree Resource Center followed the CIS model that Carter had planned for all the clusters. The emphasis on education also built a bridge between the different social classes within the Therrell Cluster because of the common interest in the educational achievement of black students and gave the white UPS executive an avenue for acceptance.[90] Of the twenty clusters, eleven developed educational programs that supplemented those offered by the school systems. Not all, however, were as successful as the Family Tree Resource Center in Therrell.

EMPOWERMENT OR PROGRAM EFFICIENCY?

The unevenness of the cluster programs and the tendency for the committees and coordinators at the top levels to dominate TAP were the main criticisms noted in an evaluation in 1995. Michael Giles, a CCEU fellow and faculty member at Emory, examined the relationship between the mission of TAP and its activities, finding the two to be largely incongruent. The one-time events did little to encourage the empowerment of residents, and the events that were the most successful were planned at the Collaboration Center rather than at the cluster level. Furthermore, although United Way was active in TAP, other nonprofit organizations in the city and counties felt left out of the collaboration process. Cluster coordinators and steering committees may have completed needs assessments of their areas, but they did not look far beyond themselves for the ability to serve the residents.[91] The nonprofit organizations that Giles spoke with claimed that TAP did not communicate its mission well and that it replicated services that they already provided.

Giles also found pockets of strength in TAP. The immunization program that brought together volunteers and residents and local initiatives that focused on education, housing, and job training were all successes and fit well with the mission.[92] Most of the funding, however, went to one-time events that offered little lasting benefit to the residents. In many clusters, few residents participated in the planning of these events. Giles' evaluation of TAP confirmed that the realization of Carter's vision was as fragmented as the programs that he had criticized in 1991.

Carter received a preliminary report from Giles and indicated that he agreed with the report's conclusions. With only one year left in TAP, he planned to help the clusters develop strategies to guide their interactions with other groups for the future. Through this effort, the leadership committees could help to ensure that the activities of the clusters were consistent with the mission of TAP as the project reorganized for Phase II.[93]

The planning for Phase II began shortly after TAP released the Giles report. United Way director Mark O'Connell chaired the study of how TAP should operate when its first five-year phase ended. By October 1995, a year before the scheduled shift in direction, Carter announced, "We had high hopes and exalted dreams for The Atlanta Project . . . I think we were overly inclined to think we could solve the generational problems in four years."[94] The study committee's report suggested that the number of clusters should be reduced and that those that were left should have "more flexibility in working with each other and with non-profit groups."[95] To solidify the program focus, the committee suggested that clusters' resources would be better directed toward programs for children and families.

The following year, TAP began the transition to Phase II with only four cluster offices and the more limited goals of "improving high school graduation rates, increasing the enrollment in pre-kindergarten programs, increasing immunizations of children younger than 2, and boosting employment."[96] Derrick Boazman, director of a neighborhood cluster, summed up the feelings of many residents when he noted, "The Atlanta Project positioned themselves as a savior. . . . Nobody ever thought they would be able to do the things they said they were going to do."[97] As with many programs in the past, TAP promised to solve problems and to bring a better life to the people of marginalized neighborhoods. The advent of the Summer Olympics in 1996 marked the end of Phase I of TAP and the Carters' direct involvement in it.

After TAP went to Phase II, many labeled it a failure. It was, however, a first attempt for a holistic approach to the numerous problems that the poor in Atlanta faced. The acknowledgment that the students in the public schools felt the stresses of poverty had the potential to bring educational reform into the venue of community development. The opportunity was lost through the fragmentation of effort and the limited time to achieve TAP's goals. The failures for Carter and for TAP resulted from using the 1996 Summer Olympics as a timeline for completion of their efforts in the neighborhoods and assuming that goodwill and collaboration would solve the problems of economic isolation and poverty in the southern neighborhoods of the Atlanta metropolitan area.

CONCLUSION

After leaving office for life as a private citizen, Carter looked for ways to continue the work he began as president. By focusing the work of the Carter Center on peace, health, and agriculture, he hoped to help the poor all over the world improve the conditions in which they lived. Through collaboration with other global organizations, the research fellows at the CCEU designed and implemented educational programs that reached out to rural communities through their governments. This approach to education involved awareness of the culture of local communities, the use of technologies that were readily available in rural areas, and the distillation of information into simple, easily understood messages. Education became a means for the immediate improvement of the health and living conditions of people in the countries where the CCEU and its partners worked.

Although CCEU representatives worked with the health and agricultural ministries in third world countries to design the "curriculum" for the educational initiatives, information quickly moved to the rural areas where, through its use, individuals could gain more control over the quality of their lives. By focusing on a single issue and thoroughly planning their implementation efforts, the CCEU was quite successful in the developing nations that participated in its projects. However, the single-issue focus could not be duplicated in the impoverished neighborhoods of south Atlanta. The vast area, urban blight, and the history of distrust that characterized relations between the mostly black residents and the mostly white business community in Atlanta stood as barriers to communication and planning. The sheer complexity of the problems involving poverty, drug abuse, crime, and teenage pregnancy meant that they could not be solved in a short amount of time. Convincing people to filter their water, while difficult, was much less complicated than rebuilding the infrastructure of areas long abandoned by cities and counties.[98]

As with the people in the southern neighborhoods of Atlanta, the schools had been neglected as well. Some had established partnerships with businesses in the past, but the programs were limited in scope and seldom addressed the conditions in which the students lived. Perhaps because of his involvement in public educational policy, Carter understood that the specific problems that TAP sought to address were present in the public schools that served the children who lived in poverty. Rather than blame the schools because they had not "fixed" the children, Carter rightfully blamed poverty. Children brought the strengths and the weaknesses of their neighborhoods with them to school and his selection of the Cities in Schools model demonstrated that he appreciated the complexity of the lives of these children. While his compassion for the children motivated many to become part of TAP, few of the middle-class volunteers understood as he did the pressures on the schools and the children within the clusters.

Conclusion

FROM 1955 TO 1996, efforts to ensure equal educational opportunity and increase the efficiency and performance of the nation's schools shifted educational policymaking responsibilities from the local districts to the state and federal levels. Jimmy Carter's involvement in educational policy followed a similar path, but diverged at the end with his "involuntary retirement" from the presidency. Carter's successes and failures on all policy levels offer potential insights into what it takes to develop effective educational policy and the challenges policymakers at all levels face as a result of the changing social and political environments in which they operate. By tracing the events that contributed to the development of Carter's educational priorities, both as an elected official and a private citizen, this analysis highlights the complex constellation of factors confronting today's educational policymakers and the conditions under which policy initiatives such as the No Child Left Behind Act will likely succeed or fail.

In his early years, as the chair of the Sumter County Board of Education in rural Georgia, Carter's efforts reflected the goals of the National Defense Education Act and corresponded with those proposed by national leaders like James B. Conant and John Gardner.[1] His attempts to streamline the delivery of public education and to spur greater achievement by offering at least the white students an improved curriculum represented a technocratic approach driven by the national trend of enhancing educational offerings by consolidating small schools. The residents of Sumter County, however, resisted these changes because of their attachment to their local high schools and the broader racial implications associated with school desegregation. Providing equal access to educational services for all students had significant social and political ramifications, threatening the existing political balance of power and generating a white backlash that endangered the very existence of the public school system. Thus, the purely technical reasoning Carter sought to apply in his efforts to streamline the delivery of education ran counter to the social and political realities of the divided South.

In the state senate and as the governor of Georgia, Carter continued to develop his technocratic approach to educational reform in an atmosphere of unrelenting resistance to desegregation. As a state senator, he focused on the relationship between educational achievement and economic development, believing that state educational policies could be instrumental in lifting many citizens out of poverty. Increasing educational achievement levels across Georgia had the further objective of making the state more attractive to businesses seeking to relocate. This association of education and economic development placed schools within a state bureaucratic structure that in many ways distanced them from the social and economic conditions of the communities whose children they taught. The assumption that the problems facing the schools could be addressed in isolation, without also considering the people they served and the larger social issues they faced, continued to dominate policymakers' thinking as political bodies at the state and federal levels assumed more dominant roles in educational policymaking in the last half of the twentieth century.

The idea that education was the key to the alleviation of poverty culminated in 1965 with Lyndon Johnson's "War on Poverty," which launched federal programs intended to address the educational needs of children attending the "most challenged high-poverty elementary and secondary schools."[2] These compensatory educational programs, defined by Title I of the Elementary and Secondary Education Act (ESEA) and Head Start, addressed real educational needs for many poor children, but neither the schools nor the children had created the poverty in their communities. City, state, and federal economic policies that encouraged the isolation of poor communities in urban areas were largely to blame.[3] Attempting to cure poverty through educational programs merely reinforced the notion that the schools could function as independent institutions, separate and apart from the social fabric of their surrounding communities.

On many levels, Carter's actions reflected a belief that good educational programming and increased funding with a just distribution of resources could address the educational needs of all students. His educational reform package, Adequate Program for Education in Georgia, changed the structure of funding, encouraged consolidation of small districts, and addressed the curriculum requirements of students with special needs, those who did not intend to go to college, and teens who were pregnant or parents. The APEG also allowed the state to support enrichment programs in impoverished districts. In exchange, the districts would test the students annually to make sure that they met state standards.

This exchange of achievement by students for increased support by the state was both a technical and a political decision. Like the federal programs in the 1960s, APEG's creators assumed that schools were part of a bureaucratic structure that could intervene in communities and dissolve the barriers to education faced by children living in poverty.[4] Politically, the testing program assured the middle-class, both black and white, that the schools would make efficient use of the increased funding they received. For Carter, APEG was both a rational solution to the problem of poverty in Georgia and a way of meeting the federal mandate to provide equal educational opportunity for disadvantaged groups.

Despite his support for equal educational opportunity in APEG, Carter opposed efforts by the federal courts to give African American students free access to all public schools. The inconsistency of his position against busing versus his use of educational policy to address poverty and provide equal educational opportunity reflected the confusion in the nation as a whole. Because most neighborhoods were segregated in the United States, desegregation could only be accomplished by moving students across neighborhoods.[5] The larger social goal of equal education and access demanded state action in the face of local resistance, yet Carter argued that busing was a mistake and that discrimination had ended "because all Georgians accepted desegregation." His denial that racism was part of the opposition to busing reflected the resistance of the Nixon administration and Congress to court-ordered busing. His well-publicized preference for the Atlanta settlement may have provided support for neighborhood schools, emphasizing the important relationship between the schools and the communities they serve, but it also undermined the larger social goal of ending discrimination by reinforcing the racial isolation of the African American students in the Atlanta public schools.

The policy that offered the most promise for addressing the needs of families, children, and schools was Carter's Early Childhood Development Program. Following the example of the federal Head Start program, his administration wished to coordinate social services through the schools for children with special needs from the age of three and for those living in poverty at age five. The program included medical, dental, and early academic intervention for these children, and its designers planned to assist their parents as well, offering them parenting classes and access to job training. Although the Early Childhood Development Program could not address the conditions of the neighborhoods where the children lived, it attempted to cut across bureaucratic offices to facilitate access to governmental services for children and their parents. Unfortunately, this structural coordination of effort represented a new organization of services that the established bureaucracy rejected. School services were educational; welfare services were social. Additionally, in the early 1970s, southern voters rejected the social policies of the War on Poverty and the economic pressures of inflation meant that state budgets could support fewer programs. Therefore, after the General Assembly passed the Early Childhood Development Program, the educational bureaucracy resisted implementing it because of the competing budgetary needs of the existing schools and educational programs.

As president of the United States, Carter continued to demonstrate his faith in solutions to educational access and achievement based on logical—though often simplistic—assumptions about the ability of schools to solve social problems. For example, the addition of a basic skills title to ESEA and his advocacy for voluntary national standardized testing were programmatic responses to the gap in achievement between students of different races and income levels; both were grounded in the assumption that, if students were held accountable for their own achievement, they would strive to learn more in school.[6] In concert with members of Congress, Carter pushed for the development of a national test, despite the protest of Joseph Califano, the secretary of Health, Education, and Welfare. After Califano demonstrated that experts in the testing field questioned the value of such a test, Carter let the issue of national testing drop, shifting his support to those advocating state level testing.[7]

Carter's policy objectives, however, limited his deference to experts and his willingness to compromise on issues of educational policy. His position on the transfer of Impact Aid Grant funds to Title I of the ESEA and student financial aid remained firm, despite the protests of Patricia Harris, the secretary of Housing and Urban Development. Carter believed that expanding Title I programs, which focused on the education of poor children, during a period of economic stress was more important than the blanket application of Impact Aid. Harris argued that that the loss of Impact Aid funding for areas with public housing threatened the schools that served children of the urban poor as well as the continued existence of public housing.[8] For Harris, affordable housing was critical to the quality of life of the children in the Title I program.

The isolation of educational policy from other social welfare programs was also an issue in the creation of the Department of Education. Politically, Carter needed to create a cabinet-level department to fulfill his campaign promise to the National Education Association. The consolidation of educational programs in a single department also appealed to his desire for administrative efficiency. By placing the majority of the educational programs in the new department, the federal government could, theoretically, manage the programs more efficiently.

Although Carter and his staff intended the new department to house all the federal educational programs, many of them remained in their original departments following protests by various constituent groups mobilized by the bureaucracy. More important, although education was the smallest office in HEW, the separation of HEW's compensatory education programs from the other offices further isolated federally sponsored educational programs from the social agencies that addressed the broader needs of families. With the exception of Head Start, which remained in the Office of Welfare, quality-of-life programs for the poor in the United States were completely isolated from the programs that focused on the education of their children. Thus, even administratively, educational programs operated in a vacuum, stressing achievement without so much as casting a glance at the environment in which the child lived.[9]

Carter lost his reelection bid and his influence on official local, state, and federal educational policy. Under President Reagan, national educational policy with its support for state-level minimum competency testing emphasizing basic skills in math, reading, and writing continued the process of isolating educational programs from social welfare. Funding for programs that addressed the needs of the poor, like Title I of ESEA, was reduced and pooled to allow states to apply for block grants.[10] Carter was no doubt aware of the Reagan administration's direction in educational policy, but the creation of the Carter Center of Emory University (CCEU) claimed the majority of his attention. Through CCEU, Carter had an opportunity to create new educational programs, unencumbered by the strictures of an existing bureaucracy or vested political interests. From 1986 to 1991, the CCEU designed educational programs to improve the quality of life of people in developing countries through agricultural demonstration and health-related initiatives. In the United States, the specialists at the CCEU also assisted in the development of secondary curricula in health and social studies in the Atlanta metropolitan area. Because of the larger "commitment to human rights and the alleviation of human suffering," education served as a means for communicating information, sometimes formally as in curriculum development for schools and sometimes informally as in culturally appropriate health education in villages.[11] The CCEU approach was quite successful because the center's staff designed outreach efforts with careful attention to the cultural and social backgrounds of the villagers; as a result, the community could integrate the information presented by CCEU field advisors into its day-to-day activities.

When Carter reengaged with the local schools to address the problems faced by poor children and their families in the Atlanta metropolitan area, this integrated approach to education became the center of The Atlanta Project (TAP). In the excitement of preparing for the 1996 Olympics, Carter challenged corporations, the upper middle-class, city and state governments, and the residents of the distressed, mostly African American neighborhoods, to devote themselves to his own "War on Poverty." In this massive five-year project to improve education, housing, and employment in south Atlanta, Carter continued to apply scientific management principles, organizing TAP in a hierarchical structure. To avoid the impression that changes were imposed from the outside, however, he deliberately involved the residents of the neighborhoods where TAP operated.

His plan was to empower the residents of the distressed areas to improve their lives in much the same way as the CCEU supported the empowerment of citizens in developing countries. As with his reorganization of the departments in state government and the creation of the federal Department of Education, Carter wished to restructure the delivery of services to families and individuals. By making schools the center of TAP's organizational structure, he sought to recreate the neighborhood schools that he had attempted to protect from busing as the governor of Georgia. Despite his history of supporting standardized testing and the increasingly important role it had in state and national policy, Carter resisted placing undue emphasis on testing in his interactions with the schools. Based on his contact with the people who lived in public housing and the teachers who worked in the schools, he focused on volunteers in the classrooms to help students learn the daily curriculum. In this environment, testing seemed superfluous; finishing high school was the major achievement.

By most accounts, Carter's holistic approach to the social and educational problems of the poor in Atlanta failed to achieve lasting change in the city. Racial and class tensions divided the volunteers from the residents and TAP's leaders from one another. The time needed to build relationships among constituents far exceeded the time available for the entire project. Community building demands sustained attention by business elites, government officials, residents of the area, and volunteer agencies. The fixed timeline of the Olympics added urgency to the work of TAP, but it also set an unrealistic deadline for achieving the goal. No city can rebuild in five years what has taken decades to destroy, especially if what was destroyed were neighborhoods that at one time were communities.[12]

Despite the failure to change the institutional racism and class discrimination in Atlanta in five years, Carter's vision for the city demonstrated what is necessary when academic achievement is seriously pursued. In their analyses of urban educational policy, Jean Anyon and Clarence Stone point out that the redevelopment of our urban centers is directly connected to the renewal of our schools and the educational attainment of the children they serve.[13] While No Child Left Behind sets goals for children, parents, and teachers on the state and federal levels, support of the communities in which the children live is an important requirement that is often ignored. The scope of the problems facing the poor in a city like Atlanta demands federal and state invention for job creation, expansion of economic opportunity, and social stability. In all distressed areas, there is also a need to address safe, affordable housing and economic development if the federal government is serious about closing the achievement gap between children living in poverty and those living in affluent neighborhoods who attend schools that assume that they will be successful.[14]

The tendency to treat education as somehow separate from the life and conditions of a community has hampered educational policy initiatives over the past fifty years. Children bring the strengths and the weaknesses of their communities to the schools that they attend. Furthermore, with the current trend to return to neighborhood schools, the economic and social problems of a community will continue to affect the ability of schools to function. For educational policy to offer equal opportunity for excellence, Carter learned as a private citizen that the quality of life in communities must receive as much attention as the quality of the schools. Poverty affects the ability of students to succeed, parents to participate, and teachers to teach.[15] Only by addressing the broader needs of the communities where students live and learn can educational policymakers offer truly equal educational opportunity and support the academic success of children as members of families and communities rather than merely as students.

Epilogue

EDUCATIONAL POLICY in the United States still displays Jimmy Carter's influence as an educational policymaker. Each presidential administration following his has addressed student aid, compensatory education focusing on basic skills, the functions of the Department of Education, and accountability for good or ill. All but Ronald Reagan have claimed to be educational reformers either before they entered the Oval Office or shortly after they arrived there. All have continued the centralization of control for educational services within the bureaucratic offices of the state and federal departments of education. None, including Carter, have acknowledged that their policies have little to do with teaching or learning.

During the second half of the twentieth century, educational policy moved from a local concern to a federal political issue culminating in the No Child Left Behind Act of 2001. The progress of this movement, however, reflects more of what policy specialist Richard Elmore refers to as starts and stops than a continuum.[1] The starts are reflected in presidential policy initiatives and the stops are in funding and implementation.

Carter's educational policies as the governor of Georgia were part of the movement of progressive southern governors to strengthen their educational systems to attract businesses from the northeastern states and other countries. Most of these governors sought to minimize public conflict over desegregation by proclaiming their states desegregated or requesting that white citizens accept desegregation. They also promoted educational reform through state standards for curriculum and minimum competency testing. By 1978, thirty-three states required these tests.[2]

By concentrating on educational reform rather than on efforts to desegregate the schools, the governors perpetuated the belief that all students had received an equal education in the past. In the southern states, this fiction affected elementary schools as well as high schools. In Florida, Mississippi, and Georgia, testing for minimum competency began as early as the third grade. Because many public school districts began school with first grade rather than kindergarten, children from poor families began school a year behind their middle-class peers, who had attended private kindergartens. The tests used to measure achievement in the southern states during the 1970s and 1980s also measured the effect of access to early literacy training, but the analyses seldom revealed that student performance reflected socioeconomic privilege on such a basic level.

The theme of accountability through testing went to the White House with Carter. Joseph Califano depicts the president as having a naïve faith in testing in his account of Carter telling him that voluntary testing in each state would help "every third grader read on the third grade level."[3] The National Academy of Education's study for the Department of Health, Education, and Welfare reported much different findings: testing could potentially caused more problems than it could solve.[4] This report, combined with lagging interest in testing by Congress, resulted in Carter's administration abandoning national voluntary standardized testing. Instead, his administration inserted support for states to develop achievement tests in the reauthorization of the Elementary and Secondary Education Act (ESEA). Modifications of ESEA became the norm for implementing educational policy after Carter left office.

When Carter pushed for the cabinet-level Department of Education, he was accused of creating an executive department to pay off a political debt and of attempting to create a ministry of education. Although educational services in the United States were (and are) decentralized, the existence of the department put educational issues at the cabinet level and gave the secretary of education more opportunities to push the states for favored educational reforms through the enforcement of civil rights legislation and federal regulations. Unfortunately, the increased awareness of educational issues served to further politicize educational policy rather than to increase equal access.

During Reagan's administration, key members of his staff viewed federal compensatory education programs as social welfare and marked them for reduction along with the dissolution of the department. Terrell Bell, the second secretary of education and former commissioner of education under President Nixon, fought to maintain the department and used the report of the National Commission on Excellence in Education, A Nation at Risk, to propel education back into the limelight. This report achieved Bell's purpose by criticizing current educational efforts by the states and advocating that the entire country adopt curriculum reforms measured by standardized testing. The data to support the spread of reforms advocated in A Nation at Risk was anecdotal rather than summative of current research on educational achievement, but the report and the Department of Education served important symbolic functions in both Reagan administrations.[5]

Under Presidents George H. W. Bush and Bill Clinton, the Department of Education took a back seat to presidential initiatives. Bush met with the nation's governors, led by Bill Clinton, to establish six national educational goals for the country to reach by the year 2000. Called *America 2000*, these goals included preschool preparation, top international test scores in math and science, adult literacy, basic skills, and safe schools. How schools reached these goals was left up to the state departments of education. Essentially, *America 2000* continued the symbolic role of the federal government in educational policy.

Like Carter, Clinton tied his educational policies to the reauthorization of ESEA. *Goals 2000*, the Educate America Act, included the six goals from the Bush administration as well as the two additional ones of support for parent involvement and teacher preparation. The 1994 Improving America's Schools Act contained requirements for states to adopt content standards, coordinate curriculum to the standards, and implement rigorous student assessments. The alignment of educational effort, known as systemic reform, focused on preparing students for economic productivity.[6] The content of the curriculum belonged to the states, and the Department of Education functioned as an advisor more than an enforcer in the process.

The enforcement role of the department has dominated George W. Bush's No Child Left Behind Act (NCLB), a bipartisan addition to ESEA. Intended to force states to close the achievement gap between middle-class white students and all other students—minority, poor, exceptional, and English language learners—NCLB mandates that all states accepting funds for Title I of ESEA demonstrate Adequate Yearly Progress (AYP) for all students in all districts. While the standards and assessments are left up to the states, the federal Department of Education monitors the progress of students. Those schools that do not demonstrate AYP face sanctions ranging from cuts in federal funding to school closure. The idea that assessment can make teachers teach and students learn has culminated in a bill that demands that all students perform at grade level by 2014.

Although in NCLB the states are still responsible for standards and assessment, federal educational policy now focuses on testing for purposes of accountability, justified by statements of equal educational opportunity. In this model, efficiency and equal educational opportunity serve the pursuit of excellence, if excellence is defined as test scores and winning the competition for the highest ones. On the other hand, if excellence is defined as critical and imaginative thought, then testing serves only a minor purpose and classroom interaction and quality of the educative experience of the student become the dominant model.[7]

The focus of educational policy on the state and federal levels must turn to the quality of the educational experience for teachers and students, the environments where teaching and learning occur, as well as the community support that teachers and students receive. This definition of excellence would also affect what policymakers would consider efficient—small classes, safe and clean facilities, well-compensated teachers, and students with enough economic support to concentrate on learning. In his 2005 book *Our Endangered Values*, Carter points out that greatest challenge of the new millennium is the gap between the rich and the poor.[8] Simultaneous with the accountability in NCLB, the Bush administration has cut domestic spending—schools continue to be isolated from the communities where the children attending them live.

Strengthening efficiency and equal opportunity to achieve excellence requires investment in the revitalization of neighborhoods that maintain residents rather than forcing them out of the area. In this model, efficiency and excellence would support equity. Expectations of learning would be rigorous, but students and teachers would have the institutional and community foundations necessary for achievement. Students would be children in their communities, rather than students isolated in schools.

Carter sought such an effort in TAP, but the structure of social services, school bureaucracies, and even charitable organizations were obstacles that even a supporter of integrated services could not overcome. Class and cultural differences among the groups involved also prevented TAP from realizing its potential. Only long-term, committed coordination of effort could overcome these obstacles of bureaucratic tradition, race, and class. Although TAP's successes were mixed at best, an important conclusion can be drawn from it as a model—if the federal government is serious about the equal opportunity goals of NCLB, then the leaders of our federal, state, and local governments and educational systems must accept responsibility for the coordination of social policies with educational services, especially in distressed areas with high rates of poverty, single-parent homes, unemployment, and teenage parenting. At the least, the federal government must support students and the teachers in holistic approaches to quality education. Until educational policymakers learn what Jimmy Carter learned, albeit too late—that students live in communities and are part of them—student achievement will remain erratic and bound in most cases by economic status. It is the commitment to the child that will bring achievement. Accountability will be found in our society's will to meet that responsibility.

Notes

INTRODUCTION

1. In Sumter County, the Grand Jury was the local governing body and had the authority to appoint school board members.

2. David Tyack and Larry Cuban, *Tinkering Toward Utopia: A Century of Public School Reform*, Reprint (Cambridge: Harvard University Press, 1997). Tyack and Cuban offer the argument that policymakers seldom repeal a reform. Instead, they layer school reforms on top of one another.

3. Raymond E. Callahan, *Education and the Cult of Efficiency: A Study of the Social Forces That Have Shaped the Administration of the Public Schools* (Chicago: University of Chicago Press, 1962), 5, 25–28.

4. Ibid., 61.

5. There are many studies on the testing movement in the United States. One that directly addresses the use of intelligence testing and social efficiency is Marvin Lazerson, Judith Block McLaughlin, Bruce McPherson, and Stephen K. Bailey, *An Education of Value: The Purposes and Practices of Schools* (New York: Cambridge University Press, 1985). Two works of particular value on the development of scientific management techniques in school systems are Callahan, *Education and the Cult of Efficiency* and David Tyack, *The One Best System: A History of American Urban Education* (Cambridge: Harvard University Press, 1974).

6. Ellwood P. Cubberley, *Public Education in the United States: A Study and Interpretation of American Educational History*, Rev. ed. (New York: Houghton Mifflin, 1934), 527.

7. Lazerson et al., *An Education of Value*, 9.

8. Tyack, *One Best System*, 206–10.

9. John Dewey, *Democracy and Education* (New York: Macmillan, 1916; repr., New York: Free Press, 1966), 85–87, 119.

10. Arthur E. Wise, *Legislated Learning: The Bureaucratization of the American Classroom* (Berkeley: University of California Press, 1979), 14.

11. An example is in Sumter County, Georgia, where the board built a high school for African American students in 1958. Until then, Sumter County only provided schooling for black students up to age fourteen, the age that compulsory schooling ended. Any black student in the county district who wanted to attend high school had to commute or move to the nearby Americus City School District, which did have a high school for black students. Transportation to the high school was left up to the parents of the student.

12. Larson et al., *An Education of Value*, 49–61.

CHAPTER ONE. THE RESISTANCE TO EQUAL OPPORTUNITY AND EFFICIENCY

1. For a description of southern politics during the early part of the twentieth century, see V. O. Key, Jr., *Southern Politics in the State and Nation* with assistance of Alexander Heard (New York: Vintage Books, 1949), 5. Also see Numan Bartley, *From Thurmond to Wallace: Political Tendencies in Georgia, 1948–68* (Baltimore: Johns Hopkins University Press, 1970).

2. Leland C. Thomas, "Some Aspects of Biracial Education in Georgia, 1900–1954" (EDD diss., George Peabody College for Teachers, 1960), 85–94; Michael Fultz, "African American Teachers in the South, 1890–1940: Powerlessness and the Ironies of Expectations and Protest," *History of Education Quarterly* 35, no. 4 (Winter 1995): 406.

3. Richard Kluger, *Simple Justice: The History of Brown v. Board of Education and Black America's Struggle for Equality* (New York: Alfred A. Knopf, 1975), 321.

4. Thomas V. O'Brien, *The Politics of Race and Schooling: Public Education in Georgia, 1900–1961* (New York: Lexington Books, 1999), 53–71, and Thomas, "Biracial Education in Georgia," 112.

5. Thomas, "Biracial Education in Georgia," 112; an example is in Sumter County where the attendance of black children decreased dramatically in the spring planting season. In 1944, the board made the comment that "it is almost impossible to operate (schools for black children) 8 months because of falling off in attendance in work season." See Minutes, Sumter County Board of Education, April 19, 1944.

6. Richard O. Johnson, "Desegregation of Public Education in Georgia—One Year Afterwards," *Journal of Negro Education* 24, no. 3 (1955): 228.

7. "Talmadge Attacks Negro School Suit," *New York Times*, October 23, 1949. http://proquest.umi.com.proxy.usf.edu/.

8. O'Brien, *The Politics of Race and Schooling*, 77–78.

9. Ibid., 69–71; Mark V. Tushnet, *The NAACP's Legal Strategy Against Segregated Education, 1925–1950* (Chapel Hill: University of North Carolina Press, 1987), 130–37, and Kluger, *Simple Justice*, 353–57.

10. "Talmadge Defiant; Others Hail Court Decision," *New York Times*, June 6, 1950. http://proquest.umi.com.proxy.usf.edu/.

11. O'Brien, *The Politics of Race and Schooling*, 84–85.

12. Ibid., 91.

13. Jimmy Carter, *Why Not the Best?* (New York: Bantam Books, 1976), 65.

14. Peter Bourne, *Jimmy Carter: A Comprehensive Biography from Plains to Post-presidency* (New York: Lisa Drew/Scribner, 1997), 88–92; Rosalynn Carter, *First Lady from Plains* (New York: Fawcett Gold Medal Books, 1984), 37, 40–41.

15. Carter, *First Lady from Plains*, 43–44.

16. Kluger, *Simple Justice*, 319.

17. Carter, *First Lady from Plains*, 42.

18. Ibid.

19. The minutes of the Sumter County Board of Education only mentioned desegregation once during the six years that Carter served on it. The superintendent at that time, W. W. Foy, recounted that his lack of opposition to the desegregation in Sumter County cost him the election for county superintendent in 1964. He then became the principal of a school in the Americus City District, which desegregated without conflict. W. W. Foy (Superintendent Sumter County Schools, 1953–1964) interview by author, May 13, 1994.

20. Jimmy Carter, *Turning Point: A Candidate, a State, and a Nation Come of Age* (New York: Times Books, 1992), 42–43.

21. Foy, interview.

22. Ibid.

23. Carter, *Turning Point*, 43.

24. Carter, *Why Not the Best?*, 72–73.

25. Minutes, Sumter County Board of Education, December 6, 1955.

26. Ibid., January 2, 1957. The board called for a study of the "possible means of providing transportation for colored pupils next fall upon the completion of the new buildings."

27. Ibid., September 24, 1956.

28. Ibid.

29. Ibid.

30. Ibid., October 22, 1956.

31. Ibid., February 7, 1961, and Carter, *First Lady from Plains*, 43.

32. Foy, interview. Foy said that he spoke with Jimmy Carter about the educational needs of the students with special needs in the district, and they agreed to work on a classroom for exceptional students. See Minutes, Sumter County Board of Education, May 1, 1956.

33. Minutes, Sumter County Board of Education, May 1, 1956.

34. Ibid., July 2, 1957.

35. Ibid., November 5, 1957.

36. Ibid., June 3, 1958.

37. Ibid., June 11, 1958.

38. Ibid., June 3, 1958. The principals requested that the board drop the condition that students pass the required units for promotion. High school students' promotion required passing grade averages. Ibid., February 3, 1959.

39. Ibid., June 11, 1958. The principals accepted the grading scale with the re-examination possibility for students with averages in the "conditional range."

40. *Americus Times Recorder*, July 14, 1961, and Foy, interview.

41. Minutes, Sumter County Board of Education, July 14, 1959, October 6, 1959, and February 7, 1961.

42. S. Ernest Vandiver, "Vandiver Takes the Middle Road," in *Georgia Governors in an Age of Change: From Ellis Arnall to George Busbee*, ed. Harold P. Henderson and Gary L. Roberts, 157–66 (Athens: University of Georgia Press, 1988), 159.

43. For the final decision in the case see *Calhoun v. Cook*, 362 F. Supp.1249, 1252 (N.D. Ga. 1973).

44. Ernest Vandiver, Interview by Cliff Kuhn, January 25, 1994, transcript 14–15, Georgia Government Documentation Project, Georgia State University, and Jeff Roche, "A Reconstruction of Resistance: The Sibley Commission and the Politics of Desegregation in Georgia" (MA thesis, Georgia State University, 1995), 122–23.

45. Vandiver, "Vandiver Takes the Middle Road," 160.

46. Ibid., 159; Roche, "A Reconstruction of Resistance," 1, 155, and O'Brien, *The Politics of Race and Schooling*, 176–79.

47. Carter, *First Lady from Plains*, 42, 46.

48. O'Brien, *The Politics of Race and Schooling*, 180–81.

49. Minutes, Sumter County Board of Education, June 7, 1960.

50. Ibid., July 5, 1960.

51. Thomas V. O'Brien, "Georgia's Response to *Brown v. Board of Education*: The Rise and Fall of Massive Resistance, 1949–1961" (PhD diss., Emory University, 1992), 146.

52. Foy, interview.

53. Rockefeller Brothers Fund, *The Pursuit of Excellence* (New York: Doubleday, 1958) and John Gardner, *Excellence: Can We Be Equal and Excellent Too?* (New York: Harper and Row, 1960).

54. Gardner, *Excellence*, 37.

55. James B. Conant, *The American High School Today* (New York: McGraw-Hill, 1959), 37–38, 44–76.

56. James R. Blair, "Our Children's Education," *Americus Times Recorder*, July 14, 1961. In his editorial, Blair claims that there are "approximately 300" students in the

county high schools. The Sumter County Board of Education recorded 411 total high school students at its meeting on January 16, 1961.

57. Minutes, Sumter County Board of Education, December 8, 1960. The estimated number of students in both county high schools for white students varied in board minutes and in newspaper stories from 254 to 425.

58. Ibid., January 3, 1961.

59. Ibid., February 7, 1961.

60. O. C. Hanes, "Weird, Wild Developments Recorded in Ga. Last Year," *Americus Times Recorder*, January 4, 1961; Vandiver, "Vandiver Takes the Middle Road," 161.

61. *Americus Times Recorder*, January 9, 1961, and Vandiver, "Vandiver Takes the Middle Road," 160–61. Vandiver claims that he closed the University of Georgia. He did cut off funding as the law dictated, but within three days, Judge Bootle enjoined Vandiver from cutting off funding to the university. See O'Brien, *The Politics of Race and Schooling*, 186–89.

62. O'Brien, *The Politics of Race and Schooling*, 190–91.

63. Minutes, Sumter County Board of Education, February 7, 1961. Jack Nix, the state superintendent when Carter was governor, was the head of the subcommittee on agricultural education.

64. Clarence Graddick, "Merger of City and County School Systems Recommended in Report by Survey Committee: 600 Persons Attend Public Session Here," *Americus Times Recorder*, March 29, 1961.

65. Ibid.

66. Ibid.

67. Minutes, Sumter County Board of Education, March 3, 1953. Earl Carter Sr. was on the Sumter County Board of Education during the 1953 attempt to consolidate the districts. When the city board rejected the county's administrative proposal, he moved that the county board proceed to plan independently.

68. Graddick, "Merger of City and County School Systems."

69. Ibid.

70. "Questions Answered on School Proposals," *Americus Times Recorder*, March 29, 1961.

71. C. O. Fitzwater, "A New Commission Looks at an Old Problem," *American School Board Journal* 135 (July 1957): 19.

72. Minutes, Sumter County Board of Education, April 4 and May 27, 1961.

73. "City-County School Consolidation Votes Scheduled July 18; Points Outlined by Board Chairman," *Americus Times Recorder*, July 1, 1961.

74. Ibid.

75. *Americus Times Recorder*, July 10–14, 1961. Although the articles were run without an author, the May 27, 1961, minutes of the Sumter County board meeting

stated that "the series of newspaper articles, which are to be drafted by Jimmy Carter, chairman, will be approved by all Board members and Mr. Foy. There will be 6 or 7 articles in all." Minutes, Sumter County Board of Education, May 27, 1961.

76. "Reasons Outlined for Merger of School Systems," *Americus Times Recorder*, July 10, 1961.

77. "Pro, Con on School Merger," *Americus Times Recorder*, July 13, 1961.

78. "School Merger Advantages Given," *Americus Times Recorder*, July 14, 1961.

79. "Disadvantages of Proposed Merger," *Americus Times Recorder*, July 17, 1961. Also see Carter, *Turning Point*, 59.

80. Rudy Hayes and Clarence Graddick, "Merger Beaten, Boards to Proceed with Plans: School Proposal Loses by Slim 84–vote Margin in County; Ok'ed in City," *Americus Times Recorder*, July 19, 1961.

81. Ibid.

82. Betty Glad, *Jimmy Carter: In Search of the Great White House* (New York: W. W. Norton, 1980), 79; Carter, *Turning Point*, 58, and Carter, *Why Not the Best?*, 88.

83. Glad, *Jimmy Carter*, 79.

84. Foy, interview.

85. Carter, *First Lady from Plains*, 46.

86. Carter, *Why Not the Best?*, 88.

87. Johnson, "Desegregation of Public Education in Georgia," 228.

88. Minutes, Sumter County Board of Education, February 6, 1962.

89. Ibid., March 6, 1962.

90. "Sumter Schools Show Drop in Enrollment," *Americus Times Recorder*, September 6, 1962.

91. Minutes, Sumter County Board of Education, June 5, 1962, and September 4, 1962.

CHAPTER TWO. THE END OF OPEN RESISTANCE

1. Taylor Branch, *Parting the Waters: America in the King Years, 1954–63* (New York: Touchstone, 1988), 420–30. For a historical account of the freedom rides see Raymond Arsenault, *Freedom Riders: 1961 and the Struggle for Racial Justice, Pivotal Movements in American History* (New York: Oxford University Press, 2006).

2. Betty Glad, *Jimmy Carter: In Search of the Great White House* (New York: W. W. Norton, 1980), 93. Glad compares Carter's gubernatorial activities with those of Sanders and finds that Carter followed Sanders's reform platforms.

3. Charles Pou, "New Chief Urges Aid for Consolidation," *Atlanta Journal*, January 16, 1963.

4. Jimmy Carter, *Turning Point: A Candidate, a State, and a Nation Come of Age* (New York: Times Books, 1992), 60.

5. Ibid., 49, 60.

6. Peter Bourne, *Jimmy Carter: A Comprehensive Biography from Plains to Post-presidency* (New York: Lisa Drew/Scribner, 1997), 109; Carter, *Turning Point*, 46–57.

7. Carter, *Turning Point*, 56, 60, 68–71.

8. For a full description of the events surrounding Carter's first election to the Georgia state senate see Carter, *Turning Point*. Also see James F. Cook, *Carl Sanders: Spokesman of the New South* (Macon, GA: Mercer University Press, 1993), 321.

9. Carter, *Turning Point*, 178 and Thomas V. O'Brien, "Georgia's Response to *Brown v. Board of Education*: The Rise and Fall of Massive Resistance, 1949 to 1961" (PhD diss., Emory University, 1992), 280.

10. Carter, *Turning Point*, 178–79.

11. Ibid. The Board of Regents of the University System of Georgia was (and is) a constitutional body. Although the governor appointed the members and the legislature allocated the budget, the governance of higher education in the state was the responsibility of the Board of Regents.

12. Pou, "New Chief Urges Aid for Consolidation."

13. Fred Powledge, "Tuition Grant Faces Action Next Week," *Atlanta Journal*, February 6, 1963.

14. Ibid.

15. "Tuition Grant Law to Face Showdown," *Atlanta Journal*, February 13, 1963.

16. Fred Powledge, "Sanders Gets Bill on County Merger," *Atlanta Journal*, February 14, 1963.

17. Ibid.

18. Fred Powledge, "Need Tuition Bill Okayed in Senate," *Atlanta Journal*, February 20, 1963.

19. Ibid.

20. Bourne, *Jimmy Carter*, 134–35, and Branch, *Parting the Waters*, 540–61.

21. "Sanders Gets Most Bills Passed Solons," *Atlanta Journal*, February 14, 1963.

22. Charles Pou, "The Trees' Last Gasp," *Atlanta Journal*, February 19, 1963.

23. Ibid.

24. Cook, *Carl Sanders*, 321.

25. Glad, *Jimmy Carter*, 93.

26. Quoted from Governor's Commission to Improve Education, *Educating Georgia's People: Investment in the Future* (Atlanta, 1963), 13.

27. "School Study Panel Named," *Atlanta Journal*, June 13, 1963 and Associated Press, "Sanders Seeking Education Plan," *Atlanta Journal*, July 1, 1963.

28. Southern Regional Education Board, *Within Our Reach: Report of the Commission on Goals for Higher Education in the South* (Atlanta: Southern Regional Educa-

tion Board, 1961), 9; Governor's Commission to Improve Education, *Educating Georgia's People*, 10.

29. Governor's Commission to Improve Education, *Educating Georgia's People*, 10.

30. Ibid., 10–11.

31. Ibid., 15.

32. Ibid.

33. Ibid., 17.

34. Ibid.

35. Ibid., 22.

36. Ibid., 23.

37. Ibid.

38. Ibid., 25.

39. Ibid., 32.

40. Ibid., 39, 40; "Governor Pushes Education Plan," *Atlanta Journal*, September 30, 1963.

41. Governor's Commission to Improve Education, *Educating Georgia's People*, 43.

42. Ibid., 15, 41–44.

43. Ibid., 45.

44. Ibid., and University System Board of Regents, *University System of Georgia Annual Report: For Fiscal Year July 1, 1962–June 30, 1963* (Atlanta, 1963), 27. Future references to this series of publications will be cited as Board of Regents, *Annual Reports* with the appropriate dates.

45. Board of Regents, *Annual Report, July 1, 1963–June 30, 1964,* 7.

46. Cook, *Carl Sanders*, 321; Jimmy Carter, *Why Not the Best?*, 110, and Bourne, *Jimmy Carter*, 108.

47. For examples of SREB programs see Board of Regents, *Annual Report, July 1, 1961–June 30, 1962*, 30–32; Board of Regents, *Annual Report, July 1, 1962–June 30, 1963*, 34–35, and Board of Regents, *Annual Report, July 1, 1963–June 30, 1964*, 27–28.

48. William O. Smith, "Education Solons Rap New Coliseum," *Atlanta Journal*, December 29, 1963.

49. Carter, *Why Not the Best?*, 39; Quoted in Bourne, *Jimmy Carter*, 144.

50. Quoted in Bourne, *Jimmy Carter*, 144.

51. Carter, *Why Not The Best?*, 99, 101, 105.

52. Branch, *Parting the Waters*, 864–65.

53. Ibid., 865; Bourne, *Jimmy Carter*, 146–47.

54. Bourne, *Jimmy Carter*, 147.

55. Ibid., 146–47.

56. Ibid., 148.

57. Gary Fink, *Prelude to the Presidency: The Political Character and Legislative Leadership Style of Governor Jimmy Carter* (Westport: Greenwood Press, 1980), 10.

CHAPTER THREE. THE COMPROMISE OF EQUAL EDUCATIONAL OPPORTUNITY

1. Peter Bourne, *Jimmy Carter: A Comprehensive Biography from Plains to Post-presidency* (New York: Lisa Drew/Scribner, 1997), 152–63; Jimmy Carter, *Why Not the Best?* (New York: Bantam Books, 1976), 110–11; Betty Glad, *Jimmy Carter: In Search of the Great White House* (New York: W. W. Norton, 1980), 104–107, and James Wooten, *Dasher: The Roots and the Rising of Jimmy Carter* (New York: Summit Books, 1978), 259–62.

2. Quoted in Bourne, *Jimmy Carter*, 157.

3. William O. Smith, "Programs Unveiled in Carter's Blueprint," *Atlanta Journal-Constitution*, July 24, 1966. *Jimmy Carter, 1962–1976, A Comprehensive Newsfile on Microfiche*. In cooperation with *Atlanta Constitution* and *Atlanta Journal* (Glen Rock, NJ: Microfilming Corporation of America, 1976). Most of the articles in this collection are marked *Atlanta Journal* or *Atlanta Constitution*; however, when the designation is unclear, I have used *Atlanta Journal-Constitution*.

4. Ibid.

5. Bourne, *Jimmy Carter*, 158, 161–62. Brooks Pennington, Carter's campaign manager, created the fictitious "Voter Research Institute" and sent out its poll results weekly to the media. Ibid.

6. Ibid., 164.

7. Wooten, *Dasher*, 261.

8. Carter, *Why Not the Best?*, 112.

9. Bourne, *Jimmy Carter*, 166–67, 174–75.

10. Wooten, *Dasher*, 262, 275, 281–82.

11. Ibid., 282; E. J. Dionne, *Why Americans Hate Politics* (New York: Touchstone, 1991), 91, 116–44.

12. Wooten, *Dasher*, 291–92.

13. Bourne, *Jimmy Carter*, 188–96.

14. Bill Montgomery, "Fly-by-Night Type: Carter Opposed Private Schools," *Atlanta Journal*, July 27, 1970.

15. "Mediocrity Assailed by Carter," *Atlanta Constitution*, March 8, 1969. For a discussion of conservatism, see Clinton Rossiter, *Conservatism in America: The Thankless Persuasion*, 2d ed. (New York: Knopf, 1962), 5–15. On Carter's conservatism and

liberalism as governor, see Gary M. Fink, *Prelude to the Presidency: The Political Character and Legislative Leadership Style of Governor Jimmy Carter* (Westport, CT: Greenwood Press, 1980), 6–9.

16. Elizabeth Gray Bowden, "The Gubernatorial Administration of Jimmy Carter" (MA thesis, University of Georgia, 1980), 18, and quoted in Wooten, *Dasher*, 289.

17. J. Harvie Wilkinson III, *From Brown to Bakke: The Supreme Court and School Integration, 1954–1978* (New York: Oxford University Press, 1979), 109–11.

18. *Green v. County School Board of New Kent County*, 391 U.S. 430 (1968) as discussed in Gary Orfield, *Must We Bus? Segregated Schools and National Policy* (Washington, D.C.: Brookings Institution, 1978), 242.

19. Gene Stephens, "Kindergartens Backed in Carter's Platform," *Atlanta Journal-Constitution*, July 30, 1970.

20. "Carter and Sanders Give Stands on 19 Key Issues," *Atlanta Journal*, September 20, 1970.

21. Stephens, "Kindergartens Backed."

22. Jimmy Carter, *Addresses of Jimmy Carter (James Earl Carter) Governor of Georgia, 1971–1975*, comp. Frank Daniel (Atlanta: Georgia Department of Archives and History, 1975), 79–80, 81.

23. Jack Bass and Walter DeVries, *The Transformation of Southern Politics: Social Change and Political Consequences Since 1945* (New York: Basic Books, 1976), 12.

24. Ibid., 145; Prentice Palmer, "'Sorry' School Busing Is Hit," *Atlanta Journal*, February 25, 1972, and Bowden, "Gubernatorial Administration," 35.

25. Michael Harrington, *The Other America: Poverty in the United States* (New York: Collier Books, 1962). Harrington's book was widely read by public policymakers in the early 1960s. Quoted from Bill Shipp, "One Thing Is Sure: He'll Be Moderate," *The Atlanta Constitution*, October 27, 1970.

26. Quoted from Bill Shipp, "One Thing Is Sure: He'll Be Moderate."

27. Bowden, "Gubernatorial Administration," 23.

28. *Acree v. County Board of Education of Richmond County, Georgia*, 294 F. Supp. 1034 (U.S. Dist. 1968). http://web.lexis-nexis.com.proxy.usf.edu/; Faith Johnson, "Lawsuit Prompted Changes," *The Augusta Chronicle*, February 28, 1999.

29. *Acree v. County Board of Education of Richmond County, Georgia.*

30. *Acree v. County Board of Education of Richmond County*, 336 F. Supp. 1275 (U.S. Dist. 1972). http://web.lexis-nexis.com.proxy.usf.edu/.

31. Randall H. Harris, "Augusta Schools in Hassle over Busing," *Atlanta Daily World*, February 17, 1972.

32. "Nix Calls School Boycott Illegal," *Atlanta Daily World*, February 20, 1972.

33. Dr. Larry Gess (education advisor to Governor Jimmy Carter), interview by author, April 28, 1997.

34. "Carter Says Edicts Harm Education," *Atlanta Journal*, October 14, 1971.

35. Bill Montgomery and Junie Brown, "Boycott Backed as Last Resort," *Atlanta Journal*, February 16, 1972.

36. Palmer, "'Sorry' School Busing is Hit."

37. David Nordan, "Carter Praises HHH Busing View," *Atlanta Journal*, February 23, 1972.

38. Jon Nordheimer, "Gov. Carter Buoys Georgia Busing Foes by Saying He May Endorse Boycott," *New York Times* (1857–Current File), February 17, 1972. http://www.newsbank.com/.

39. "Bitter Confrontation Over Augusta's Busing," *Atlanta Daily World*, February 29, 1972.

40. Thomas V. O'Brien, *The Politics of Race and Schooling: Public Education in Georgia, 1900–1961* (New York: Lexington Books, 1999), 146, 160, 171.

41. Wilkinson, *From Brown to Bakke*, 84.

42. O'Brien, *The Politics of Race and Schooling*, 191–93.

43. Orfield, *Must We Bus?*, 355.

44. "NAACP Shuts School Talk Door to Press," *Atlanta Journal*, January 28, 1972.

45. Wilkinson, *From Brown to Bakke*, 233.

46. Memo, Larry Gess to Governor Carter, February 20, 1972, "Governor's Incoming Correspondence," Record Group 1, Sub Group 1, Series 5, Governor Carter Papers, Georgia Department of History and Archives. Hereafter cited as Governor Carter Papers.

47. "Carter's School Plan Will Be Popular Here," *Augusta Chronicle*, reprinted in *Atlanta Constitution*, March 5, 1972.

48. Wilkinson, *From Brown to Bakke*, 233; Orfield, *Must We Bus?*, 400.

49. Orfield, *Must We Bus?*, 25.

50. Ibid., 369–70, 400–401. The Detroit NAACP continued with its case, *Milliken v. Bradley*, for metropolitan busing and lost before the U.S. Supreme Court in 1974.

51. Prentice Palmer, "Carter Hits Busing," *Atlanta Journal*, March 23, 1972.

52. See *Adams v. Richardson*, 356 F. Supp. 92 (D.D.C. 1973).

53. John B. Williams, III, "Title VI Regulation of Higher Education," in *Desegregating America's Colleges and Universities: Title VI Regulation of Higher Education*, ed. John B. Williams, III (New York: Teacher's College Press, 1988), 8.

54. Ibid.

55. University System Board of Regents, *University System of Georgia Annual Report: For Fiscal Year July 1, 1973–June 30, 1974* (Atlanta: University System of Georgia, 1974), 20–22. Future references to this series of publications will be cited as Board of Regents, *Annual Reports* with the appropriate dates.

56. Ibid., 18, 20–22.

57. Ibid., 21.

58. Ibid.

59. Ibid.

60. Board of Regents, *Annual Reports, July 1, 1974–June 30, 1975*, 21.

61. Ibid., 19. In the totals for fall semester 1974 were 9 Native American, 17 Asian American, 53 "Spanish Surname," and 3,634 Other (mostly Caucasian). Ibid.

62. Ibid., 20.

63. Ibid.

64. Ibid.

65. Ibid., 21.

66. Ibid., 20.

67. Carter, *Addresses*, 202.

68. James Wooten, "'Too Late Now' To Buck Integration in South," *New York Times* (1857–Current File), September 5, 1971. http://www.newsbank.com/.

69. Carter, *Addresses*, 202.

CHAPTER FOUR. EQUAL EDUCATIONAL OPPORTUNITY THROUGH SYSTEM REFORM

1. Gary M. Fink, *Prelude to the Presidency: The Political Character and Legislative Leadership Style of Governor Jimmy Carter* (Westport, CT: Greenwood Press, 1980), 10, and Elizabeth Gray Bowden, "The Gubernatorial Administration of Jimmy Carter" (MA thesis, University of Georgia, 1980), 52. For information about the southern progressive governors of the early 1970s, see Jack Bass and Walter DeVries, *The Transformation of Southern Politics: Social Change and Political Consequences Since 1945* (New York: Basic Books, 1976).

2. Press Release, March 26, 1974, Press Releases 2/1/74–3/26/74, Record Group 1, Sub Group 10, Series 43, Governor Jimmy Carter Papers, Georgia Department of Archives and History, Atlanta, Georgia. Hereafter cited as Governor Carter Papers.

3. Minimum Foundation Program of Education Study Committee, *APEG: Adequate Program for Education in Georgia* (Atlanta: State of Georgia, 1973).

4. For an explanation of the power relationships between governors and state superintendents in the 1970s, see Ronald F. Campbell and Tim L. Mazzoni, Jr., *State Policy Making for the Public Schools: A Comparative Analysis of Policy Making for the Public Schools in Twelve States and a Treatment of State Governance Models* (Berkeley: McCutchan, 1976). This study includes Georgia in 1972 and 1973.

5. James Wooten, *Dasher: The Roots and the Rising of Jimmy Carter* (New York: Summit Books, 1978), 291–92.

6. Gene Stephens, "Kindergartens Backed in Carter's Platform," *Atlanta Journal-Constitution*, July 30, 1970, *Jimmy Carter, 1962–1976, A Comprehensive Newsfile on*

Microfiche. In cooperation with *Atlanta Constitution* and *Atlanta Journal* (Glen Rock, NJ: Microfilming Corporation of America, 1976). Most of the articles in this collection are marked *Atlanta Journal* or *Atlanta Constitution*; however, when the designation is unclear, I have used *Atlanta Journal-Constitution.*

7. "Carter and Sanders Give Stands on 19 Key Issues," *Atlanta Journal,* September 20, 1970.

8. Jimmy Carter, *Addresses of Jimmy Carter (James Earl Carter) Governor of Georgia, 1971–1975,* comp. Frank Daniel (Atlanta: Georgia Department of Archives and History, 1975), 82.

9. Ibid., 84.

10. Ibid., 84–85.

11. Ibid., 85.

12. Southern Regional Education Board, *Fact Book on Higher Education in the South* (Atlanta: Southern Regional Education Board, 1971).

13. Fink, *Prelude to the Presidency,* 35.

14. Ibid., 42. Before 1978, the governor of Georgia could not run for consecutive terms. After his term as governor expired, Maddox ran for and won the office of lieutenant governor. The lieutenant governor is the presiding officer of the Georgia State Senate.

15. Ibid., 45–47.

16. Ibid., 50, 46, 56–57.

17. Ibid., 56.

18. Ibid., 36.

19. Ibid., 95. Ben Fortson was the brother of Warren Fortson, the attorney forced to leave Americus, Georgia, after he tried to organize a biracial committee to mediate the racial violence in the city.

20. Ibid., 98.

21. Bradley R. Rice, "Lester Maddox and the Politics of Populism," in *Georgia Governors in an Age of Change: From Ellis Arnall to George Busbee,* eds. Harold Henderson and Gary L. Roberts, 193–210 (Athens: University of Georgia Press, 1988), 202.

22. Ibid., 201.

23. Memo to All Department Heads from Governor Jimmy Carter, November 15, 1971, Governor, Record 12, Sub Group 2, Series 27, Box 35, State Superintendent Papers, Georgia Department of Archives and History, Atlanta, Georgia. Hereafter cited as State Superintendent Papers.

24. Ibid.

25. Memo 1D-2, Findings and Recommendations of Committees Studying Agency Organization: Education, Record Group 1, Sub Group 15, Series, 151, Box 1, Governor Office of Reorganization, Governor Carter Papers.

26. Ibid.

27. Ibid.

28. Ibid.

29. Ibid and Fink, *Prelude to the Presidency*, 57.

30. General Assembly, Record Group 12, Sub Group 2, Series 27, Box 9, State Superintendent Papers.

31. January 1972, Public Information, Record Group 12, Sub Group 4, Series 6, State Superintendent Papers.

32. Memo 1D-2, Findings and Recommendations of Committees Studying Agency Organization: Education.

33. Carter, *Addresses*, 115.

34. University System Board of Regents, *University System of Georgia Annual Report: For Fiscal Year July 1, 1971–June 30, 1972* (Atlanta: University System of Georgia, 1974), 15. Future references to this series of publications will be cited as Board of Regents, *Annual Reports* with the appropriate dates.

35. Carter, *Addresses*, 82.

36. Education, Governor's Press Secretary Reference File, Record Group 1, Sub Group 1, Series 98, Box 2, Governor Carter Papers and Dr. Larry Gess (education advisor to Governor Jimmy Carter), interview by author, April 28, 1997. For a discussion of the Early Childhood Education Program and its legislative battles, see Deanna Michael, "The Politics Behind the Establishment of Kindergartens in Georgia," *Journal of the Georgia Association of Historians* 25 (2004): 1–22.

37. Bill Jordan, "Childhood Development Plan in Trouble, Floyd Reports," *Atlanta Constitution*, January 27, 1972.

38. Ibid.

39. Georgia Congress of Colored Parents and Teachers, Resolutions—1970 Session, Education, Record Group 12, Sub Group 2, Series 27, Box 28, State Superintendent Papers.

40. Speech for Governor's Conference on Education, 1969, Education, Record Group 12, Sub Group 2, Series 27, Box 27, State Superintendent Papers.

41. Ibid.

42. Jordan, "Childhood Development Plan in Trouble." An example of Carter's opinion that lobbyists represent only their constituents is his statement that "The lobbyists who represent teachers work for what is best for their own employers. They would not try to cut teachers' salaries or retirement benefits in order to finance a new kindergarten program." Jimmy Carter, *Why Not the Best?* (New York: Bantam Books, 1976), 105.

43. January 1972, Public Information, Record Group 12, Sub Group 4, Series 6, State Superintendent Papers.

44. Education, Governor's Press Secretary Reference Files, Record Group 1, Sub Group 10, Series 98, Box 2, Governor Carter Papers.

45. Henry J. Perkinson, *The Imperfect Panacea: American Faith in Education, 1865–1990*, 3rd ed. (New York: McGraw-Hill, 1991), 152–59.

46. Junie Brown, "Carter Says Edicts Harm Education," *Atlanta Journal*, October 14, 1971.

47. Education, Governor's Press Secretary Reference Files, Record Group 1, Sub Group 10, Series 98, Box 2, Governor Carter Papers.

48. Junie Brown, "School Aid for Poor Blocked, Carter Says," *Atlanta Constitution*, September 17, 1972.

49. Ibid.

50. Carnegie Council on Policy Studies in Higher Education. *The Federal Role in Post-Secondary Education: Unfinished Business* (San Francisco: Jossey-Bass, 1975).

51. Memo 1B, Findings and Recommendations of Committees Studying Agency Organization: Education, Record Group 1, Sub Group 15, Series, 151, Box 1, Governor Office of Reorganization, Governor Carter Papers.

52. Ibid.

53. Board of Regents, *Annual Reports, July 1, 1972–June 30, 1973*, 18–19.

54. While the coordination of services for student financial aid was necessary, student loans and grants were changing during this period. In 1972, loans began to go directly to the students rather than to the institutions of higher education. See chapter 5.

55. Board of Regents, *Annual Reports, July 1, 1974–June 30, 1975*, 17.

56. Ibid.

57. Carter, *Addresses*, 84–85.

58. Board of Regents, *Annual Reports, July 1, 1970–June 30, 1971*, 12.

59. Board of Regents, *Annual Reports, July 1, 1972–June 30, 1973*, 16.

60. Board of Regents, *Annual Reports, July 1, 1970–June 30, 1971* through *July 1, 1974–June 30, 1975*.

61. Letter to Jack Nix from Jimmy Carter, March 6, 1973, Education, Governor's Incoming Correspondence, Record Group 1, Sub Group 1, Series 5, Box 59, Governor Carter Papers.

62. Ibid.

63. Ibid.

64. Ibid.

65. Letter to Jimmy Carter from Jack Nix, March 7, 1973, Education, Governor's Incoming Correspondence, Record Group 1, Sub Group 1, Series 5, Box 59, Governor Carter Papers.

66. Ibid.

67. Campbell and Mazzoni, *State Policy Making for the Public Schools*, 102–109. Larry Gess also addressed this issue and pointed out the power of the Georgia state superintendent in rural areas. Gess, interview with author, May 8, 1997.

68. Press Releases 6/9/73–7/25/73, Record Group 1, Sub Group 10, Series 43, Box 4, Governor Carter Papers.

69. Ibid., 11–52 and Minimum Foundation Program for Education Study Committee, APEG.

70. Ibid., 16–17.

71. *Ordway v. Hargraves*, 323 F. Supp, 1155 (D. Mass. 1971); Martha M. McCarthy, Nelda H. Cambron-McCabe, and Stephen B. Thomas, *Public School Law: Teachers' and Students' Rights* (Boston: Allyn and Bacon, 2003), 157–59 and William C. Thompson, Jr., *Undercounted and Underserved: New York City's 20,000 School-Aged Young Mothers* (New York: Office of Comptroller and Office of Policy Management, 2003), 6. http://www.comptroller.nyc.gov/bureaus/opm/reports/Teen_Mothers.pdf.

72. Minimum Foundation Program of Education Study Committee, APEG, 15, 17.

73. Ibid., 21.

74. Ibid., 22.

75. Ibid., 23, 24.

76. Ibid., 27.

77. Ibid.

78. Ibid., 45.

79. Ibid.

80. Ibid., 46–47.

81. Ibid., 57–74.

82. Ibid., 59.

83. Ibid., 70.

84. Arthur E. Wise, *Legislated Learning: The Bureaucratization of the American Classroom* (Berkeley: University of California Press, 1979), 2.

85. Minimum Foundation Program of Education Study Committee, APEG, 79.

86. *Minimum Foundation Program of Education*, SB 180, Georgia State Senate, sec. 2, quoted in ibid., 80.

87. Minimum Foundation Program for Education Study Committee, APEG, 82.

88. Gess, interview, April 28, 1997.

89. Memo to Jimmy Carter from Larry Gess, 12/28/73, Education, Governor's Incoming Correspondence, Record Group 1, Sub Group 1, Series 5, Box 59, Governor Carter Papers.

90. Ibid.

91. On the problems in the evaluation of Head Start, see Edward Zigler and Susan Muenchow, *Head Start: The Inside Story of America's Most Successful Educational Experiment* (New York: Basic Books, 1992), 69–98.

92. Carter, *Addresses*, 242–43.

93. Gess, interview, April 28, 1997.

94. Memo from Larry Gess to Jimmy Carter, 2/8/73, Governor's Incoming Correspondence, Record Group 1, Sub Group 1, Series 5, Box 59, Governor Carter Papers. In current terms $12 or $15 per student does not seem significant, but, in 1973, the local effort per student in Average Daily Attendance ranged from $23 to $182. See APEG, 77–79.

95. Senate Bill 672, APEG Governor Busbee 74–75, Legislative Review Files, Record Group 1, Sub Group 7, Series 96, Box 19, Governor George Busbee Papers, Georgia Department of Archives and History, Atlanta, Georgia.

96. Carter, *Addresses*, 264–95.

CHAPTER FIVE. AN OPPORTUNITY MISSED

1. See E. J. Dionne, Jr., *Why Americans Hate Politics* (New York: Touchstone/Simon & Schuster, 1991) and Dan T. Carter, *The Politics of Rage: George Wallace, the Origins of the New Conservatism, and the Transformation of American Politics* (New York: Simon & Schuster, 1995) on the reaction against federal social programs and the alienation of the middle-class from the political process during the 1970s.

2. Jimmy Carter, *Addresses of Jimmy Carter (James Earl Carter) Governor of Georgia, 1971–1975*, comp. Frank Daniel (Atlanta: Georgia Department of Archives and History, 1975), 286.

3. Ibid., 286–88.

4. Ibid.

5. Peter Bourne, *Jimmy Carter: A Comprehensive Biography from Plains to Postpresidency* (New York: Lisa Drew/Scribner, 1997), 264.

6. John Dumbrell, *The Carter Presidency: A Re-evaluation* (New York: Manchester University Press, 1993), 88. Drumbell gives the number as 94 percent of black voters in the 1976 election.

7. Jimmy Carter, *Keeping Faith: Memoirs of a President* (New York: Bantam Books, 1982), 71–74.

8. William Van Til, "Education and Jimmy Carter," *Phi Delta Kappan* 58 (November 1976): 277.

9. NEA Reporter (June 1976), quoted in Erwin Hargrove, *Jimmy Carter as President: Leadership and the Politics of the Public Good* (Baton Rouge: Louisiana State University Press, 1988), 60.

10. Joseph Califano, Jr., *Governing America: An Insider's Report from the White House and the Cabinet* (New York: Simon & Schuster, 1981), 19.

11. Jimmy Carter, "The Sun Is Rising on a Beautiful New Day," *A Government as Good as its People* (Fayetteville: University of Arkansas Press, 1996), 217.

12. Message to Congress from President Jimmy Carter, "2/28/78" folder, Box FG 236, White House Central Files (WHCF), Jimmy Carter Library, Atlanta, Georgia. Hereafter cited as Jimmy Carter Library.

13. Bourne, *Jimmy Carter*, 369.

14. Ibid.

15. Carter, *Keeping Faith*, 74. Betty Glad described Carter's populism as more of "an attempt to articulate the deeper feelings and frustrations of the small people—their suspicions of the urban centers, the rich, the big interests—than a fundamental challenge to the established center of power." See Betty Glad, *Jimmy Carter: In Search of the Great White House* (New York: W. W. Norton, 1980), 139.

16. Bourne, *Jimmy Carter*, 365. Ernest L. Boyer became the commissioner of education on March 15, 1977. The commissioner of the Office of Education had little political power and all policy suggestions from the Office of Education went through the secretary of HEW's office. For a description of the commissioner's political position, see Samuel Halperin, "Some Diagnoses and Prescriptions," in Christopher T. Cross et al., *Education in the Carter Years* (Washington, D.C.: Institute for Educational Leadership, 1978), 64.

17. Califano, *Governing America*, 272–73.

18. John B. Williams, III, "Title VI Regulation of Higher Education," in *Desegregating America's Colleges and Universities: Title VI Regulation of Higher Education*, ed. John B. Williams, III (New York: Teachers College Press, 1988), 9. The states involved in the *Adams* suit were Arkansas, Georgia, Florida, Louisiana, Maryland, Mississippi, North Carolina, Oklahoma, Pennsylvania, and Virginia. See *Adams v. Califano*, 1977, 430 F. Supp. 118 (D.D.C. 1977).

19. Williams, "Title VI Regulation of Higher Education," 9.

20. Ibid., 9–10, and HEW News, 7/5/77, Box 183, Subject Files, Stuart Eizenstat, Domestic Policy Staff (DPS), Jimmy Carter Library.

21. Williams, "Title VI Regulation of Higher Education," 13 and HEW News, 7/5/77. On the desegregation of North Carolina's colleges and universities, see Robert A. Dentler, D. Catherine Baltzell, and Daniel J. Sullivan, *University on Trial: The Case of the University of North Carolina* (Cambridge: Abt Books, 1983).

22. Carnegie Council on Policy Studies in Higher Education, *The Federal Role in Post Secondary Education: Unfinished Business* (San Francisco: Jossey-Bass, 1975), 22.

23. Memo, HEW to OMB, 2/15/77, "HEW [Health, Education, and Welfare], Dept of" folder, Box 212, Subject Files, Stuart Eizenstat, DPS, Jimmy Carter Library and "NEA Encouraged: Carter Education Budget 1.5 Billion More for Schools," *NEA Reporter* 16 (April 1977): 4.

24. Letter, Joseph Califano to Warren Magnuson, 5/20/77, "HEW Dept. of" folder, Box 212, Subject Files, Stuart Eizenstat, DPS, Jimmy Carter Library; The House also increased HEW's total appropriations.

25. Memo, HEW to OMB, 2/15/77.

26. Letter, Joseph Califano to Warren G. Magnuson, 5/20/77.

27. Memo, From HEW to OMB, 2/15/77.

28. John Brademas, *The Politics of Education: Conflict and Consensus on Capital Hill* (Norman: University of Oklahoma Press, 1987), 77.

29. Letter, Joseph Califano to Warren Magnuson, 5/20/77, and Memo, Bert Lance to President Carter, n.d., "Handicapped [1]" folder, Box 213, Subject Files, Stuart Eizenstat, DPS, Jimmy Carter Library.

30. Hyamn Rickover, *Education and Freedom* (New York: E. P. Dutton, 1959), 136. For the reaction of Congress and the academic community to Sputnik, see Barbara Barksdale Clowse, *Brain Power for the Cold War: The Sputnik Crisis and National Defense Education Act of 1958* (Westport, CT: Greenwood Press, 1981) and Jurgen Herbst, *The Once and Future School: Three Hundred and Fifty Years of American Secondary Education* (New York: Routledge, 1996), 176–79.

31. Califano, *Governing America*, 295.

32. Letter, Senator S. I. Hayakawa to President Jimmy Carter, 11/21/77, "Competency Testing/Federal Role" folder, Box 172, Subject Files, Stuart Eizenstat, DPS, Jimmy Carter Library.

33. Ibid.

34. Ibid.

35. Califano, *Governing America*, 273.

36. Memo, Beth Abramowitz to Stuart Eizenstat, 10/13/77, "Competency Testing/Federal Role" folder, Box 172, Subject Files, Stuart Eizenstat, DPS, Jimmy Carter Library.

37. Letter, President Carter to Joseph Califano, 11/28/77, "Competency Testing/Federal Role" folder, Box 172, Subject Files, Stuart Eizenstat, DPS, Jimmy Carter Library.

38. Memo, Beth Abramowitz to Stuart Eizenstat, 10/13/77.

39. Memo, Joseph Califano to President Carter, 12/2/77, "Competency Testing/Federal Role" folder, Box 172, Subject Files, Stuart Eizenstat, DPS, Jimmy Carter Library.

40. Ibid.

41. Letter, President Carter to Joseph Califano, 12/5/77, "Competency Testing/Federal Role" folder, Box 172, Subject File, Stuart Eizenstat, DPS, Jimmy Carter Library.

42. Memo, Joseph Califano to President Carter, 12/5/77, "Competency Testing/Federal Role" folder, Box 172, Subject File, Stuart Eizenstat, DPS, Jimmy Carter Library.

43. Memo, Joseph Califano to President Carter, 12/28/77, HEW News, "Competency Testing/Federal Role" folder, Box 172, Subject Files, Stuart Eizenstat, DPS, Jimmy Carter Library.

44. Ibid.

45. The NEA had supported a cabinet-level department of education since 1917 and moved its offices to Washington, D.C., to promote it.

46. Senator Ribicoff informed Joseph Califano of his intention to create a separate department of education before Califano was sworn in as the secretary of HEW.

See Califano, *Governing America*, 273, and Congress, Senate, Committee in Governmental Affairs, *The Legislative History of Public Law 96–88 Department of Education Organization Act*, 96th Cong., 2d sess., 1980, Committee Print, 46.

47. Memo, Vice President Mondale to President Carter, 6/22/77, "Education, Depart. Of (Separate) [5]" folder, Box 195, Subject Files, Stuart Eizenstat, DPS, Jimmy Carter Library; Note on Memo, Bert Carp to Stuart Eizenstat, 6/15/77, "Education, Depart. Of (Separate) [5]" folder, Box 195, Subject Files, Stuart Eizenstat, DPS, Jimmy Carter Library, and Memo, Bert Carp to Stuart Eizenstat, 11/23/77, "Education, Depart. Of (Separate) [5]" folder, Box 195, Subject Files, Stuart Eizenstat, DPS, Jimmy Carter Library.

48. Memo, Vice President Mondale to President Carter, 6/22/77.

49. Memo, Hamilton Jordan to President Carter, n.d., "Education, Department of, 1978" folder, Box 34, Hamilton Jordan, Chief of Staff Files, Jimmy Carter Library.

50. James McIntyre became the director of OMB in November 1977 after Bert Lance resigned.

51. Memo, James T. McIntyre, Jr. to President Carter, n.d., "Establishing a Cabinet Level Department of Education" folder, Box FG-236, Subject Files, White House Central Files (WHCF), Jimmy Carter Library.

52. Memo, Stuart Eizenstat to President Carter, 12/2/77, "Education, Dept. of (Separate)" folder, Box 195, Subject Files, Stuart Eizenstat, DPS, Jimmy Carter Library.

53. Ibid.

54. Jimmy Carter, "State of the Union Address, 1/19/78," *Public Papers of the Presidents of the United States: Jimmy Carter* (Washington, D.C.: Government Printing Office, 1980), 104.

55. Carter, "Message to Congress, 2/28/78," *Public Papers of the Presidents, Jimmy Carter*, 425.

56. Ibid.

57. Cross et al. *Educational Policy in the Carter Years*, 24, 93. The FY 1978 budget for Title I was $2.735 billion, and the FY 1979 budget was $3.379 billion.

58. Califano, *Governing America*, 293. In the ensuing discussion of Carter's interest in basic skills and achievement testing, documents from the Jimmy Carter Library are used. Joseph Califano's account in *Governing America* does not contain citations for the documents quoted in his text. Therefore, his account will only be used for his interpretation of events.

59. Carter, "Message to Congress, 2/28/78," *Public Papers of the Presidents, Jimmy Carter*, 427.

60. Memo, Secretary Califano to President Carter, 12/3/77, "Education—ESEA" folder, Box 195, Subject File, Stuart Eizenstat, DPS, Jimmy Carter Library, and Memo, Stuart Eizenstat and Bert Carp to President Carter, 12/5/77, "Education—ESEA" folder, Box 195, Subject File, Stuart Eizenstat, DPS, Jimmy Carter Library.

61. Carter, "Message to Congress, 2/28/78," *Public Papers of the Presidents, Jimmy Carter*, 425 and Brademas, *The Politics of Education*, 22.

62. Brademas, *The Politics of Education*, 22, 21.

63. Ibid., 22, and Carter, "Message to Congress, 2/28/78," *Public Papers of the Presidents, Jimmy Carter*, 425.

64. Brademas also noted that Carter never gave the members of the House credit for their help in the development of the Middle Income Student Assistance Act, see Brademas, *The Politics of Education*, 22.

65. Memo, Patricia Roberts Harris to Stuart Eizenstat, 2/24/78, "ESEA [2]" folder, Box 191, Subject Files, Stuart Eizenstat, DPS, Jimmy Carter Library.

66. National Academy of Education, *Improving Educational Achievement: Report of the National Academy of Education, Committee on Testing and Basic Skills to the Assistant Secretary for Education* (Washington, D. C.: Department of Health, Education, and Welfare, 1978), iv, 9 and Califano, *Governing America*, 299.

67. Memo, Stuart Eizenstat to President Carter, 5/18/78, "Education (General) [1]" folder, Box 196, Subject Files, Stuart Eizenstat, DPS, Jimmy Carter Library.

68. Memo, Stuart Eizenstat and Beth Abramowitz to President Carter, 11/1/78, "ESEA [Elementary and Secondary Education Act] [1]" folder, Box 191, Subject Files, Stuart Eizenstat, DPS, Jimmy Carter Library.

69. Maurice R. Berube, *American Presidents and Education* (Westport, CT: Greenwood Press, 1991), 51; Califano, *Governing America*, 279, and Charles O. Jones, *The Trustee Presidency: Jimmy Carter and the United States Congress* (Baton Rouge: Louisiana State University Press, 1988), 185.

70. Jones, *The Trustee Presidency*, 185; Hargrove, *Jimmy Carter*, 61–63, and Memo, James McIntyre, Jr. to President Carter, n.d., "Education, Establishing a Cabinet Department of" folder, Box 44, Hamilton Jordan, Chief of Staff Files, Jimmy Carter Library.

71. Carter, *Keeping Faith*, 75.

72. Ibid., 76.

73. Jones, *The Trustee Presidency*, 185 and Hargrove, *Jimmy Carter*, 64.

74. Congress, Senate, *Legislative History of Public Law 96–88, Department of Education Organizational Act*, 1042.

75. Ibid., 1048–49.

76. Carter, Message to Congress, *Public Papers of the Presidents, Jimmy Carter*, 264.

77. Congress, Senate, *Legislative History of Public Law 96–88, Department of Education Organizational Act*, 1230.

78. Ibid., 1233 and Harry L. Summerfield, *Power and Process: The Formation and Limits of Federal Educational Policy* (Berkeley: McCutchen, 1974), 155.

79. Joan Hutchon King, "Establishing the U.S. Department of Education During the Carter Administration, 1978–1979" (PhD diss., Clairmont Graduate School,

1980), 109. Albert Shanker, the president of the American Federation of Teachers, opposed the creation of the department of education and lived in New York. According to King, his opposition may have influenced the *New York Times*. "An Idea Whose Time Has Not Come," *Change* (May 1978) quoted in King, "Establishing the U.S. Department of Education," 109.

80. "What's In and Out of the New Department of Education," *Academe* (December 1979), 470–71; Califano, *Governing America*, 264, and Jones, *The Trustee Presidency*, 185. In July 1979, Joseph Califano resigned from his position as the secretary of HEW at Carter's request. Carter's advisors viewed Califano as too liberal and independent to effectively serve the president. See Bourne, *Jimmy Carter*, 445–46.

81. Memo, Jack Watson and Arnie Miller to President Carter, "9/28/79" folder, Box 149, Staff Secretary Handwriting Files, Jimmy Carter Library.

82. Spencer Rich, "Congress Passes Bill to Establish Education Dept.," *Washington Post*, September 28, 1979, and Memo, Vice President Mondale to President Carter, "10/9/79 [1]" folder, Box 150, Staff Secretary Handwriting Files, Jimmy Carter Library.

83. Memo, Jack Watson and Arnie Miller to President Carter, n.d., "10/15/79" folder, Box 151, Staff Secretary Handwriting Files, Jimmy Carter Library.

84. Shirley M. Hufstedler, "What the Courts Cannot Do," *Washington Post*, January 1, 1978.

85. Ibid.

86. Congress, Senate, Committee on Labor and Human Resources, *Hearing on Shirley M. Hufstedler*, 96th Cong., 1st sess. 1979, 21.

87. Memo, Stuart Eizenstat and Beth Abramowitz to President Carter, 11/1/78.

88. Ibid.

89. Ibid.

90. William A. Kaplin, *The Law of Higher Education: A Comprehensive Guide to Legal Implications of Administrative Decision Making* (San Francisco: Jossey-Bass, 1988), 365.

91. Cameron Fincher, *A Study of Title III Impact on Historically Black Institutions* (Atlanta: Southern Education Foundation, 1980), 6.

92. Congress, Senate, Subcommittee on Education, Arts and Humanities of the Committee on Labor and Human Resources, *S. 1839: To Extend the Higher Education Act of 1965, and for Other Purposes*, 96th Cong., 1st sess., 1979, 15.

93. Ibid.

94. Memo, Secretary of Education from Don Boselovic, "6/3/80" folder, Box 6, Subject Files, Shirley M. Hufstedler Collection, Jimmy Carter Library, Atlanta, Georgia. Hereafter cited as Shirley M. Hufstedler Collection.

95. Ibid.

96. Edward P. St. John, *Public Policy and College Management: Title III of the Higher Education Act* (New York: Praeger, 1981), 23–28. The protest from other institutions was so great that HEW delayed the use of the criteria for a year. Ibid., 28.

97. Carter, *Addresses*, 202.

98. Memo, From Shirley M. Hufstedler to James McIntyre, Jr., 12/3/79, "FY 81 Agency Budget Appeals to OMB Director" folder, Box 8, Subject Files, Shirley M. Hufstedler Collection.

99. Carter, *Why Not the Best?*, 150; Carter, *Keeping Faith*, 526.

CHAPTER SIX. RETURN TO LOCAL LEADERSHIP: THE CARTER CENTER AND ATLANTA PROJECT

1. Peter Bourne, *Jimmy Carter: A Comprehensive Biography from Plains to Post-presidency* (New York: Lisa Drew/Scribner, 1997), 457. The ABC news television show *Nightline* counted off the days that Iranian students held the hostages in Tehran.

2. Jimmy Carter, *Keeping Faith: Memoirs of a President* (New York: Bantam Books, 1982), 471–76.

3. Ibid, 490–96.

4. Ibid., 530–33.

5. Ibid., 568, and Bourne, *Jimmy Carter*, 471.

6. Herbert Hoover was an exception to the rule of quiet retirement.

7. Dylan Thomas, "Do Not Go Gentle into That Night," Internal.Org, http://www.internal.org/view_poem.phtml?poemID=92.

8. Bourne, *Jimmy Carter*, 479.

9. Douglas Brinkley, *The Unfinished Presidency: Jimmy Carter's Journey to the Nobel Peace Prize* (New York: Penguin Books, 1999), 84–86.

10. Ibid., 84, and Bourne, *Jimmy Carter*, 480–82.

11. Bourne, *Jimmy Carter*, 479–80, and Brinkley, *Unfinished Presidency*, 76.

12. Brinkley, *Unfinished Presidency*, 76–77.

13. Ibid., 77.

14. Ibid., 90, 87–88.

15. Ibid., 87–90.

16. Ibid., 90.

17. Ibid., 91–92, 94.

18. William Schmidt, "Mideast Conference in Atlanta Draws Arab and U.S. Officials," *New York Times* (1857–Current File) November 9, 1983. Proquest Historical Newspapers: *The New York Times* (1851–2002). http://proquest.umi.com.proxy.usf.

19. Brinkley, *Unfinished Presidency*, 117–23; Bourne, *Jimmy Carter*, 481.

20. Francesca Lyman, "Atlantans Label It the Exprezway, "*New York Times* (1857–Current File) September 1, 1984; "A Day of Cameras and Hammers Ex-President," *New York Times* (1857–Current File) September 4, 1984, and William Schmidt, "Panel Refuses to Block Parkway to Carter Library," *New York Times* (1857–Current File) September 21, 1984.

21. The Carter Center, "About Us, The Carter Center FAQS—Answers to Frequently Answered Questions," http://www.cartercenter.org/aboutus/faqs.htm.

22. Ibid.

23. In his series titled *American Education*, Lawrence Cremin explained that once researchers step beyond the schools, other institutions such as "families, churches, libraries" serve educational functions within the community. See Lawrence A. Cremin, *American Education: The Colonial Experience, 1607–1783* (New York: Harper and Row, 1970), xi.

24. The Carter Center News, "Mental Illness and the Media: A Rosalynn Carter Symposium" (Fall 1988): 12–13. http://www.cartercenter.org/documents/1140.pdf.

25. The Carter Center News, "Teaching the Teachers" (Summer 1987): 8. http://www.cartercenter.org/documents/1138.pdf.

26. The Carter Center News, "Education a Major Objective" (Spring 1988): 7 http://www.cartercenter.org/documents/1139.pdf.

27. The Carter Center News, "Teachers Brush Up On Middle East" (Fall 1989): 13. http://www.cartercenter.org/documents/1142.pdf.

28. Ibid.

29. The Carter Center News, "Global 2000: Feeding the Future: A Conversation with Nobel Laureate Norman Borlaug" (Fall 1988): 14. http://www.cartercenter.org/documents/1140.pdf.

30. Frederick W. Haberman, ed., *Nobel Lectures, Peace 1951–1970* (Amsterdam: Elsevier, 1972). http://nobelprize.org/peace/laureates/1970/borlaug-bio.html.

31. The Carter Center News, "Global 2000: Norman Borlaug," 15.

32. Kelly Callahan via Lauren S. Kent-Delany, e-mail message to author, February 14, 2006. Some governments elected to use national radio broadcasts and, at times, local dance and theater productions.

33. The Carter Center, *Annual Report, 1998–1999*, 19. http://cartercenter.org/documents/520.pdf

34. Ibid. By 1999, the efforts of the CCEU and other organizations like the World Health Organization and UNICEF had reduced the cases of guinea worm from 8 million to fewer than 90,000. The main obstacle they faced was the civil war in Sudan and the sheer number of cases in Nigeria and Ghana. Ibid., 18.

35. Habitat for Humanity, "History of Habitat." http://www.habitat.org/how/historytext.aspx.

36. Ibid.

37. Jimmy Carter and Rosalynn Carter, *Everything to Gain: Making the Most of the Rest of Your Life* (Fayetteville: University of Arkansas Press, 1995), 86.

38. Ibid., 80.

39. Ibid., 82–86.

40. Habitat for Humanity, "Jimmy Carter and Habitat for Humanity." http://www.habitat.org/how/carter.aspx.

41. Quoted in Carter and Carter, *Everything to Gain*, 88.

42. Bruce Adams, "Atlanta: Where Success Is Not Enough," *Boundary Crossers: Case Studies of How Ten of America's Metropolitan Regions Work* (College Park, MD: Academy of Leadership, 1998), 4, 19. http://www.academy.umd.edu/publications/Boundary/CaseStudies/bcsatlanta.htm.

43. The Annie E. Casey Foundation, City KIDS COUNT: Data on the Well-Being of Children in Large Cities, "City Profiles: Atlanta," http://www.aecf.org/kidscount/city/atla_ga.htm. The definition for a "distressed neighborhood" is a census tract with all of the following characteristics: high poverty rate (over 24.7%), high percent of female-headed families (above 36.8%), high percent of males unattached to the labor force (above 45.4%), high percent of families receiving public assistance (above 17.6%). Ibid., "Definition and Data Sources," http://www.aecf.org/kidscount/city/def_ sou.htm.

44. The Annie E. Casey Foundation, City KIDS COUNT: Data on the Well-Being of Children in Large Cities, "City Profiles: Atlanta."

45. Research Atlanta, "The Metro Atlanta Statistical Profile," http://raweb2003.brinkster.net/FullReports/01_reportCard.htm.

46. The Annie E. Casey Foundation, City KIDS COUNT: Data on the Well-Being of Children in Large Cities, "City Profiles: Atlanta."

47. It should be noted that there were two black Atlantas as well—one poor and one wealthy enough to move to the suburbs.

48. Alexander Von Hoffman, *House by House, Block by Block: The Rebirth of America's Urban Neighborhoods* (New York: Oxford University Press, 2003), 162–63.

49. Ibid.

50. "Goal: Minimum Funds, Maximum Volunteers," *Atlanta Journal* and *Atlanta Constitution*, October 25, 1991. http://www.newsbank.com/. All articles 1985 to the present from the *Atlanta Journal* and the *Atlanta Constitution* are from Newsbank database.

51. Ibid.

52. Ibid., and Elizabeth Kurylo, "Analysis: Can Carter's Third World Successes Work at Home?" *Atlanta Journal* and *Atlanta Constitution*, October 26, 1991.

53. Brinkley, *Unfinished Presidency*, 358, and Bourne, *Jimmy Carter*, 500.

54. By the time he announced the Atlanta Project, Carter had already recruited the president of the Summerhill CDC to participate on the task force to plan the initiative. See Adams, "Atlanta," 7–8, 11–14; Joan Walsh, *Stories of Renewal: Community Building and the Future of Urban America* (New York: Rockefeller Foundation, January 1997), 45–56. http://www.rockfound.org/Library/Stories_of_Renewal_Community_Building_and_the_Future_of_Urban_America.pdf.

55. Scott Bronstein, "A Pound of Despair: The Baby that Moved President Carter to Tears," *Atlanta Journal* and *Atlanta Constitution*, October 26, 1991, and Phyllis Thompson, "Technology and The Atlanta Project," *Georgia Tech Alumni Magazine Online* (Spring 1993) http://gtalumni.org/news/magazine/spr93/hood.html.

56. Bronstein, "A Pound of Despair."

57. Bronstein, "A Pound of Despair" and Brinkley, *Unfinished Presidency*, 356–57. Brinkley reports that she died at the age of two.

58. Brinkley, *Unfinished Presidency*, 357.

59. Ibid.

60. Chet Fuller, "Carter Goes to the People for Atlanta Project Ideas: Starting to Focus 2-week-old Plan to Help Inner City," *Atlanta Journal* and *Atlanta Constitution*, November 8, 1991.

61. Kurylo, "Analysis: Can Carter's Third World Successes Work at Home?"

62. Douglas Blackmon, "Carter Visits East Lake: Former President Says Curing Ills May Take Years," *Atlanta Journal* and *Atlanta Constitution*, November 27, 1991.

63. Ibid.

64. Clarence N. Stone, "Civic Capacity and Urban School Reform," in *Changing Urban Education*, ed. Clarence N. Stone, 250–73 (Kansas City: University of Kansas Press, 1998), 262–63. Stone explains that systemic change is only possible when business, teachers, school administrators, and parents come together to work for school improvement.

65. Douglas Blackmon, "On Board for Atlanta Project: Carter Names Effort's Leaders," *Atlanta Journal* and *Atlanta Constitution*, November 16, 1991.

66. Promising Practices Network on children, families and communities, "Programs That Work: Communities In Schools." http://www.promisingpractices.net/program.asp?programid=65#overview.

67. Jimmy Carter, *Turning Point: A Candidate, a State, and a Nation Come of Age* (New York: Times Books, 1992), 207–208.

68. Ibid., 209.

69. Maria Saporta, "Carter Has Spark to Make Project Work, Leader Says," *Atlanta Journal* and *Atlanta Constitution*, November 19, 1991.

70. Michael W. Giles, "The Atlanta Project: A Community-Based Approach to Solving Urban Problems," *National Civic Review* 82, no. 4 (Fall 1993): 357, http://infotrac.galegroup.com.proxy.usf.edu/ and Von Hoffman, *House by House*, 165.

71. Betsy White, "Atlanta Promise Leaders Vow to Lose Egos," *Atlanta Journal* and *Atlanta Constitution*, November 22, 1991.

72. National Neighborhood Indicators Partnership (NNIP), "NNIP Partner Spotlight, Atlanta: Office of Data and Policy Analysis," http://www2.urban.org/nnip/desc_atl.html, and Phyllis Thompson, "Technology and The Atlanta Project."

73. Giles, "The Atlanta Project," under The Clusters.

74. Ibid.

75. Ibid., under The Collaboration Centers.

76. Ibid., under Governance Structure.

77. Julie K. Miller, "Clayton School Board's Response Stings Atlanta Project," *Atlanta Journal* and *Atlanta Constitution*, September 17, 1992.

78. Bernadette Burden, "The Atlanta Project: Family Matters, the Class of '92: Graduates of Carver High Have Reason to be Proud," *Atlanta Journal* and *Atlanta Constitution*, November 29, 1992.

79. The Atlanta Project, Mission Statement. http://www2.gsu.edu/~wwwtap/about/mission.htm.

80. Gary Pomerantz, "Atlanta Project Official Quits, Alleging Racism: Black Member of Secretariat Accuses Whites of 'Arrogance,'" *Atlanta Journal* and *Atlanta Constitution*, September 17, 1992.

81. Ibid.

82. Ibid.

83. Ibid.

84. Ibid.

85. Jean Anyon, *Ghetto Schools: A Political Economy of Urban Education Reform* (New York: Teachers College Record, 1997), 130–34. Anyon's description of the distance between the economic elite and of the urban poor in Newark, NJ, is reflective of the problems faced by TAP.

86. Walsh, *Stories of Renewal*, 49.

87. Ibid., 48–53.

88. Von Hoffman, *House by House*, 167; Giles, "The Atlanta Project," under The First TAP-Wide Initiative, and The Carter Center News, "Thousands Immunized Through Atlanta Project Children's Health Initiative" (Spring 1993):1–3, http://www.cartercenter.org/documents/1149.pdf.

89. Von Hoffman, *House by House*, 168; Giles, "The Atlanta Project," under The First TAP-Wide Initiative.

90. The Atlanta Project, "Stories: Therrell Cluster: Transition to The Family Tree Resource Center" http://www2.gsu.edu/~wwwtap/about/stories/story30.html; Walsh, *Stories of Renewal*, 48–53.

91. Von Hoffman, *House by House*, 170–71; Walsh, *Stories of Renewal*, 48; Brinkley, *Unfinished Presidency*, 363; Jill Vejnoska, "Legislature '95: The Atlanta Project: Group Has Abandoned Mission, Report Finds; Audit: Resources Spent on Programs Not Linked to Goals," *Atlanta Journal* and *Atlanta Constitution*, February 16, 1995.

92. Walsh, *Stories of Renewal*, 48; Vejnoska, "Group has Abandoned Mission."

93. Von Hoffman, *House by House*, 170; Brinkley, *Unfinished Presidency*, 363; John Blake, "TAP has Big Plans and the Clusters Each Put Them in Writing," *Atlanta Journal* and *Atlanta Constitution*, September 21, 1995.

94. John Blake, "Carter: Atlanta Project Must Focus on Families," *Atlanta Journal* and *Atlanta Constitution*, October 19, 1995.

95. Ibid.

96. John Blake, "Atlanta Project Lowers Its Goals: Five Years Later; Effort to Help Poor May Have Tried to do Too Much," *Atlanta Journal* and *Atlanta Constitution*, August 27, 1996.

97. Ibid.

98. Anyon, *Ghetto Schools*, 168–71.

CONCLUSION

1. See James B. Conant, The *American High School Today* (New York: McGraw-Hill, 1959) and John Gardner, *Excellence: Can We Be Equal and Excellent Too?* (New York: Harper and Row, 1960).

2. Geoffrey D. Borman, "National Efforts to Bring Reform to Scale in High-Poverty Schools: Outcomes and Implications," *Review of Research in Education* 29 (2005): 1.

3. Jean Anyon, *Ghetto Schools: A Political Economy of Urban Education Reform* (New York: Teachers College Press, 1997), 163–80, and Alexander Von Hoffman, *House by House, Block by Block: The Rebirth of America's Urban Neighborhoods* (New York: Oxford University Press, 2003), 162–63.

4. Arthur E. Wise, *Legislated Learning: The Bureaucratization of the American Classroom* (Berkeley: University of California Press, 1979), 106.

5. Gray Orfield, *Must We Bus? Segregated School and National Policy* (Washington, D.C.: Brookings Institution, 1978), 12–19.

6. Wise, *Legislated Learning*, 14.

7. Steven Brint, *In the Age of Experts: The Changing Role of Professionals in Politics and Public Life* (Princeton: Princeton University Press, 1994), 136–37.

8. Memo, From Patricia Roberts Harris to Stuart Eizenstat, 2/24/78, "ESEA [2]" folder, Box 191, Subject Files, Eizenstat, DPS, Jimmy Carter Library.

9. See Anyon, *Ghetto Schools*, 168–70, 180.

10. For Reagan's educational policies during his first term, see Catherine A. Lugg, *For God and Country: Conservatism and American School Policy*, Counterpoints 32 (New York: Peter Lang, 1996).

11. The Carter Center, "About Us, The Carter Center FAQS—Answers to Frequently Answered Questions," http://www.cartercenter.org/aboutus/faqs.htm.

12. Clarence N. Stone, "Civic Capacity and Urban School Reform," in *Changing Urban Education*, ed. Clarence N. Stone, 250–73 (Kansas City: University of Kansas Press, 1998), 269.

13. Ibid., 267–71, and Anyon, *Ghetto Schools*, 164–84.

14. Anyon, *Ghetto Schools*, 164–65.

15. Ibid., 180, and Gary Orfield and Chungmei Lee, *Why Segregation Matters: Poverty and Educational Inequality* (Cambridge: The Civil Rights Project, Harvard University, 2005), 6–9. http://www.civilrightsproject.harvard.edu/research/deseg/Why_Segreg_Matters.pdf.

EPILOGUE

1. Richard F. Elmore, "Change and Improvement in Educational Reform," in *A Nation Reformed? American Education 20 Years after A Nation at Risk*, ed. David T. Gordon (Cambridge: Harvard Education Press, 2003), 23–38.

2. Arthur Wise, *Legislated Learning: The Bureaucratization of the American Classroom* (Berkeley: University of California Press, 1979), 2.

3. Joseph Califano, *Governing America: An Insider's Report from the White House and the Cabinet* (New York: Simon & Schuster, 1981), 293.

4. National Academy of Education, *Improving Educational Achievement: Report of the National Academy of Education, Committee on Testing and Basic Skills to the Assistant Secretary for Education* (Washington, D. C.: Department of Health, Education, and Welfare, 1978), iv, 9.

5. Terrel Bell, *The Thirteenth Man: A Reagan Cabinet Memoir* (New York: Free Press, 1988), 114–43, and Catherine A. Lugg, *For God and Country: Conservatism and American School Policy*, Counterpoints 32 (New York: Peter Lang, 1996), 134–40, 203–205.

6. Maris Vinovskis, *History and Educational Policymaking* (New Haven: Yale University Press, 1999). In this collection of essays, Vinovskis argues that most of the reforms over the past fourty years are based on policitical decisions that have little relationship to research concerning student learning.

7. Marvin Lazerson, Judith Block McLaughlin, Bruce McPherson, and Stephen K. Bailey, *An Education of Value: The Purposes and Practices of Schools* (New York: Cambridge University Press, 1985), 116.

8. Jimmy Cater, *Our Endangered Values: America's Moral Crisis* (New York: Simon & Schuster, 2005), 178–80, 190–97.

Bibliography

SPECIAL COLLECTIONS

Carter, James E. Presidential Papers. Jimmy Carter Library, Atlanta, Georgia.

Carter, James E. Papers. Georgia Department of Archives and History, Atlanta, Georgia.

Carter, James E. Collection. Lake Blackshear Memorial Library, Americus, Georgia.

Georgia Government Documentation Project. Special Collections, Georgia State University, Atlanta, Georgia.

Hufstedler, Shirley M. Collection. Jimmy Carter Library, Atlanta, Georgia.

State Superintendent of Schools Papers. Georgia Department of Archives and History, Atlanta, Georgia.

GOVERNMENT DOCUMENTS

Bachtel, Douglas C., and Susan R. Boatright, eds. *The Georgia County Guide*. 11th ed. Athens: University of Georgia Cooperative Extension Service.

Carter, Jimmy. *Addresses of Jimmy Carter (James Earl Carter) Governor of Georgia, 1971–1975*. Frank Daniel, Compiler. Atlanta: Georgia Department of Archives and History, 1975.

Carter, Jimmy. *Public Papers of the Presidents of the United States: Jimmy Carter, 1977–81*. 9 vols. Washington, D.C.: Office of the Federal Register, National Archives and Records Service, 1977–1982.

Georgia Department of Archives and History. *A State in Action: Georgia 1971–1975*. Atlanta, 1975.

Governor's Commission to Improve Education. *Educating Georgia's People: Investment in the Future*. Atlanta, 1963.

Minimum Foundation Program of Education Study Committee. *APEG: Adequate Program for Education in Georgia*. Atlanta, 1973.

Sumter County Board of Education. Minutes. Americus, Georgia, 1953–1963.

Thompson, William C., Jr. *Undercounted and Underserved: New York City's 20,0000 School-Aged Young Mothers.* New York: Office of Comptroller and Office of Policy Management, 2003.

U.S. Congress. Senate. Committee on Governmental Affairs. *The Legislative History of Public Law 96–88, Department of Education Organizational Act.* 96th Cong., 2d sess., 1980.

———. Committee on Labor and Human Resources. *Hearing on Shirley M. Hufstedler.* 96th Cong., 1st sess., 1979.

———. Subcommittee on Education, Arts and Humanities of the Committee on Labor and Human Resources. *S. 1839: To Extend the Higher Education Act of 1965, and for Other Purposes.* 96th Cong., 1st sess., 1979.

University System Board of Regents. *University System of Georgia Annual Report,* 1962–1965 and 1971–1976.

NEWSPAPERS

Americus Times-Recorder, Americus, Georgia
Atlanta Constitution
Atlanta Daily World
Atlanta Journal
Augusta Chronicle
New York Times
Washington Post

BOOKS, CHAPTERS, ARTICLES, AND UNPUBLISHED MATERIALS

Abernathy, M. Glenn. "The Carter Administration and Domestic Civil Rights." In *The Carter Years: The President and Policy Making,* edited by M. Glenn Abernathy, Dilys M. Hill, and Phil Williams, 106–22. New York: St. Martin's Press, 1984.

Adams, Bruce. "Atlanta: Where Success Is Not Enough." In *Boundary Crossers: Case Studies of How Ten of America's Metropolitan Regions Work.* College Park, MD: Academy of Leadership, 1998. http://academy.umd.edu/publications/Boundary/CaseStudies/bcsatlanta.htm.

Anderson, James. *The Education of Blacks in the South 1860–1935.* Chapel Hill: University of North Carolina Press, 1988.

Anyon, Jean. *Ghetto Schools: Political Economy in Urban School Reform.* New York: Teachers College Press, 1997. http://www.netlibrary.com.

Ariail, Dan, and Cheryl Heckler-Feltz. *The Carpenter's Apprentice: The Spiritual Biography of Jimmy Carter.* Grand Rapids: Zondervan, 1996.

Arsenault, Raymond. *Freedom Riders: 1961 and the Struggle for Racial Justice. Pivotal Movements in American History.* New York: Oxford University Press, 2006.

Barber, James. *The Lawmakers: Recruitment and Adaptation to Legislative Life.* New Haven: Yale University Press, 1965.

Bartley, Numan V. *The Creation of Modern Georgia.* 2d ed. Athens: University of Georgia Press, 1990.

———. *From Thurmond to Wallace: Political Tendencies in Georgia, 1948–1968.* Baltimore: Johns Hopkins University Press, 1970.

———, and Hugh Davis Graham. *Southern Politics and the Second Reconstruction.* Baltimore: Johns Hopkins University Press, 1975.

Bass, Jack, and Walter DeVries. *The Transformation of Southern Politics: Social Change and Political Consequences Since 1945.* New York: Basic Books, 1976.

Bell, Terrell. *The Thirteenth Man: A Reagan Cabinet Memoir.* New York: Free Press, 1988.

Berube, Maurice R. *American Presidents and Education.* Westport, CT: Greenwood Press, 1991.

———. *American School Reform: Progressive, Equity, and Excellence Movements, 1883–1993.* Westport, CT: Praeger, 1994.

———. *Teacher Politics: The Influence of Unions.* Westport, CT: Greenwood Press, 1988.

Borman, Geoffrey. "National Efforts to Bring Reform to Scale in High-Poverty Schools: Outcomes and Implication." In "The Elementary and Secondary Education Act at 40: Reviews of Research, Policy Implementation, Critical Perspectives, and Reflections," edited by Laurence Parker, Special issue, *Review of Research in Education* 29 (2005): 1–27.

Bourne, Peter. *Jimmy Carter: A Comprehensive Biography from Plains to Postpresidency.* New York: Lisa Drew Books/Scribner, 1997.

Bowden, Elizabeth Gray. "The Gubernatorial Administration of Jimmy Carter." MA thesis, University of Georgia, 1980.

Brademas, John. *The Politics of Education: Conflict and Consensus on Capital Hill.* Norman: University of Oklahoma Press, 1987.

Branch, Taylor. *Parting the Waters: America in the King Years, 1954–63.* New York: Touchstone, 1988.

Brinkley, Douglas. *Unfinished Presidency: Jimmy Carter's Journey to the Nobel Peace Prize.* New York: Penguin Books, 1999.

Brint, Stephen. *In an Age of Experts: The Changing Role of Professionals in Politics and Public Life.* Princeton: Princeton University Press, 1994.

Califano, Joseph A., Jr. *Governing America: An Insider's Report from the White House and the Cabinet.* New York: Simon and Schuster, 1981.

Callahan, Raymond E. *Education and the Cult of Efficiency: A Study of the Social Forces that Have Shaped the Administration of the Public Schools.* Chicago: University of Chicago Press, 1962.

Campbell, Ronald F., and Tim L. Mazzoni, Jr. *State Policy Making for the Public Schools: A Comparative Analysis of Policy Making for the Public Schools in Twelve States and a Treatment of State Governance Models.* Berkeley: McCutchan, 1976.

Carnegie Commission on Higher Education. *Quality and Equality: New Levels of Federal Responsibility for Higher Education: A Special Report and Recommendations by the Commission.* New York: McGraw-Hill, 1968.

Carnegie Council on Policy Studies in Higher Education. *The Federal Role in Post-Secondary Education: Unfinished Business.* San Francisco: Jossey-Bass, 1975.

Carnegie Foundation for the Advancement of Teaching. *The States and Higher Education: A Proud Past and a Vital Future.* San Francisco: Jossey-Bass, 1976.

The Carter Center. *Annual Report, 1998–1999.* http://cartercenter.org/documents/520.pdf.

The Carter Center News, Fall 1987–92. http://www.cartercenter.org.

Carter, Dan T. *The Politics of Rage: George Wallace, the Origins of the New Conservatism, and the Transformation of American Politics.* New York: Simon & Schuster, 1995.

Carter, Hugh. *Cousin Beedie and Cousin Hot: My Life with the Carter Family of Plains, Georgia.* As told to Frances Spatz Leighton. Englewood Cliffs, NJ: Prentice-Hall, 1978.

Carter, Jimmy. *A Government as Good as Its People.* Fayetteville: University of Arkansas Press, 1996.

———. *An Hour Before Daylight: Memories of a Rural Boyhood.* New York: Touchstone/Simon & Schuster, 2001.

———. *Keeping Faith: Memoirs of a President.* New York: Bantam Books, 1982.

———. *Our Endangered Values: America's Moral Crisis.* New York: Simon & Schuster, 2005.

———. *Turning Point: A Candidate, a State, and a Nation Come of Age.* New York: Times Books, 1992.

———. *Why Not the Best?* New York: Bantam Books, 1976.

———, and Rosalynn Carter. *Everything to Gain: Making the Most of the Rest of Your Life.* Rev. ed. Fayetteville: University of Arkansas Press, 1995.

Carter, Rosalynn. *First Lady from Plains.* New York: Fawcett Gold Medal Books, 1984.

Cartisano, O. Joseph. "School Boards as an Alternative Vehicle for Entry into Politics." EDD diss., Columbia University, Teachers College, 1987.

Chambers, John W. "The Agenda Continued: Jimmy Carter's Post-Presidency." In *The Carter Presidency: Policy Choices in the Post New Deal Era,* edited by Gary M. Fink and Hugh Davis Graham, 267–85. Lawrence: University Press of Kansas, 1999.

———. "Jimmy Carter's Public Policy Ex-Presidency." *Political Science Quarterly* 113, no. 3 (Autumn 1998): 405–25.

Chancey, Andrew S. "Race, Religion, and Agricultural Reform: The Communal Vision of Koinonia Farm." In *Georgia in Black and White: Explorations in the Race Relations of a Southern State, 1865–1950,* edited by John Inscoe, 255–75. Athens: University of Georgia Press, 1994.

Clowse, Barbara Barksdale. *Brain Power for the Cold War: The Sputnik Crisis and National Defense Education Act of 1958*. Westport, CT: Greenwood Press, 1981.

Coleman, James, Sara D. Kelly, and John A. Moore. *Trends in School Segregation, 1968–73*. Washington, D.C.: Urban Institute, 1975.

Conant, James Bryant. *The American High School Today*. New York: McGraw-Hill, 1959.

Cook, James F. *Carl Sanders: Spokesman of the New South*. Macon: Mercer University Press, 1993.

Cremin, Lawrence A. *American Education: The Colonial Experience, 1607–1783*. New York: Harper and Row, 1970.

Cross, Christopher T., William Blakey, Samuel Halperin, Gregory A. Humphrey, John F. Jennings, George R. Kaplan, Alms C. McGuinness, Jr., Michael O'Keefe, and Charles B. Sanders, Jr. *Educational Policy in the Carter Years*. Washington, D.C.: Institute of Educational Leadership, George Washington University, 1978.

Cubberley, Ellwood P. *Public Education in the United States: A Study and Interpretation of American Educational History*. Rev. ed., New York: Houghton Mifflin, 1934.

Dentler, Robert A., D. Catherine Baltzell, and Daniel J. Sullivan. *University on Trial: The Case of the University of North Carolina*. Cambridge: Abt Books, 1983.

Dewey, John. *Democracy and Education: An Introduction to the Philosophy of Education*. New York: Macmillan, 1916. Reprinted New York: Free Press, 1966.

Dionne, E. J. *Why Americans Hate Politics*. New York: Touchstone/Simon & Schuster, 1991.

Dobelle, Samuel Evans. "A Study of the Creation of a Federal Cabinet-Level Department of Education, 1857–1979; with an Analysis of Executive Branch Public Policy, 1977–1979." EDD diss., University of Massachusetts, 1988.

Dumbrell, John. *The Carter Presidency: A Re-evaluation*. New York: Manchester University Press, 1993.

Elmore, Richard. "Change and Improvement in Educational Reform." In *A Nation Reformed? American Education 20 Years after A Nation at Risk*, edited by David T. Gordon, 23–38. Cambridge: Harvard Education Press, 2003.

Fincher, Cameron. *A Study of Title III Impact on Historically Black Institutions*. Atlanta: Southern Education Foundation, 1980.

Fink, Gary M. *Prelude to the Presidency: The Political Character and Legislative Leadership Style of Governor Jimmy Carter*. Westport, CT: Greenwood Press, 1980.

Fitzwater, C. O. "A New Commission Looks at an Old Problem." *American School Board Journal* 135 (July 1957): 19–31.

Fultz, Michael. "African American Teachers in the South, 1890–1940: Powerlessness and the Ironies of Expectations and Protest." *History of Education Quarterly* 35, no. 4 (Winter 1995): 401–22.

Gardner, John. *Excellence: Can We be Equal and Excellent Too?* New York: Harper and Row, 1960.

Glad, Betty. *Jimmy Carter: In Search of the Great White House*. New York: W. W. Norton, 1980.

Goodwyn, Lawrence. *The Populist Moment: A Short History of the Agrarian Revolt in America*. New York: Oxford University Press, 1978.

Haberman, Frederick W., ed. *Nobel Lectures, Peace 1951–1970*. Amsterdam: Elsevier, 1972. http://nobelprize.org/peace/laureates/1970/borlaug-bio.html.

Halperin, Samuel. "Some Diagnoses and Prescriptions." In Christopher T. Cross et al., *Education in the Carter Years*. Washington, D.C.: Institute for Educational Leadership, 1978.

Hargrove, Erwin C. *Jimmy Carter as President: Leadership and the Politics of the Public Good*. Baton Rouge: Louisiana State University Press, 1988.

Harrington, Michael. *The Other America: Poverty in the United States*. New York: Collier Books, 1962.

Henderson, Harold P., and Gary L. Roberts, eds. *Georgia Governors in an Age of Change: From Ellis Arnall to George Busbee*. Athens: University of Georgia Press, 1988.

Herbst, Jurgen. *The Once and Future School: Three Hundred and Fifty Years of American Secondary Education*. New York: Routledge, 1996.

Hertzberg, Hendrik. "Jimmy Carter, 1977–1981." In *Character Above All: Ten Presidents from FDR to George Bush*, edited by Robert A. Wilson. New York: Simon & Schuster, 1995.

Hill, Dilys M. "Domestic Policy." In *The Carter Years: The President and Policy Making*, edited by M. Glenn Abernathy, Dilys Hill, and Phil Williams, 24–62. New York: St. Martin's Press, 1984.

Johnson, Lyndon Baines. *The Vantage Point*. New York: Holt, Rinehart and Winston, 1971.

Johnson, Richard O. "Desegregation of Public Education in Georgia—One Year Afterwards." *Journal of Negro Education* 24, no. 3 (1955): 228–47.

Jones, Charles O. *The Trustee Presidency: Jimmy Carter and the United States Congress*. Baton Rouge: Louisiana State University Press, 1988.

Kaestle, Carl F., and Marshall S. Smith. "The Federal Role in Elementary and Secondary Education, 1940–1980." *Harvard Educational Review* 52, no. 4 (November 1982): 384–408.

Kaplin, William A. *The Law of Higher Education: A Comprehensive Guide to Legal Implications of Administrative Decision Making*. San Francisco: Jossey-Bass, 1988.

Key, V. O., Jr. *Southern Politics in State and Nation*. With the assistance of Alexander Heard. New York: Vintage Books, 1949.

King, Joan Hutchon. "Establishing the U.S. Department of Education During the Carter Administration, 1978–1979." PhD diss., Claremont Graduate School, 1980.

Klarman, Michael J. "How *Brown* Changed Race Relations: The Backlash Thesis." *Journal of American History* 81, no. 1 (June 1994): 81–118.

Kluger, Richard. *Simple Justice: The History of Brown v. Board of Education and Black America's Struggle for Equality.* New York: Knopf, 1975.

Knott, Jack, and Aaron Wildavsky. "Jimmy Carter's Theory of Governing." *Wilson Quarterly* I (Winter 1977): 49–67.

Lazerson, Marvin, Judith Block McLaughlin, Bruce McPherson, and Stephen K. Bailey. *An Education of Value: The Purposes and Practices of Schools.* New York: Cambridge University Press, 1985.

Lewis, Finlay. *Mondale: Portrait of an American Politician.* New York: Harper & Row, 1980.

Light, Paul. "Vice-Presidential Influence under Rockefeller and Mondale." *Political Science Quarterly* 98, no. 4 (Winter 1983–84): 617–40.

Mazzoni, Tim L., Jr. "Jimmy Carter: An 'Education President'?" *Phi Delta Kappan* 58 (1977): 547–49.

McCarthy, Martha M., Nelds Cambron-McCabe, and Stephen B. Thomas. *Public School Law: Teachers' and Students' Rights.* Boston: Allyn and Bacon, 2003.

McDonnell, Lorraine M. "Assessment and Accountability from the Policymaker's Perspective." In *Uses and Misuses of Data for Educational Accountability and Improvement: The 104th Yearbook of the National Society for the Study of Education, Part 2,* edited by Joan L. Herman and Edward H. Haertel, 35–51. Malden, MA: Blackwell, 2005.

Michael, Deanna. "The Politics Behind the Establishment of Kindergartens in Georgia." *Journal of the Georgia Association of Historians* 25 (2004): 1–22.

Morris, Kenneth. *Jimmy Carter: American Moralist.* Athens: University of Georgia Press, 1996.

Motter, Russell D. "Jimmy Carter in Context." *Mississippi Quarterly* 45 (Fall 1992): 467–82.

Murphy, Jerome. "Progress and Problems: The Paradox of State Reform." In *Policy Making in Education: Eighty-first Yearbook of the National Society for the Study of Education, Part 1,* edited by Ann Lieberman and Milbrey W. McLaughlin, 195–214. Chicago: University of Chicago Press, 1982.

National Academy of Education. *Improving Educational Achievement: Report of the National Academy of Education, Committee on Testing and Basic Skills to the Assistant Secretary for Education.* Washington, D.C.: Department of Health, Education, and Welfare, 1978.

"NEA Encouraged: Carter Education Budget 1.5 Billion More for Schools." *NEA Reporter* 16 (April 1977): 4.

Newberry, Anthony L. "Without Urgency or Ardor: The South's Middle-of-the-Road Liberals and Civil Rights, 1945–1960." PhD diss., Ohio University, 1982.

Nuestadt, Richard E. *Presidential Power: The Politics of Leadership from FDR to Carter.* Rev. ed. New York: Wiley, 1980.

O'Brien, Thomas V. "Georgia's Response to *Brown v. Board of Education*: The Rise and Fall of Massive Resistance, 1949–1961." PhD diss., Emory University, 1992.

——— . *The Politics of Race and Schooling: Public Education in Georgia, 1900–1961.* New York: Lexington Books, 1999.

Orfield, Gary. *Must We Bus? Segregated Schools and National Policy.* Washington, D.C.: Brookings Institution, 1978.

——— , and Chungmei Lee. *Why Segregation Matters: Poverty and Educational Inequalities.* Cambridge: The Civil Rights Project, Harvard University, 2005. http://www.civilrightsproject.harvard.edu/research/deseg/Why_Segreg_Matters.pdf.

Perkinson, Henry. *The Imperfect Panacea: American Faith in Education 1865–1990.* 3rd ed. New York: McGraw-Hill, 1991.

Plank, David N., and Marcia E. Turner. "Contrasting Patterns in Black School Politics: Atlanta and Memphis, 1865–1985." *Journal of Negro Education* 60, no. 2 (Spring 1991): 203–18.

Rice, Bradley R. "Lester Maddox and the Politics of Populism." In *Georgia Governors in an Age of Change: From Ellis Arnall to George Busbee,* edited by Harold Henderson and Gary L. Roberts, 193–210. Athens: University of Georgia Press, 1988.

Rickover, Hyman. *Education and Freedom.* New York: E. P. Dutton, 1959.

Roche, Jeff. "A Reconstruction of Resistance: The Sibley Commission and the Politics of Desegregation in Georgia." MA thesis, Georgia State University, 1995.

Rockefeller Brothers Fund. *The Pursuit of Excellence.* New York: Doubleday, 1958.

Rossiter, Clinton. *Conservatism in America: The Thankless Persuasion.* 2d ed. New York: Knopf, 1962.

Smith, Hunter H. "'What Did It All Mean': Jimmy Carter and Civil Rights in Georgia." MA thesis, Georgia State University, 1995.

Southern Regional Education Board. *Fact Book on Higher Education in the South.* Atlanta: Southern Regional Education Board, 1971.

——— . *Within Our Reach: Report of the Commission on Goals for Higher Education in the South.* Atlanta: Southern Regional Education Board, 1961.

Spring, Joel. *Education and the Rise of the Corporate State.* Boston: Beacon Press, 1972.

St. John, Edward P. *Public Policy and College Management: Title III of the Higher Education Act.* New York: Praeger, 1981.

Steed, Robert P., Laurence W. Moreland, and Todd A. Baker, eds. *The Disappearing South? Studies in Regional Change and Continuity.* Tuscaloosa: University of Alabama Press, 1990.

Stephens, David. "President Carter, the Congress, and NEA: Creating the Department of Education." *Political Science Quarterly* 98 (Winter 1983–84): 641–63.

Stone, Clarence. "Civic Capacity and Urban School Reform." In *Changing Urban Education. Studies in Government and Public Policy,* edited by Clarence N. Stone, 250–73. Lawrence: University of Kansas Press, 1998.

Street, Paul. *Segregated Schools: Educational Apartheid in Post-Civil Rights America. Positions: Education, Politics, and Culture.* New York: Routledge/Taylor & Francis Group, 2005.

Summerfield, Harry L. *Power and Process: The Formation and Limits of Federal Educational Policy.* Berkeley: McCutchen, 1974.

Sundquist, James L. *Politics and Policy: The Eisenhower, Kennedy, and Johnson Years.* Washington, D.C.: Brookings Institution, 1969.

Thomas, Leland C. "Some Aspects of Biracial Educational in Georgia, 1900–1954." EDD diss., George Peabody College for Teachers, 1960.

Thompson, Phyllis. "Technology and The Atlanta Project." *Georgia Tech Alumni Magazine Online* (Spring 1993). http://gtalumni.org/news/magazine/spr93/hood.html.

Tushnet, Mark V. *The NAACP's Legal Strategy Against Segregated Education, 1925–1950.* Chapel Hill: University of North Carolina Press, 1987.

Tyack, David. *The One Best System: A History of American Urban Education.* Reprint. Cambridge: Harvard University Press, 1974.

———, and Larry Cuban. *Tinkering Toward Utopia: A Century of Public School Reform.* Reprint. Cambridge: Harvard University Press, 1997.

Urban, Wayne J. *Black Scholar: Horace Mann Bond 1904–1972.* Athens: University of Georgia Press, 1992.

Vandiver, S. Ernest. "Vandiver Takes the Middle Road." In *Georgia Governors in an Age of Change: From Ellis Arnall to George Busbee,* edited by Harold P. Henderson and Gary L. Roberts, 157–66. Athens: University of Georgia Press, 1988.

Van Til, William. "Education and Jimmy Carter." *Phi Delta Kappan* 58 (November 1976): 277.

Vinovski, Maris. *History and Educational Policymaking.* New Haven: Yale University Press, 1999.

Von Hoffman, Alexander. *House by House, Block by Block: The Rebirth of America's Urban Neighborhoods.* New York: Oxford University Press, 2003. http://www.netlibrary.com

"What's In and Out of the New Department of Education." *Academe* (December 1979): 470–71.

Wilkinson, J. Harvie, III. *From Brown to Bakke: The Supreme Court and School Integration 1954–1978.* New York: Oxford University Press, 1979.

Williams, John L., III. "Title VI Regulations of Higher Education." In *Desegregating America's Colleges and Universities: Title VI Regulation of Higher Education,* edited by John B. Williams, III. New York: Teacher's College Press, 1988.

Williford, William B. *Americus Through the Years: The Story of a Georgia Town and Its People, 1832–1975.* Atlanta: Cherokee Publishing, 1975.

Wise, Arthur E. *Legislated Learning: The Bureaucratization of the American Classroom.* Berkeley: University of California Press, 1979.

Woodward, C. Vann. *Tom Watson: Agrarian Rebel.* 2d ed. Savannah: Beehive Books, 1973.

Wooten, James. *Dasher: The Roots and the Rising of Jimmy Carter.* New York: Summit Books, 1978.

Zigler, Edward, and Susan Muenchow. *Head Start: The Inside Story of America's Most Successful Educational Experiment.* New York: Basic Books, 1992.

Index